Advancing Governance in the South

What Roles for International Financial Institutions in Developing States?

Pia Riggirozzi

Research Associate, Department of Politics, University of Sheffield, UK

palgrave
macmillan

First published 2009 by
PALGRAVE MACMILLAN

Palgrave Macmillan in the UK is an imprint of Macmillan Publishers Limited, registered in England, company number 785998, of Houndmills, Basingstoke, Hampshire RG21 6XS.

Palgrave Macmillan in the US is a division of St Martin's Press LLC, 175 Fifth Avenue, New York, NY 10010.

Palgrave Macmillan is the global academic imprint of the above companies and has companies and representatives throughout the world.

Palgrave® and Macmillan® are registered trademarks in the United States, the United Kingdom, Europe and other countries.

ISBN-13: 978-0-230-22011-9 hardback
ISBN-10: 0-230-22011-8 hardback

This book is printed on paper suitable for recycling and made from fully managed and sustained forest sources. Logging, pulping and manufacturing processes are expected to conform to the environmental regulations of the country of origin.

A catalogue record for this book is available from the British Library.

Library of Congress Cataloging-in-Publication Data
Riggirozzi, Pia, 1971–
    Advancing governance in the South : what roles for international financial institutions in developing states? / Pia Riggirozzi.
        p. cm. — (International political economy series)
    Includes bibliographical references and index.
    ISBN 978-0-230-22011-9 (alk. paper)
    1. Financial institutions, International—Developing countries.
    2. Financial institutions, International—Argentina. 3. Developing countries—Economic policy. 4. Argentina—Economic policy. I. Title.
HG3881.R47 2009
    332.1′5091724—dc22   2008030470

10   9   8   7   6   5   4   3   2   1
18   17   16   15   14   13   12   11   10   09

Printed and bound in Great Britain by
CPI Antony Rowe, Chippenham and Eastbourne

International Political Economy Series

General Editor: **Timothy M. Shaw**, Professor and Director, Institute of International Relations, The University of the West Indies, Trinidad & Tobago

Titles include:

Angela W. Little
LABOURING TO LEARN
Towards a Political Economy of Plantations, People and Education in Sri Lanka

John Loxley (*editor*)
INTERDEPENDENCE, DISEQUILIBRIUM AND GROWTH
Reflections on the Political Economy of North–South Relations at the Turn of the Century

Don D. Marshall
CARIBBEAN POLITICAL ECONOMY AT THE CROSSROADS
NAFTA and Regional Developmentalism

Susan M. McMillan
FOREIGN DIRECT INVESTMENT IN THREE REGIONS OF THE SOUTH AT THE END OF THE TWENTIETH CENTURY

S. Javed Maswood
THE SOUTH IN INTERNATIONAL ECONOMIC REGIMES
Whose Globalization?

John Minns
THE POLITICS OF DEVELOPMENTALISM
The Midas States of Mexico, South Korea and Taiwan

Philip Nel
THE POLITICS OF ECONOMIC INEQUALITY IN DEVELOPING COUNTRIES

Pia Riggirozzi
ADVANCING GOVERNANCE IN THE SOUTH
What Roles for International Financial Institutions in Developing States?

Lars Rudebeck, Olle Törnquist and Virgilio Rojas (*editors*)
DEMOCRATIZATION IN THE THIRD WORLD
Concrete Cases in Comparative and Theoretical Perspective

Benu Schneider (*editor*)
THE ROAD TO INTERNATIONAL FINANCIAL STABILITY
Are Key Financial Standards the Answer?

Howard Stein (*editor*)
ASIAN INDUSTRIALIZATION AND AFRICA
Studies in Policy Alternatives to Structural Adjustment

William Vlcek
OFFSHORE FINANCE AND SMALL STATES
Sovereignty, Size and Money

International Political Economy Series
Series Standing Order ISBN 978–0–333–71708–0 hardcover
Series Standing Order ISBN 978–0–333–71110–1 paperback
(*outside North America only*)

You can receive future titles in this series as they are published by placing a standing order. Please contact your bookseller or, in case of difficulty, write to us at the address below with your name and address, the title of the series and one of the ISBNs quoted above.

Customer Services Department, Macmillan Distribution Ltd, Houndmills, Basingstoke, Hampshire RG21 6XS, England

This book is dedicated to John and Delfina.

Contents

List of Table and Figures

Table

Figures

Acknowledgements

The origins and motivation of this book are part of many years of research which began as a doctoral project at the University of Warwick. My gratitude is due to the many people involved in its evolution for their invaluable time, support and patience. Their readings of various early drafts of the manuscript provided suggestions, criticism and comments that gave the work fresh impetus. I am particularly thankful to Jan Aart Scholte, Diane Stone, Bill Smith, Diana Tussie, friends and colleagues at FLACSO/Argentina, and to the many interviewees cited in the study. Since I extended this project to cover current issues in political economy in Latin America I have also benefited immensely from the shared work, conversations and exchange with Jean Grugel, Ben-Thirkell White and Paul Mosley in the context of the ESRC-funded project 'Political Economy of Pro-poor Adjustment Policies' at the University of Sheffield. I owe particular thanks to Jean Grugel for reading the entire manuscript at different points and for advising me on both its overall arguments and the substance of specific chapters. Funding from an ESRC Post-doctoral Fellowship is also gratefully acknowledged; this made possible the updating and completion of the work. Thanks also to Liz Thompson for her editing suggestions. Last but not least, I would like to thank Alexandra Webster, Gemma D'Arcy-Hughes and Tim Shaw at Palgrave for their professionalism and support, as well as to the anonymous reviewer whose comments helped to improve this study.

List of Abbreviations

ADC	Asociación por los Derechos Civiles (Civil Rights Association)
CAS	Country Assistance Strategy
CDF	Comprehensive Development Framework
CELS	Centro de Estudios Legales y Sociales (Centre for Legal and Social Studies)
CIPPEC	Centro de Implementación de Políticas Públicas para la Equidad y el Crecimiento (Centre for the Implementation of Public Policies promoting Equity and Growth)
DECRG	Development Economics Research Group
FARN	Fundación Ambiente y Recursos Naturales (Environment and Natural Resources Foundation)
FIEL	Fundación de Investigación Económica Latinoamericana (Latin American Economic Research Foundation)
FOCAL	Canadian Foundation for the Americas
FORES	Foro de Estudios sobre Administración y Justicia (Forum for the Study of Justice Administration)
FREPASO	Frente del País Solidario (Front for a Solidary Country)
IACC	Inter-American Convention against Corruption
IDB	Inter-American Development Bank
IDEA	Instituto para el Desarrollo Empresario en la Argentina (Business Development Institute)
IDF	Institutional Development Facility
IMF	International Monetary Fund
INECIP	Instituto de Estudios Comparados en Ciencias Penales y Sociales (Institute of Comparative Studies in Criminal and Social Sciences)
IPE	International Political Economy
IR	International Relations
JUFEJUS	Junta Federal de Cortes y Superiores Tribunales de Justicia de las Provincias Argentinas (Federal Board of Judicial Courts of the Provinces of Argentina)
NGOs	Non-governmental Organizations
OECD	Organisation for Economic Cooperation and Development
OED	Operations Evaluation Department

ONEP   Oficina Nacional de Etica Pública (National Public Ethics
            Office)
ONTI   Oficina Nacional de Tecnología de la Información
            (National Office for Information Technologies)
PREM   Poverty Reduction and Economic Management
PREJUD   Programa Integral de Reforma Judicial (Integral Programme
            of Judicial Reform)
PROJUM   Proyecto Juzgado Modelo (Model Court Project)
UCR   Union Cívica Radical Party
UNECA   United Nations Economic Commission for Africa
UNDP   United Nations Development Programme
US   United States of America
USAID   United States Agency for International Development
WBI   World Bank Institute
WDR   World Development Report
WTO   World Trade Organization

1
Introduction

International Financial Institutions (IFIs) have consistently exercised considerable influence over policy-making in Latin America and they have traditionally been able to call upon a range of tools in order to uphold their authority and to standardize and reproduce hegemonic projects of development. The neoliberal response to debt crisis in Latin America during the 1980s and 1990s was held in place by the formulation of global rules around governance and development which were backed by the International Monetary Fund (IMF) and the multilateral development banks, in particular the World Bank. However, as this book will argue, despite having apparently little room for dissent from the global rule, IFIs have had to work with domestic actors over policy implementation in developing countries. Reforming governance institutions for development is entrenched in social relations and political realities and thus is likely to lead to either support or contestation. As such, advancing 'good' governance takes more than the financial and intellectual authoritative stance of the IFIs. Local knowledge and legitimacy are critical aspects in the politics of governance reforms. This is becoming a more pressing matter since Latin America is currently capitalizing in an enabling international context to build alternative and more autonomous governance in stark contrast to the neoliberal models promoted for more than two decades in the region.

At the core of this book is the unfolding power relations and the conditions under which the IFIs promoted governance reforms in Argentina since the 1990s. Equally, the study is concerned with the challenges and dilemmas for the IFIs in the face of the most recent re-definition of political and economic governance at the regional scale. This study suggests, first, that power should not simply be reduced to the coercive authority

1

of international organizations over developing countries. Power in the global political economy works through social relations of interaction which, in turn, provide resources to actors at different points in the policy chain (see Barnett and Duvall 2005). Consequently, the implementation of, and outcomes from, IFI-promoted reforms and projects of good governance is not a simple consequence of the dominance of the lender, acting in the interest of powerful states, but rather an outcome of negotiation, conflict and contested paradigms. Moreover, the ways IFIs engage with local actors can enhance or limit their ability to advance policy change. Second, when IFIs are able to draw on their financial and knowledge power to consolidate pro-reform networks with local actors, they are more likely to ensure the implementation of governance reforms in client countries.

The current backlash within Latin America and elsewhere against both neoliberalism and the IFIs supports these arguments and raises doubts as to whether the IFIs can continue to shape global rules in a prescriptive way. Whilst the debt crisis in the 1980s and early 1990s increased the leverage of the IFIs *vis-à-vis* borrower governments, the political and economic crises that beset most of Latin America at the end of the 1990s revealed, first, the extent to which power and compliance are highly political processes and, second, the fluidity of power relations between domestic and international actors. Events in Argentina from the 1990s to the contemporary period provide a revealing mirror of the changing relationships between IFIs and developing countries.

This introductory chapter begins by tracing the embodiment of governance within the development agenda of the IFIs. It also speculates on the place of power politics and policy change in advancing the norm of 'good governance' in developing countries. The chapter is divided into four sections. The first section explores the agenda of governance as a normative goal that adds new attempts to modify state institutions, such as the judiciary, to traditional market-oriented goals championing what is called 'good governance'. The analysis of governance, however, raises critical questions: to what extent can the IFIs affect models of the state and development? Can 'good governance' be imposed from outside? Taking up these questions, the second section discusses the structure of IFIs' power resources in advancing policy implementation of politically sensitive reforms on the ground, including the way 'knowledge' became an element of these power resources. The third section focuses on this knowledge component as a powerful resource in the promotion of 'good' governance. Among the IFIs, the World Bank provides the greatest financial and technical support for good governance programmes. According to the 2006 World Bank Annual Review (33), 'nearly half of the prior actions for development policy operations are related to governance, particularly public financial management'. The wider range of instruments, financial and knowledge-related, that the World Bank deploys compared to other multilateral institutions positions it as the major source of funds and ideas for governance reforms. Its renewed focus as a 'Knowledge Bank' has helped to shape, justify and legitimate new goals in development assistance and new instruments for its promotion (see Gilbert *et al.* 2000). Nevertheless, it is argued that the ability of the World Bank, and of the IFIs in general, to translate ideas into policies and institutional forms depends on their capacity to act as an effective 'norm-broker' engaging with local actors to reproduce ideas and practices in developing countries. This section discusses these issues to be further developed in the empirical analysis of governance reform in Argentina. The chapter closes with the content description of the book.

Crafting governance for development

Since the late 1980s, the terms 'governance' and 'good governance' have increasingly become part of the development discourse among IFIs. Strong arguments have been proffered that without 'good governance' developing countries cannot achieve economic growth or effective poverty reduction. Amongst economists in general, there was increasing interest in the institutional foundations of growth. This included theoretical exploration of the ways in which stable institutions could create investor confidence under conditions of imperfect information (Stiglitz 1994), the insights of the 'new institutional economics' (North 1990) and empirical studies demonstrating the importance of institutions for growth and data reproduced in several World Bank reports since its influential 2001 World Development Report (WDR) *Building Institutions for Markets*.

The discussion about stability, growth and institutional foundations for effective development within the IFIs was led by a combination of pressures from within and outside the institutions. In particular, critical reports on the performance of the World Bank, the IMF and the regional banks in the achievement of development goals led powerful voices within major donors to revisit development assistance since the 1980s (Woods 2006: 201). In particular, the failures mainly in Africa and Latin America after more than a decade of intensive and profound reforms, and the contrasting experience in those East Asian countries that experienced rapid levels of economic growth without following the blueprint promoted by the World Bank and the IMF, confirmed the need to rethink the development agenda (Stiglitz 1998a).

In the case of Latin America, the economic reforms introduced to alleviate the deep economic crisis in the 1980s triggered a radical process of privatization of public services, changes in regulations and an administrative decentralization that dismantled the old state-centric economic model of the 1950s and 1960s (Cavarozzi 1994; Haggard and Kaufman 1994). These reforms, which followed the international financial institutions' economic paradigm known as Washington Consensus, were effective in leading the economies of developing countries towards financial restoration and a measure of economic recovery. However, high levels of poverty and inequality failed to fulfil the promise of the 'virtuous circle' of macroeconomic reforms (Morley 1995; Birdsall and Graham 2000). Within a decade, the levels of poverty and inequality in Latin America showed an alarming increase: from 1982 to 1993 the overall number of persons living in poverty increased from 78 to 150 million (Korzeniewicz and Smith 2000: 8–9). Throughout the 1990s Latin America registered the highest levels of inequality in the world (*ibid.*: 12).

In a different context, but also facing adverse economic realities, the World Bank's adjustment policies in Africa were under scrutiny by international non-governmental organizations (NGOs) such as Development Gap and the African Women's Economic Policy Network, Oxfam and the Structural Adjustment Participatory Review International Network, which claimed that structural adjustment programmes supported by the World Bank and the IMF failed to transform critical contexts into economic growth. Instead, NGOs' campaigns claimed, the economic reforms led by the IFIs increased poverty, undermined food security, led to unsustainable resource exploitation and provoked environmental and social unrest. These conclusions were highlighted by the United Nations Economic Commission for Africa (UNECA), which reiterated the claims (UNECA 1998).

Among the IFIs, the World Bank was quick to recognize the negative results after a decade of the Washington Consensus. In its 1992 WDR it acknowledged that macroeconomic and structural reforms had proved insufficient to meet the aim of poverty reduction in developing countries during the 1980s. The World Bank's report shows, in effect, that all poverty measures worsened in sub-Saharan Africa, the Middle East and North Africa and in Latin America and the Caribbean. At the same time, while the number of the poor increased in these regions, the experience in East Asia, where governments did not follow the path prescribed by the Washington Consensus, was remarkably different (World Bank 1989; Boeninger 1992: 42). In Japan and the East and South East Asian countries state intervention was the motor of economic development, and government action a key element in directing policies to enhance international competitiveness. At odds with the conservatism of the Washington Consensus, these experiences showed that the state can work *for* the market rather than *against* it (Bresser-Pereira 1995). In this context, the debate in regard to effective conditions for sustainable development on economic development in general was reopened among development economists, practitioners and scholars, and with it a new consideration of the role of state institutions in economic development (Fernandez-Arias and Montiel 1997; Stewart 1997; Stiglitz 1998a,b, 2000; Easterly 2001).

The multilateral development banks responded first to these challenges in a way that opened productive new spheres of action to them. The IMF followed suit in a more conservative fashion. A new consensus emerged asserting that politically feasible and sustainable development needed legitimacy of governments; adequate regulatory frameworks; active participation by those most directly affected; a capable and transparent civil service; and a decentralized system of policy implementation that generated accountability. Put together, these new conditions became increasingly packaged under the catch-all word 'governance' (Casaburi *et al.* 2000: 495). Increasingly, lending operations and overall financial support extended towards new policy-based loans, and with it a new conditionality, to help to improve the governance of borrowing countries.

But rather than constituting a drastic break with the past, the good governance agenda was constructed to complement the macroeconomic reforms supported by the Washington Consensus. That is, instead of accepting that failure in development outcomes was part and parcel of the neoliberal economic policies undertaken in the developing world, the IFIs emphatically shifted the blame to the institutional environment in which politics evolved in developing countries. Poor and unreliable institutions were the focus of unsustainable policies, and thus enhancing transparency and the rule of law became part and parcel of effective and sustainable development. This paradigm was outlined in the World Bank's 1992 report *Governance and Development*:

Good governance is central to creating and sustaining an environment which fosters strong and equitable development, and it is an essential complement to sound economic policies. Governments play a key role in the provision of public goods. They establish the rules that make markets work efficiently and, more problematically, they correct for market failure. In order to play this role, they need revenues, and agents to collect revenues and produce the public goods. [...] This in turn requires systems of accountability, adequate and reliable information, and efficiency in resource management and the delivery of public services.

(Boeninger 1992: 1)

Underlying the new approach was the idea that market reforms were not working in developing countries in part due to a lack of 'market-enhancing' institutional underpinnings, fostering corruption and a general disregard for the rule of law (World Bank 1994). The governance agenda thus became a manifestation of the new development thinking subsequently decoded into a framework that broadened the paradigm of liberalization, deregulation and privatization by placing new emphasis on an effective and reliable legal system and the rule of law, efficient and transparent management of public funds, political accountability and the participation of citizen organizations (Burki and Perry 1998; Kaufmann *et al.* 1999, 2002; World Bank 2000a, 2001a, 2002a). Among the IFIs, the World Bank and the Inter-American Development Bank (IDB) championed this 'post-Washington Consensus' and a new operational agenda that supported the institutional infrastructure that reduces 'transaction costs' for effective investment, production and trade (Paliwala 2000: 4).

By attributing failure to 'poor institutions', the IFIs paved the way for more intrusive and politically sensitive reforms in borrowing countries. Legal and state reforms became part of a new mantra oriented towards securing private property rights, enforcing contracts and expansion of the private sector. Beyond development economics, promoting the goal of good governance became a means of institutionalizing neoliberal globalization in the developing world. Moreover, the technical, a-political definition of a pro-market institutional environment left aside a more profound debate about the political implications of institutional reforms. Issues such as the quality of democracy and human rights, for instance, have been omitted from the governance loop. Even within the agenda of the 'rule of law and transparency', which became a World Bank landmark, the emphasis was on what makes markets work rather than on the conditions that enhance broader access to justice for the population and institutional accountability. Consequently, the promotion of good governance is an integral part of the emergent global economic order and a technical aspect of the development agenda.

But to what extent can the IFIs really affect models of the state and development? Can 'good governance' be imposed from outside? Who is governance good for? These are the key questions at the core of this book. Their answers call for a critical analysis of power relations and policy processes with particular focus on the dynamics of engagement between IFIs and local actors for the implementation of politically sensitive reforms. The ensuing chapters pick up on the argument that the agenda of governance advanced by the IFIs represents a green light for the use of more intrusive conditionality advancing, willingly or not, new political tasks (Kapur and Webb 2000; Santiso 2002). They also concur with claims that by promoting certain types of state institutions the IFIs are active components in the construction of new neoliberal global architecture. This study, however, argues strongly that the promotion of systems of governance involves more than a hierarchical transfer of norms and best practice from the IFIs to developing countries. Existing literature on IFIs and power relations tends to put too much emphasis on the power of 'hegemonic forces' to either impose development agendas (Payer 1982) or co-opt local actors by engaging primarily in institutional reforms (Harrison 2004). I argue instead that the implementation of politically sensitive reforms such as those of governance create spaces not only for dissent but also for negotiation between local and external actors. Moreover, as this analysis suggests, local politics affect the power of the IFIs in their attempts to organize systems of governance on the ground.

These claims are particularly relevant for middle-income countries such as Argentina, where not only is there a strong base of local experts, politically involved in the design of reform programmes prior to the involvement of international agencies in governance reforms, but the economy also has gradually become less dependent on international funds, in particular from 2003 following the post-crisis recovery. There may be compelling arguments to the contrary with reference to Africa, for instance, as these countries are highly dependent on external funding and technical support (Mosley *et al.* 1995; Harrison 2004). But the experience of middle-income countries in Latin America is rather different, as their position in the global economy allows them access to private financial markets and their policy outcomes are the result of more complex policy processes, in which a highly mobilized and articulated civil society can influence the course of decision-making. As shown in the analysis of governance reforms in Argentina since the

1990s developed in subsequent chapters, politically sensitive reforms are entrenched in a complex policy process in which the dominance of a particular actor or paradigm *vis-à-vis* other contending actors or ideas is not reinforced simply by the coercive position of the lender over the borrower, but rather by its capacity to integrate contesting impulses into a broader consensus for policy change. This argument becomes even more pressing, as suggested towards the end of this book, as the current dynamics of regional politics and resource management are shaping a new regionalism in an attempt to contest the global rule.

As a result, we suggest, first, that any understanding of policy change involving the IFIs and local actors in developing countries needs to play special attention to the social relations of interaction through which power relations manifest. Equally, the modality of influence involving the IFIs and local politics in developing countries require more than simply coercive and authoritative power. Conveying IFIs-promoted good governance reforms into local realities requires acceptance and legitimacy. Politically sensitive reforms cannot be uncritically transferred in a linear process. Once they enter the domestic policy domain they are subject to negotiation, conflict and contestation. From this perspective, the ways in which IFIs engage with local actors are critical for advancing policy change in client countries. That is, when IFIs are able to draw on their financial and knowledge power to engage in networks with local actors they are more likely to ensure policy change.

With both funds to disburse and technical advice to give, IFIs are therefore in a better position to advance development paradigms and to empower certain actors who can get the project through by facilitating resources for putting them into practice. Networks of academic and professional elites, often influential within the policy-making bureaucracy and with links to international institutions such as the World Bank and IMF, have played an important role in the diffusion of ideas about development (Babb 2001). However, policy diffusion does not guarantee policy implementation. This is even more so in the case of governance reforms which involve and affect a wider range of constituencies at the local level. Legitimacy is a compelling component in the achievement of policy change.

The case of Argentina's governance reforms since the 1990s helps to focus on these processes as multiple spaces of contestation in which competing interests, incentives, resources and institutional capabilities affected power relations between the IFIs and the local actors. It also helps to draw lessons for the current regional reaction against neoliberal governance. With regard to the 1990s, governance was embodied mainly within ambitious judicial reform and anti-corruption programmes, both of which were promoted by and identified with the World Bank. After the 2001 crisis, governance became a broader project, calling for a new beginning in the relationship between state, civil society and the IFIs. Governance, therefore, was not simply a matter of 'getting the policies or the institutions right' but was rather a broader project in which social policies became a priority and part of an economic strategy of stabilization. As explained in Chapter 6, in addition to its obvious economic aspects, the crisis was a crisis of neoliberal governance and public confidence in the political class as much as it was a crisis of legitimacy of the policy-expertise that emanated from the IFIs. In this context, the role of the IMF and the World Bank in the reconstruction of post-crisis governance was secured only when they tailored their advice and aspirations to fit within the domestic political agenda.

Certainly, the normative compound generated within the IFIs was a critical resource that had the potential to affect incentives and policy choices within and outside the IFIs. In particular, the current emphasis on knowledge as an important instrument in the advancement of policy ideas in developing countries, especially in the World Bank, has become a powerful mechanism to justify and legitimize specific policy ideas, while de-legitimizing others (George and Sabelli 1994; Williams and Young 1994; Mehta 2001; Wade 2002). Often, as recognized in an independent IMF study, preconceived ideas are taken as templates for developing countries 'based on a theoretical or textbook model, housed in Washington' (IMF 1999: 36; see also Rodrik 2008). But, as the empirical analysis in this book explores, powerful resources such as funds and knowledge are context-dependent and thus once they enter a local domain they are affected by the encounter with other ideas held by local actors. The current trend in the regional political economy reinforces these arguments and calls for more profound analysis on the ways and extent to which the search for autonomy in Latin America challenges the financial and intellectual power of the IFIs.

Power politics and reform processes

The agenda of governance embraced by the IFIs for the last two decades has been politically more intrusive than their traditional macroeconomic approach. As such, the promotion of governance necessitated considerable rethinking inside the IFIs. Technocratic training for staff was consistent with the traditional way of promoting policy change via conditionality, and this was an effective mechanism for enforcing externally promoted policy change in areas of macroeconomic reform such as trade liberalization, structural adjustment and privatization. During the 1980s in particular, the leverage of conditionality as an enforcing mechanism was enabled by the circumstances of debt crisis and by the much restricted international financial markets which reduced the access of developing countries to private capital (Stallings 1992: 43–44). Ideologically, there was also a generalized belief in the failure of state-led development projects of the 1940s–1960s. This has been particularly the case among governing elites in the newly democratized Latin American countries. But the promotion of neoliberal governance by the IFIs has seriously challenged the rationale of their mission and mandate. Therefore it is not surprising that, in turn, in addition to the debate generated amongst the international development community outside the IFIs, within the organizations themselves senior management also has an ambivalent attitude towards engaging with local actors for the definition and implementation of governance reforms. Moreover, within the IFIs the dominance of economists, many recruited from academia and having little practical experience in public policy decision-making, has resulted in a poor appreciation of these non-economic factors in the development equation. What this suggests is that the international organizations are by no means monolithic institutions and thus they must not be analysed as acting and impacting in a uniform way.

From the perspective of the IFIs' work in the field – from negotiation to implementation of programmes in developing countries – there are two factors that have affected the engagement of staff managers with local experts on the ground. The first is related to the discretionary capacity of the task managers of the World Bank and the IMF to use local expertise, for instance. The decision to engage in efforts to coordinate local knowledge and policy is reserved to the discretion of each manager. Despite the new participatory policies adopted within the IFIs, in particular the World Bank, since the mid-1990s (World Bank 1996a; also Nelson 2000), there are no binding operational directives that enforce the use of knowledge-related activities and engagement with local expertise for the negotiation and implementation of programmes. Second, in the case of the World Bank, despite corporate efforts to establish a 'Knowledge Bank', sharing knowledge within and outside the Bank is not a standard for task managers' internal performance evaluation or promotion. In this context, articulation and amalgamation of knowledge(s) is left to a task manager's personal commitment, informal relationships with borrowers and professional practices. Some scholars have claimed that the IFIs' approach to lending operations tend to simplify and standardize not only knowledge but also the contextual specificity in project design, implementation, supervision and evaluation (Pincus 2002: 78). These circumstances leave IFI managers a large amount of discretion to manage the gap between global knowledge and country-specific needs. These observations confirm not only that the IFIs are not monolithic institutions, but also that different patterns of implementation of governance-related programmes emerge as the IFIs engage with certain actors and the terrain of domestic polices.

Reforms of state and legal institutions are undoubtedly rooted in a political and historical context and thus are likely to raise support and opposition among the local actors. Opposition to these reforms can draw from local actors that oppose reform programmes that resemble an 'orthodox solution' imposed by external actors, or from the lack of political will on the part of those at the centre of the policy-making process, even after loan approval (see Chapter 4). In the 1980s, the debate on developing countries' bargaining power *vis-à-vis* international lenders and creditors was defined by the focus on uneven leverage in favour of the latter. Inequality of power was part of the paucity of international funds and restricted access to external money for developing countries. In this context, dependency on external finance, marked by a deep debt crisis, secured compliance with the international norm. Throughout the 1990s, the adoption of neoliberal policies in Latin America confirmed an apparent standardization of international politics to which developing countries succumbed as their margin for manoeuvre *vis-à-vis* external lenders declined.

Many studies explored how credit rationing during the debt crisis in the 1980s in Latin America confined policy choices to the adoption of stabilization policies according to IFIs' prescriptions; that is, reduction of fiscal deficits, liberalization of trade and exchange rate regimes and general expansion of the role of market forces and the private sector (Nelson 1990; Stallings 1992: 43–44; Haggard and Kaufman 1994; Acuña and Smith 1994). In this case, the financial leverage of the IFIs was directly proportionate to the amount of lending provided. By adapting domestic choices to the implementation of structural, market-oriented reforms, Latin American countries gained access to further financial flows. In this context, many countries in the region surrendered important margins of national sovereignty and subordinated national priorities to the global rule (see, for instance, Weyland 1998). It was clear, for example, during the 1990s that independent political options for developing countries were severely reduced by the need to adhere to global economic norms.

Politically, these power relations were thought to reflect a 'new constitutionalism' of global capitalism in which states' choice tended to converge into neoliberal forms of state (Gill 2000).

This pattern in global governance led to a situation in which politically sensitive reforms, such as the privatization of services and the flexibilization of labour markets, were often implemented without seeking social consensus (Acuña and Tuozzo 2000). However, this very situation also undermined the long-term viability of reform implementation and hindered the effectiveness of new regulations and institutions created in the wake of those reforms. In the end, a decade of neoliberal reforms undermined both the incipient consolidation of democracy and the economic stability in many developing countries (Teichman 2004; Tuozzo 2004). Moreover, the international financial crises, in particular the socio-economic impact of these crises that spread from East Asian to South American economies from the late 1990s, came to be linked to the policy prescriptions promoted by the IFIs a decade before, especially capital liberalization and state dismantling.

The literature of Latin American studies has discussed these issues in detail, dissecting the ways in which democratization and economic adjustment intersect (Grugel 2003). Conditionality packages associated with adjustment loans functioned as the transmission link for a whole new paradigm of development. Yet, if dependence on external funding gave external donors extensive leverage over development policies, the more the economies recovered the less they were obliged to comply with the normative prescriptions of the IFIs. Moreover, as argued in the subsequent chapters, issues of implementation and compliance were made more complex in some cases by problems internal to newly democratic polities, where decision-making processes entailed parliamentary deliberation and approval of policies. In Argentina, the implementation of governance-related programmes in the mid-1990s shows that despite their funding and technical advice, the capacity of the IFIs to affect key actors' perceptions and implementation of policies was mediated by previously established interests in the local arena. In other words, local actors were not passive receptors of the policies designed and conveyed by the IFIs.

From these observations, there are a number of related issues that merit careful consideration for a discussion of the current role and power of the IFIs in their pursuit of policy changes in developing countries. First, despite the prominent role of IFIs in the global political economy, their ability to influence government policies is not always large (Kahler 1992: 100). Many empirical studies demonstrated that the power of conditionality as a bargaining tool was poor and that in some cases external conditionality was even used by governments to overcome internal opposition and accelerate government agendas, or to resist and renegotiate policies with the IFIs (Casaburi *et al.* 2000: 152; Killick 2002; Woods 2006).

Second, power should be seen as a process, rather than as an attribute of a single actor, and that process is both restrained and enabled by the context in which actors take action. This means that the external context does not determine choice but rather provides the framework and sometimes the set of choices. In other words, choices and decision-making are not external to developing countries, rather they are embedded in the particular situations within which they operate. Therefore, failure to pay sufficient attention to domestic contextual factors in shaping international and national politics limits a comprehensive understanding of empirical patterns of politics and relations in the implementation of programmes.

Although the current political economy in developing countries suggests that the power capacity of international organizations is strongly contested, it is still necessary to explore the complex dynamics of power relationships involving international organizations and local actors in developing countries. Policy outcomes are a consequence of how these power relationships evolve and thus do not follow a linear path. In Latin America, for instance, imposition – or the perception of it – has worked against externally supported policy reforms, especially in democratic societies. In order to understand the nature of power flows in development assistance, it is therefore important to disaggregate different patterns of IFI involvement in different contexts and formulate fresh analyses of the prospects of intervention by IFIs in areas where, as demonstrated currently in South America, more financial autonomy and alternative development models are emerging.

What this means is that any explanation of relations between IFIs and developing countries should not neglect the material grounding of global and local power relations. Local actors are not passive recipients of funds and policy proposals. They take, contest, modify or reject IFI proposals. Thus, different relationships unfold in different contexts of space and time from the process of negotiation between IFIs and local actors. Moreover, the attempt to 'transfer' policy paradigms and funds may sometimes impede consensus building for reform and thereby weaken the capacity of the IFIs to advance their development and ideological agendas. Power relations are, in effect, dynamic not static and power becomes context-dependent, demonstrated in the different

configurations of social relations in which the IFIs are one participant actor. Therefore, the ways IFIs engage in developing countries can
enhance or limit their ability to respond to social and political changes
and to adapt accordingly. This is particularly relevant in understanding different responses and policy outcomes and the role played by the
IFIs in Argentina's governance reform in the 1990s and during the crisis
resolution.

The claims presented in this book echo the body of critical theory
in International Political Economy (IPE), which highlights the issue
of power as a function of accommodation and compromise amongst
actors' interests, ideas and political agendas and resources (see Cox
1987, 1993). Ideas held by actors endorse differing views on policy
issues that define both the nature and legitimacy of practices and
the policy outcomes (Cox 1986: 218). For instance, by championing
development paradigms according to specific practices and ideologies,
the IFIs promote particular norms in defence of a particular project.
Local actors, for their part, may articulate a different framework. The
clash of these rival projects provides evidence for the potential for
alternative paths of development as actors in this process can compromise on certain grounds (Cox 1993). Therefore, while policy ideas and
proposals may be several and even opposed, the task of policy change
relies on the creation of a common ground in terms of discourse and
practices. The reactions against neoliberalism experienced in the developing world since the early 2000s confirm these points and in the case
of Latin America, rather than a coherent and powerful ideologically
project delivered by the IFIs, the politics of development counteract the
pressures towards externally driven neoliberal policies.

Evidence of these developments is presented in the empirical
analysis throughout the book, showing that the attempt to 'transfer'
policy paradigms and funds impedes consensus building for reform and
thereby weakens the capacity of the IFIs to advance their development
and ideological agendas. Power relations in these cases proved, in effect,
to be dynamic and context-dependent, found in different configurations
of social relations in which the IFIs are one participant actor. Therefore, failure to pay sufficient attention to domestic contextual factors
in shaping international and national politics limits a comprehensive
understanding of empirical patterns of politics and relations within the
implementation of programmes.

The search for governance in Latin America, and in particular in the
context of the current crisis of neoliberalism, shows that despite having apparently less space for dissent from the global rule, international

organizations do not exert uncontested power and thus the dominance of a particular actor or paradigm *vis-à-vis* other contending actors or ideas has not been reinforced by their coercive position as lenders. The current trends in Latin American political economy show not only that neoliberalism is not in fact inexorable but more importantly that promoting governance for the IFIs has become a pressing dilemma. How the IFIs' staff resolve the struggle over meaning and practices in the promo tion of governance reforms is inherently linked to their capacity to avoid what Rodrik (2008: 4) calls the 'best-practice trap'. That is, either they promote governance-related programmes on the basis of preconceived ideas of what constitutes good policies and good reforms, or they engage with local experts to compromise and amalgamate positions utilizing joint expertise in the framing of policy reforms and their implementation. These patterns are associated with the extent to which IFI staff either acknowledge the complex and dynamic relationships between government agents and local actors, or seek a technical, a-political institutionalization of procedures and norms in which the state is narrowly defined in terms of functionality, brushing aside the socio-political complex in which it operates. These distinctions affect the way local interests and externally driven policy ideas interact and influence the prospects of policy change in developing countries.

Conveyors and brokers of funds, knowledge and policies

The empirical analysis of policy processes involving judicial reform and anti-corruption programmes in Argentina (Chapters 4 and 5) proves that in studying the role of the IFIs in the promotion of governance-related norms it is important to consider that their leverage in a country rests not only on the volume of its portfolio or its transfer of funds, but also on its capacity to engage with local actors to amalgamate and compromise positions. Similarly, the analysis of the 2001 crisis in Argentina, and particularly the crisis resolution (Chapter 6) as well as the current regional political economic dynamics (Chapter 7), confirms that coercive power and the perception of imposition on policy choice provoked contestation among local actors widening the gap between externally driven proposals and local politics.

The policy dynamics in force in Latin America since the 1990s test the micro-relations of power and the conditions under which the IFIs have had more or less influence in governance models. The financial weight and ideological influence of IFIs in development economics and development assistance confers a unique capacity to combine knowledge with financial strategies to pursue policy reform on the ground. Yet 'knowledge transferred' does not necessarily translate into 'paradigms a-critically taken'. The contrasting experience of the World Bank in judicial and anti-corruption reform as well as that of the multilateral banks and the IMF in crisis resolution is evidence of how power relations and policy change are more viable when the IFIs engage with local actors, 'brokering' policy ideas and compromising with local proposals.

The role of the multilateral institutions as 'broker' should not be related to 'neutral' intervention, or power related simply to 'norm-building' (Payne 2001: 39). Rather, 'norm-broker' is here associated with the idea that the IFIs can engage with local experts for the amalgamation and recognition of knowledge(s) in the form of contesting ideas and policy positions, empowering certain actors who can carry through a project. There is an instrumental purpose in engaging with local experts that is related to the capacity to generate a broader consensus to ensure that the norms and institutional practices supported by external actors are not only taken up by governments but also implemented on the ground. While persuasion and transfer of normative ideas have been strongly emphasized in some accounts as important attributes in explaining how knowledge and policy paradigms translate into practice (Keck and Sikkink 1998; Barnett and Finnemore 1999), closer examination here indicates that persuasion and transfer by themselves do not make the difference. The implementation of ideas into institutions and policies is the consequence of effective compromise between the policy frameworks supported by the IFIs and those supported by the local actors. That is, integrating local experts in both the framing of the problem and the solution is central to effective implementation of policies on the ground.

In the cases of governance reforms analysed in this book, a top-down model of power imposition, specifically by the IMF in the aftermath of the 2001 crisis in Argentina, led not only to a loss of legitimacy but in turn to the disempowerment of the institution. This experience was in contrast to that of the World Bank and the IDB, which made efforts to adapt their interests and practices to the Argentine political economic reality, articulating local and external expertise for the design and implementation of policy change in the aftermath of the crisis.

However, the contrasting experience of the World Bank in its approach to and involvement in the judicial reform and anti-corruption policies in Argentina and the divergent modalities of involvement of the IFIs in the reconstruction of post-crisis governance illustrate the claim that IFIs are not uniform institutions. The flexibility experienced by the multilateral development banks in these cases, compared to the IMF, although pragmatic, related to the way the IFIs' staff resolved the technical versus political dilemma in advancing sensitive reforms. The a-political mandate that prevents the IFIs from interfering in the domestic politics of borrowing countries and a prevailing technocratic culture has led some task managers to 'seek to reduce risk in loan approval' and thus to promote consensus among policy-makers, rather than to broader exchanges with local experts, especially if these support contesting 'political' proposals.

Reflecting on such tensions and contradictions, this study claims that the role of the IFIs in advancing governance reforms has evolved into a two-pronged dynamic: in some circumstances, as in the case of the role of the World Bank in judicial reform and of the IMF in crisis management, IFIs' staff approached reform as a process of *transfer* of blueprints and 'best practices', negotiating funded projects with the government but neglecting local experts and their expertise (see Chapters 4 and 6). In other circumstances, as in the case of the role of the World Bank in anti-corruption, IFIs' staff engaged with local expertise for the framing of the problem and the implementation of the solution (Chapter 5). In the first case the World Bank's Legal Unit and the IMF mission played an important role in disseminating knowledge, yet in practice transfer of knowledge and funds proved insufficient to assure success in policy implementation. In the second case, in contrast, development assistance involved a process in which the World Bank's Poverty Reduction and Economic Management (PREM) unit acted as a *norm-broker*, integrating the World Bank's normative agenda with country-based knowledge for the design, negotiation and implementation of policies. The struggle over definition and implementation of governance programmes are the current challenge for the legitimacy and authority of the IFIs. Governance can be predicated as the institutional arrangements needed to minimize transaction costs or as an end to improve responsive and inclusive democracies. This scenario, as analysed in Chapter 7, presents a dilemma to the IFIs.

Ultimately, although conditional funds and authoritative knowledge can be important factors in explaining the power of external influence to dictate certain reforms for inclusion in a government's agenda, this does not explain the extent to which those reforms are implemented and materialized in policy change. International financial institutions can transfer ideas that legitimize certain policy preferences and the funds that can make them happen, but the ways and extent to which policy change occurs depends on pro-reform engagement with local actors in the materialization of ideas and interests on the ground.

The core argument

The remainder of the book offers a detailed empirical and theoretical discussion of the processes and politics of achieving governance in developing countries. Chapter 2 opens with a discussion of power in international politics organized around a number of key debates within the field of International Relations (IR) and IPE. The chapter brings to bear theories that help to understand power and modalities of influence involving the IFIs and local actors in developing countries. It thus attempts to bridge, as little other research has done, theories of critical IPE and actor-oriented models of policy-making, in particular the literature of policy transfer and networks. In doing so it seeks to compensate for the limitations of earlier writing in public policy literature which overemphasized evidence and patterns in the adoption of public policies at the micro-level of government behaviour, assuming rational models in which ideas, policy models and institutions are transferred mimetically from one country to another. While this literature focused mainly on policy transfer in and between member countries of the Organisation for Economic Cooperation and Development (OECD), it tended to overlook not only the interplay between multilateral institutions and developing countries, but also the nature of power relations and sources of power between actors (James and Lodge 2003). It also seeks to compensate for some caveats in critical theory in IPE as it often focuses on macro-level structures to explain developments in the global political economy brushing aside empirical questions on policy processes, dynamics of social relations and channels of interactions between actors, and their material and non-material resources (Phillips 2005). The analytical framework proposed here helps to explain the empirical patterns in spaces of cooperation and contestation in which interests, incentives, material and ideological capabilities affect policy outcomes. It also puts forward definition of 'broker', as opposed to mere 'conveyor' of funds and paradigms, to denote the ability of international organizations to 'craft consensus' engaging with local actors in *pro-reform networks* in order to carry through politically sensitive projects. The concepts of IFIs as brokers and conveyors of money and ideas depict the 'technical versus political' tension that they face in advancing governance reforms.

To understand these policy processes, power relations and tensions in grounding governance in developing countries, Chapter 3 takes us into the contextual boundaries of Argentina's political economy since the 1990s. The choice of Argentina as a leading case is not unintentional. Argentina is a middle-income country with a strong base of local experts, policy think-tanks, consultancy, academic and pressure groups involved in policy proposals – often prior to the arrival of the IFIs' mission in the country. In this context, the dynamics between funds, knowledge and policy outcomes varied as the IFIs act with or without local experts and their expertise. The chapter thus presents the grounds to explore micro-relations and the types of engagement of local and international actors in the making and implementation of politically sensitive governance reforms. This analysis helps us to understand the ways and extent to which 'good' governance can be an area of contestation and at the same time can become an area of political engagement between local actors and the IFIs. This is also particularly relevant to understand the political dynamics and the changing relationships of the IFIs and local actors in the definition and implementation of governance reforms in the aftermath of a generalized crisis of neoliberal governance, analysed later in the book.

Chapter 4 presents the first case study, which analyses power relations and policy change in the case of judicial reform in Argentina. The World Bank's involvement in judicial reform is paradigmatic in the IFIs' thrust to embed specific types of state institutions following a model in which the promotion of domestic regimes is expected to be the consequence of imported models of governance. This chapter explores how the World Bank's Legal Department tended to reduce the goal of judicial reform to a logic of loan approval, ensuring the government's agreement rather than seeking a broader consensus with local experts who had already been pushing for reforms in the sector. In this context, the chapter discusses the implications of the World Bank as 'conveyor' of funds and policy ideas, and suggests that the failure to recognize local expertise (contestation) and networking efforts with local actors inhibited the implementation process and created a situation in which the Bank lost legitimacy, autonomy and influence in the area of judicial reform. The chapter concludes that adverse power relations led the World Bank to compete rather than cooperate with local actors, failing to materialize the approval of the project into effective institutional reform. Ultimately, this context-specific analysis shows that governance-related reforms are less likely to be successfully implemented when the IFIs are reluctant or fail to engage in pro-reform networks with local actors.

A contrasting experience is presented in Chapter 5, which analyses the involvement of the World Bank in anti-corruption policies in Argentina. This chapter looks at the World Bank's Public Sector Group and World Bank Institute (WBI) 'brokering' global and local projects of governance. It concentrates on two anti-corruption initiatives supported by the World Bank in Argentina, the Anti-Corruption Office and the Crystal Government Initiative. The chapter opens with a description of the problem of corruption in Argentina and analyses actors, approaches, incentives and local initiatives to curb corruption. In particular, it focuses on the local experts and organizations that form a national 'epistemic community' that not only motivated the anti-corruption agenda in the country, but also set a theoretical precedent for a new way of making policy. It then explores the engagement of the World Bank in networking activities with local actors to advance anti-corruption on the ground. This chapter proves empirically that the power of the World Bank to advance governance norms is explained by the capacity of external actors to combine funds and networking activities to gain the consent of local actors – beyond the government – to implement policy change effectively.

Extending the discussion of power relations and governance reforms in the context of crisis of neoliberalism, Chapter 6 focuses on Argentina's post-crisis resolution. In December 2001 the crisis confirmed the comprehensive failure of neoliberalism to deliver stable and equitable growth. The rejection of neoliberalism in Argentina epitomized a general loss of faith in neoliberal politics and economics across the region that, among other consequences, led to a change in the relationship between the countries and the IFIs. The chapter looks at Argentina's attempt to reconstruct governance and the involvement of the World Bank, the IDB and the IMF in the process. Three central questions developed in this chapter bring to the analysis a more general outlook: has governance become more political than technical? To what extent can the IFIs affect models of the state and development in a context in which political and economic crisis calls for a new beginning in terms of policy-making and legitimacy? To what extent has the trend away from neoliberalism transformed power relationships between donor and recipient countries? In response to these questions and complementing previous analysis, the chapter analyses how the post-crisis political economy changed the relationship between the country and the IFIs as it facilitated a re-balancing of power in favour of sovereign decision-making, and how power relations were shaped in the reconstruction of post-crisis governance. The analysis of Argentina's governance reforms suggests that externally conceived paradigms are limited in terms of acceptance, legitimacy and success, particularly in vibrant and politically informed polities. Local actors constitute a source of power that can enhance or limit the prospects of policy change. The crisis in Argentina in 2001 demonstrated that this is even more the case if formal democracy encourages a logic of exclusion that is reinforced by top-down forms of intervention on the part of the IFIs. This is also the case when what is technical for the IFIs becomes a political matter for the local civil society.

Taking from these lessons, Chapter 7 analyses, from a broader and comparative perspective, the challenges for the IFIs in a context in which the current neoliberal model became discredited and eroded in Latin America. The regional political scenario is now very different from that of the 1990s and there is a range of elected incumbents who are not only critical of neoliberalism but willing to push for the adoption of alternative models of governance, founded on the rejection and criticism of neoliberal adjustment and externally imposed stabilization. This has been the case with Chavez in Venezuela, Kirchner in Argentina, Vasquez in Uruguay, Morales in Bolivia, Lula in Brazil, and more recently, Correa in Ecuador and Ortega in Nicaragua. The chapter thus analyses how the emergence of new financial and epistemological schemes affected the role of the multilateral financial institutions. It considers the general argument about the contextual character of power relations and the importance of the political reality of developing countries. It thus extends the analysis moving away from Argentina to a more general review of economic ideas, power relations and policy change in Latin America as a whole.

The analysis of specific cases of governance reforms before and after the crisis in Argentina, as well as the broader examination of the current political economic problem in Latin America, shows that in the promotion of politically sensitive reforms IFIs face a dilemma: either they promote governance-related programmes on the basis of preconceived ideas of what constitutes good policies and good reforms, or they engage with local experts to compromise and amalgamate positions, utilizing joint expertise in the framing of policy reforms and their implementation. These patterns are associated with the extent to which the IFIs acknowledge the complex and dynamic relationships in local politics or simply seek a technical, a-political institutionalization of norms in which the state is expected to act as a transmission mechanism for externally conceived paradigms. Based on these findings issues of power, compliance, legitimacy and policy change are then discussed within the broader context of the contemporary shift in Latin America towards a re-evaluation of the role of the state and civil society *vis-à-vis* external actors in the definition of development agendas.

In the final chapter, Chapter 8, the main arguments are summarized and some crucial questions are placed to further the discussion of what 'power' currently means in the relationship between the IFIs and the developing countries. The crisis of neoliberalism has opened the way for the generation of alternative political and economic projects, at least in Latin America, that are challenging 'Washington Consensus strategies' consciously rejecting the one-size-fits-all model of development that the Consensus was fundamentally built on. The emergent nationalism in many developing countries, it is argued, is a test for the limits of externally led models of the state and development. This does not mean that governments are seeking to move away from global integration. But it does suggest that they are searching for more strategic ways of promoting national interests. The ways the IFIs involve in this process are the essence of this book.

2
Brokers and Conveyors of Governance

A notable characteristic of development theory and practice during recent decades has been that of reinvention in response to earlier failures. Crafting and diffusing changing visions of development has been one of the tasks of international institutions such as the World Bank, the regional development banks and the IMF. The most persuasive addition to the current discourse on development is 'good governance', largely founded on the recognition that strong and accountable institutions grounded in a sound market economy are fundamental to equitable development. Good governance is now central to academic and policy debates concerning the relationship between state, markets and civil society. There is an excess of material focusing on the ways in which local governance institutions are changing combined with those analysing the global forces behind these changes. From the perspective of IFIs, good governance is presented as a technical project to discipline the role of the state in developing economies. In the World Bank's own definition, governance represents the process by which authority is exercised in the management of a country's economic and social resources for development, and the capacity of governments to design, formulate and implement policies and discharge functions (Boeninger 1992: 3). While the importance of the political dimension is recognized in the governance discourse of the World Bank, and in fact of most multilateral agencies, in practice, advancing governance goals have often been restricted to the economic boundaries of their mandates. In fact, the neoliberal understanding of the role of the state attempts to correct the 'political' bias in economic intervention. Good governance, therefore, becomes a synonym for solid, responsible development management in the direction of social relations and efficient markets, especially in avoiding misallocation of resources and corruption in politics and administration.

While policy-makers and academics agree that good governance is important for development, there is less agreement on how good governance reforms, as promoted by the IFIs, have impacted on democratic governance in developing countries. Joseph Stiglitz, former Chief Economist of the World Bank, for instance, has acknowledged the disastrous effects of advancing technical understandings of governance on developing countries. While good governance is associated with a normative of participation, ownership and transparency, reforms promoted under this umbrella have in fact been highly contradictory – at times rather anti-democratic. Even so, as recent developments in the political economy of emerging countries demonstrate, development is essentially political – in particular, *governance for development* (Boeninger 1992). As a development project, governance reforms involved designing and modifying institutional arrangements that are entrenched in the socio-political fabric of any society and thus require a great deal of legitimacy and local knowledge. The *politics* of governance thus means that advancing such reforms involves more than technical definitions and best practices. The ways IFIs deal with this aspect requires closer inspection.

To analyse the inherent contradictions between technical and political approaches to development, and between general 'one-size-fits-all remedies' and the complexities of context, politics and change, this chapter considers existing discussions on power, compliance and policy change in international politics within the field of IR and IPE. It elaborates a framework that combines theories of critical IPE and actor-oriented models of policy-making, in particular the literature of policy transfer and networks in an attempt to bridge macro-level explanations of power in the global economy and conceptual models of policy-making focusing on empirical questions on the dynamics of power relations involving external and local actors, resources and policy outcomes. In agreement with the critical analysis in IPE, this study suggests that power emerges out of the ensemble of relations and configurations of networks of actors within a political and economic context and concomitant ideologies. As such policy change should be analysed as multiple spaces of contestation in which competing interests, incentives, material and ideological capabilities affect policy outcomes. Yet, spaces of contestation can also become areas of policy engagement and even platforms for the local actors to dispute the global rule. This perspective thus directs the attention to the centrality of organizations and politics in any analysis of social processes and change. The empirical analysis of the World Bank's involvement in governance reforms in Argentina and more broadly of the policy processes currently taking place in Latin America also suggests that designing appropriate policies and institutions for development is entrenched in the social fabric of any society and thus requires local knowledge and legitimacy. In other words, the dominance of neoliberal paradigm may be unquestionable. However, it would be analytically misguided to overemphasize the material and ideological capabilities of the IFIs in shaping the course of policy change; particularly in middle-income countries where financial resources are not reduced to the multilateral donors and, equally important, there is a vibrant and politically influential local network of experts informing policy-making. In this scenario, as this study suggests, the IFIs are almost compelled to avoid what Rodrik (2008: 4) calls the 'good practices trap' and engage with the local conveyors of knowledge and policy ideas. This is a tall call for the IFIs and one that has not been evenly internalized among the staff in the organizations. As a result, IFI's quandary is how to avoid acting as mere 'conveyors of funds and knowledge' – in a top-down manner – and become 'brokers' by engaging in pro-reform networks with local actors for the definition of both the problem and the solution in the promotion of governance in developing countries.

The framework provided in this chapter is critical for an analysis of the micro-relations of power and the conditions under which the IFIs have had more or less influence in promoting governance models in developing countries. The inherent tension between the economic and the political dimension of good governance has led to the most contentious dynamics between local actors and the international development agencies. This chapter thus introduces a way of understanding how contending ideas and power relations rule the global political economy recognizing the intrinsic struggle between legitimate and effective governance.

Issues of power in the international political economy

Although the question of power is a central concern in most theoretical approaches, how power is constituted is a major cause of contention in the literature of IR and IPE (Wendt 1999: 96–97). The dynamics of power and rule setting in the IPE have been largely explained by the capacity of the IMF and the World Bank to lead the process of globalization in developing countries. They have even been referred to as 'globalizers' (Woods

2006). By extension, the general thrust of mainstream analyses of global relations involving international institutions and developing countries has been simply in terms of how global rules impacted on the choices of policy-making of developing countries (Phillips 2005: 33). Many studies have documented the influence of the major industrial states, especially the US, and more recently of northern NGOs, on directives and agendas of the IFIs (Payer 1982; Wade 1996, 2002). The main channels through which these actors exert their influence on the IFIs' rules and commitments, according to this view, include budgetary control and asymmetry of power in their governance structure, reflected in voting weight, uneven representation and biased accountability (Woods 1999, 2003).

The power of major actors as compared to that of the borrowers shaping the behaviour of the international institutions cannot be denied; yet, neither overemphasized. Despite the prominent role of IFIs in the global political economy, the ability of IFIs to influence government policies is not always substantial (Kahler 1992: 100). Many empirical studies demonstrate that the power of IFIs' conditionality as a bargaining tool has been negligible and that in some cases external conditionality was even used by governments to overcome internal opposition and accelerate government agendas, or even to resist and renegotiate policies with the IFIs (Killick *et al.* 1998; Casaburi *et al.* 2000: 152; Woods 2006).

Explanations that focus exclusively on a single actor definition, namely US national interest, or the dominance of lender of last resort underestimate the genuine importance of the linkages between local and international actors. Of course, the critical economic and political vulnerabilities that most developing countries, especially Latin America, faced in the 1980s and 1990s are key to explain the narrowed margin of manoeuvre that these countries had *vis-à-vis* the IFIs. Credit rationing at the time determined a situation in which most developing countries ultimately had little choice but to accept the well-known IFIs-led Washington Consensus. The neoliberal prescriptions encrypted in the 'consensus' meant that most developing countries had to adjust to the global rule. Several factors explained how this consensus was adopted in developing countries in the face of severe financial crises, in particular Latin America in the 1980s. In addition to external pressure, though, economically liberal ideas made sense to the new generation of rulers that came into office in the 1980s and 1990s with the (re)introduction of democracy in most Latin American countries (Grugel *et al.* 2008). Initially and perhaps surprisingly, the reforms seemed to meet with less public opposition than might have been expected; certainly far less than the less severe experiences of conditionality in the late 1970s, partly as a result of a sense, in government at least, that there was indeed little choice. In this context, the Washington institutions 'brokered' deals that emphasized the potential benefits of the reforms with like-minded local power holders (Teichman 2001). These events have led many analysts to emphasize the dominance of neoliberal paradigm and the capabilities of the most powerful conveyors of neoliberal ideas. The IFIs were defined as core elements in the formation of a 'transnational managerial class' involving the governing elites in developing countries (Cox 1987; Robinson 1996).

However, these circumstances, like all power relations, are context-dependent and thus unfold in particular circumstances enforced by the confluence of factors – financial survival of developing countries being one of them, and the position of lender of last resort of the IFIs being another. Motivations and incentives of local elites to enter into negotiations and adopt the policy prescriptions of the multilateral lenders are often considered expected consequences. This is particularly relevant in the current changes in the international political economy, where there seems to be an unprecedented repositioning of the actors, material resources and ideas that are reshaping power relations and governance arrangements at different levels of authority. As explained in Chapters 6 and 7, the changing trend in the international capital markets over the last half decade meant that the borrowers are increasingly augmenting their margin of manoeuvre *vis-à-vis* the IFIs' conditions, walking away and making other financial arrangements in the direction of new intra-regional financial institutions. As such, while for most of the recent period the IMF and the World Bank have been large recipients of repayment flows from countries in the region, more recently credit from these institutions started to decrease drastically and new sources of finance have become available in the form of bilateral aid. This trend re-defines not only power relations between developing countries and the IFIs but also intra-regional relations. For instance, oil-rich countries like Venezuela provided around US$2.5 billion to help Argentina repay its IMF loan early, and is currently offering US$500 million to reduce the debt crunch in Ecuador and US$1.5 billion to stabilize the economic situation in Bolivia. Equally, terms of trade in the region have benefited by raising demands in new centres of global power such as China and India (Chandrasekhar and Ghosh 2008: 8; also Chapter 7 in this book). The financial and trade opportunities that the 'new globalizers' bring is unquestionably important to the emergence of power dynamics as they support and encourage new configurations of social relations, relations of production and a new space for an ideological redefinition.

This brings to question not only the relevance and effectiveness of the IFIs but more importantly the extent to which new actors in the developing world can become the platform for dissent from the global rule. In these circumstances, can actors that contest policy paradigms at the local level defy externally supported reform policies on the ground? What are the implications for the policy dynamics, relations and channels of interactions between the actors that convey and those that contest policy paradigms at the local level? In fact, these questions have been something of a challenge within the field of IPE, which, as Phillips has claimed, suffers from excessive 'structuralism', relegating politics and agency to a secondary place (Phillips 2005: 47). The fields of IR and IPE have, in general, given insufficient attention to the policy processes that underlie policy reforms and outcomes in developing countries, and hence the divide between the international and the national arenas (*ibid.*: 9). What is striking is that this is still the case in relation to the critical currents in IPE theories despite their call for more attention to the agency of social forces and their focus on the social and territorial power relations, and their nature, in the global political economy (*ibid.*: 267; Cammack 2007). The approach taken in this book, therefore, takes from the notion that paradigms are not transferred from one setting to another without giving rise to contesting and conflicting relations with the local actors – and thus that local actors are not passive recipients of external funds and knowledge. The study attempts to develop a broader and more inclusive understanding, bridging the gap between politics and economics and global and domestic politics, concentrating on the role of the IFIs in politically sensitive reforms in developing countries and the dynamics of social relations between external and local actors. It thus brings to the fore new questions related to the relationships of global institutions with domestic politics in borrowing countries. These relationships are analysed in an extensive way, including not only the borrowing governments but also the local experts and other civil society organizations, whose political and normative stands as well as their access to material resources can also enhance or hinder the power of international institutions like the World Bank and the IMF to advance reforms.

Ever since Robert Cox laid the foundations for the study of structure and agency in IPE, incorporating ideational and material analysis, studies of power in IR and IPE theories have queried how the movement of capital and ideas shape interest and possibly even the interlink between local and global actors. Critical theory in IPE then provides an integrative framework for analysing the production of meanings and ideas as the basis of power relations. In his early writing, for instance, Cox (1986, 1989, 1993) explains that social actors – individuals, civil organizations, states – develop social, political and economic relationships acting upon ideas. According to Cox, ideas are powerful resources that combined with material capabilities can lead to institutional change and thus to the materialization of forms of governance consistent with dominant models in the global political economy. Ideas, therefore, are key political drivers that can help secure the grounding of rules in domestic arenas. Ideational power, from this point of view, relies on the capacity of 'rule makers' to promote ideas that become accepted as 'common sense', or 'a generic mode of thought' (Gramsci 1971: 330). It is in this manner that ideas establish the wider frameworks of thought, 'which condition the way individuals and groups are able to understand their social situation, and the possibilities of social change' (Gill and Law 1988: 74). Following Cox's definition of ideational power, it is argued that 'collective images' within power relations endorse differing views on policy issues defining both the nature and the legitimacy of practices and policy outcomes (1986: 218). According to Cox, three categories of forces shape the structure of social relations and policy outcomes – ideas, material capabilities and institutions. Ideas are composed of 'intersubjective meanings' shared by almost everyone and 'collective images' of social order held by different groups of people. Institutions reflect the power relations and tend to encourage collective images consistent with these power relations. Crucially, Cox argues that disjuncture between these two forms of ideational phenomena is a major source of structural change (1986: 138). In the interactions between lenders and developing countries, it is expected that the World Bank and the IMF promote particular norms in defence of a particular project by championing development paradigms according to specific practices and ideologies – a case in point, for instance, being good governance (Gill 1995, 2000: 4–10). The articulation of the Washington Consensus as a development strategy has been as much a political-economic tool for the promotion of open markets as a way of understanding the world. This mode of thought is grounded in a view which presumes that the primary role of the state, and of other social and institutional arrangements in general, is to minimize transaction costs to improve the investment climate and thus promote growth. The notion of governance then becomes an (economic) means without paying attention to history, ideological traditions and politics that define the nature of social relations in a society.

Crises always allow the powerful to exploit the asymmetrical power over the weak, and on these bases was explained the power of the

IFIs–US Treasury to promote compliance of highly indebted countries with the global rule. Internationally promoted ideas are thus internalized as part of a hierarchically diffuse process by which the policy-making channels of national governments and big corporations act as 'transmission belts', adjusting the domestic economy to the requirements of the global economy and creating a world order that reflects the interests of the most powerful actors in the international political economy (Cox 1987: 254).

Despite the undeniable power of international lenders over overwhelmed developing countries, it is debatable that the extent to which the linkages between the former and the local actors in the poorest nations can simply be understood as elite-led consensus-crafting. The configuration of network of actors assumed by critical IPE tends to reduce the domestic player to a state-centric approach overlooking the complexities and contradictions of the state as a space for both contesting and negotiating politics and ideas among a wider range of actors beyond the government and some powerful business groups. Critical IPE deems decision-making processes and the construction of public policy to be a special relationship between the state and the international organizations (Cammack 2007). This being so, IPE theoretical standpoints still ignore key aspects linked to actors' relationships, the intersection between power, material resources and ideas. In other words, the excessive focus on macro-level structures to explain developments in the global political economy sidelines empirical questions about dynamics, relationships and channels of interaction between key actors and their material and non-material resources. Likewise, such economic determinism ignores processes of contestation and collaboration among domestic and international actors (Gale 1998; Egan 2001; Levy and Newell 2002; also Germain and Kenny 1998). Questions as to how the interplay between actors (and their ideas) affects policy outcomes or, more importantly, how do actors *construct* common grounds based on which effective change occurs reveal the shortcomings in critical IPE's central concern about social forces and policy change.

The main aim of this book is, therefore, to bring social forces – and their ideas and policy stances – to centre stage. Debates on global power relations need to take adequate account of politics and agency, and more importantly the arenas in which they are played out. The literature of IPE, in particular, needs to portray more broadly local dynamics of power and sources of local resistance in its analyses of global trends. Thus, appropriate attention must be paid to the politics of resistance and to the engagement of external actors in domestic politics, to the nature of power relations resulting from that engagement, and to the effects of these on policy outcomes on the ground. This is, indeed, an analytical dilemma for researchers as well as a practical one for the IFIs' political action. As was the case more than two decades ago, what is at stake now is how to analyse policy processes as multiple spaces of contestation in which competing interests, incentives, material and ideological capabilities affect policy outcomes. It is our intention to show that power is not simply something that one actor uses to constrain other actors, but a factor which constrains and enables possible courses of action for all actors (Hayward 2000: 3). What this means is that when looking at issues of power in relation to international organizations and local actors in developing countries, the nature of power is never abstract. Once engaged in social relations, actors may have the ability to shape the interests of others.

The financial weight and authority of multilateral institutions gives them a unique capacity to combine financial strategies with authoritative ideas in pursuit of politically sensitive reforms in developing countries (Bøas and McNeill 2004). By and large, developing countries' dependency on financial support has empowered the IFIs to advance policy change in areas, sometimes beyond their strict economic mandate. Since the late 1970s, when many developing countries were caught progressively in crises of deepening debt and financial insolvency, they struggled to balance sovereign decisions and externally driven economic conditions. IFIs, as lenders of last resort, had a significant role in shaping the policy agenda of the region by exercising their influence through the deployment of conditional policy-based finance and technical assistance. The financial crisis of the 1980s, in particular, created an unprecedented opportunity for the IFIs to assert the importance of a global liberal trading regime, underpinned by firm international legal rules and largely responsive to Washington's demands. True, most developing countries had little choice but to accept the new policy matrix. Yet, this is only part of the story behind the global domination of neoliberalism and the IFIs in the 1980s and 1990s. It will be analytically invalid to assume that power is constructed on a static context, as if both the nature of power and the environment in which it is exercised are indeed unsusceptible to change.

We therefore consider the international context as a structure which both restrains and enables actors to take action. Global developments change the policy preferences of some actors, increase the bargaining power of others and open up new institutional options for still others.

Indeed, a realization of the power of local actors in development, and most radically in crisis management, is at last beginning to filter into the IFIs themselves, where it is increasingly argued that engaging and networking with local actors can help to institutionalize effective policies (Levy and Kpundeh 2004). The need to develop more appropriate theoretical responses, which have more nuanced understandings of power and which are able to identify the fluidity of relationships in particular policy processes, thus becomes ever more urgent.

Grounding governance in local power politics

Analyses of relationships between IFIs and developing countries emphasizing 'who rules' and 'in whose interests' were particularly strong during the 1980s and 1990s. Given the credit-rationing situation at the time, it became apparent, to Latin American countries especially, that in order to stabilize their economies and to participate in the international economy after severe debt crises, the financial assistance and support of the IFIs was key. In this context, multilateral financial agencies enjoyed influential power as lenders of last resort, and were able to condition the disbursement of scarce funds upon the adoption of certain policies (Stallings 1992; Harris 2000).

Politically, these power relations were thought to reflect the 'new constitutionalism' of global capitalism in which states' choices tended to converge into neoliberal forms of state (Gill 2005). It was clear, for example, during the 1990s that independent political options for developing countries were severely reduced by the need to adhere to global economic norms. In the aftermath of debt crises this provided the IFIs with unparallel leverage over indebted countries in need to access external capital. On the receiving end of politics this meant subjecting choices to the external discipline, surrendering important margins of national sovereignty and subordinating national priorities to the interests of external forces (see, for instance, Weyland 1998). The overwhelming acceptance of the neoliberal rule in many developing countries, in effect, cannot be interpreted without understanding the legacy of failed political and economic systems of previous decades. Consequently, a top-down pattern of politically sensitive reforms, such as the privatization of services and deregulation of labour markets, was often implemented without seeking social consensus (Acuña and Tuozzo 2000). Ironically, this very situation undermined the legitimacy of the reform process and the long-term viability of new regulations and institutions created in the wake of those reforms. In the end, a decade of neoliberal reforms undermined both the economic stability and the incipient consolidation of democracy in many developing countries (Teichman 2004; Tuozzo 2004). Furthermore, the international financial crises, particularly the socio-economic impact of these crises, affecting economies from East Asia to South America from the late 1990s, became to be linked to the policy prescriptions promoted by the IFIs, especially capital liberalization and state dismantling.

Within the IFIs, most noticeably in the World Bank, this fostered a new discourse linking more encompassing policies of good governance with sustainable economic development. The World Bank was the key advocate of a new language of intervention, based on normative ideals of governance: partnership, transparency, participation, ownership and consultation with local actors. The WBI, for instance, codified a definition of good governance based on six normative dimensions: (1) voice and accountability, which includes civil liberties and political stability; (2) government effectiveness, which includes the quality of policy-making and public service delivery; (3) the lack of regulatory burden; (4) the rule of law, which includes protection of property rights; (5) independence of the judiciary; and (6) control of corruption (Kaufmann *et al.* 1999). In turn, this normative agenda has created within the multilateral institutions a recurring tension between the recognition of the need for political and social management of globalization and the object of dismantling the state, still deemed a significant obstacle to the realization of market-oriented globalization.

For the analysis of power relations between IFIs and developing countries this suggests two things. First, that the approach to the role of the state and civil society in development is not just a divisive issue within the IFIs but also a difficult matter to grasp within the research and policy community. Very little work has been done in terms of how governance programmes are actually implemented on the ground and how staff within the IFIs compromise corporate policy frameworks and local sources of knowledge in the framing and implementation of policies. Rather, most research tended towards the abstract and generic, arising from a focus on the IFIs as global institutions rather than as more complex grouping of political actors participating in concrete sovereign politics (Harrison 2004).

Second, these claims suggest that governance discourse, supported by a wide range of knowledge-related activities such as in-house research production and dissemination, allows the World Bank and other international institutions to articulate their interventions in a way which smoothes issues of power and local contestation. The discourse of governance may thus play down the material power of conditionality, which, although a critical instrument for shaping and triggering neoliberal reforms during the 1980s and 1990s, was ineffective in assuring policy change. As noted by Weyland, though dependence on external funding gives external donors extensive leverage over development policies, it does not give them control over the implementation of policy on the ground (2006: 15). Issues of implementation and compliance have been made even more complex in some cases by problems that were internal to newly democratic polities where decision-making processes entailed parliamentary deliberation and approval of policies (*ibid.*). In short, local politics and local actors are not passive receptors of policies designed and conveyed by the IFIs.

To be sure, there are a number of related issues that merit careful consideration in a discussion of modalities of influence and power relations involving the IFIs and developing countries. Power must be seen as a process rather than as an attribute of a single actor, and that process is both constrained and enabled by the context in which the actors to take action. Despite the relative power of the IFIs in shaping developing countries' behaviour, this factor on its own cannot account for the choice of policy-making and even more for the results of policy implementation. Unexpected outcomes are part of the power game that results from the IFIs' involvement in reforming the political economy of developing countries. This is particularly so since the IFIs expanded their mission to new norms of development related to 'good' governance. In other words, choices and decision-making are not external to developing countries, rather they are embedded in the particular situations within which they operate. Therefore, failure to pay sufficient attention to domestic contextual factors in shaping international and national politics hinders a comprehensive understanding of empirical patterns of politics and relations in the implementation of programmes. To claim that international organizations exert uncontested power and that policy outcomes are anticipated by those actors who dominate the international political economy is not only narrow, but in fact analytically misguided. The implementation of policy reforms is highly political as it involves complex dynamics between a diverse range of actors and a diverse range of resources. Moreover, imposition, or the perception of it, at the level of developing countries has worked against externally supported policy reforms, especially in democratic societies. In order to understand the nature of power flows in development assistance, it is important to disaggregate different patterns of IFI involvement in different contexts.

What this means is that an explanation of relations between IFIs and developing countries should not neglect the material grounding of global and local power relations. Local actors are not passive recipients of funds and policy proposals. They take, contest, modify or reject IFI proposals. Thus, different relationships unfold in different contexts of space and time in the process of negotiation between the IFIs and local actors. Moreover, often the attempt to 'transfer' policy paradigms and funds can even impede consensus building for reform and thereby weaken the capacity of the IFIs to advance their developmental and ideological agendas. Power relations are, in effect, dynamic not static and power becomes context-dependent, found in different configurations of social relations in which the IFIs are but one participating actor. As suggested by Barnett and Duvall, power should not simply be reduced to the coercive authority of international organizations over developing countries but viewed as working through the social relations of interaction (2005: 11–17). From this perspective, the ways in which the IFIs engage in developing countries can enhance or restrict their ability to respond to social and political changes and to adapt accordingly. This is particularly relevant in understanding different responses and policy outcomes and the role played by the IFIs in the Argentine post-crisis resolution.

Some crucial aspects of the policy process, therefore, need to be taken into consideration. For instance, why certain ideas are enforced by the IFIs and implemented on domestic arenas while others are rejected; the ways in which local actors are persuaded to follow certain policy ideas within a range of policy choices; and how policy outcomes are affected by the contexts in which policy ideas are adopted or contested. Moreover, what is perceived to be politically significant in one society might not resonate as strongly in another. These observations are central to the analysis of different patterns of intervention by the IFIs in developing countries, as well as to different outcomes in terms of power and compliance with external norms. Furthermore, recent crises show that despite having seemingly less room for dissent from the global rule, the dominance of a particular actor or paradigm *vis-à-vis* other contending actors or ideas has not been strengthened by the coercive position of the lender over the borrower, but rather by the capacity of the latter to integrate contesting impulses into a broader consensus for policy change. Social relationships, in this context, are 'chronically negotiated and renegotiated' on the basis of the positions of the actors that are in turn affected by historical circumstances and the context in which they interact. As a result, power 'is contingent upon the complex interactions and [ideologically mediated] interpretations of concretely situated historical agents' (Rupert 2005: 209).

This is not to deny the unquestionable influence of the IFIs in the policy-making of developing countries. Despite the continuing strength of such influence, in particular in cases where the interests of the domestic elite converge with those of the US and the IFIs, regional trends with regard to current development show that the dynamics of the global marketplace and the balance of global economic power are changing, and in the process the power of the IFIs and the established rules is increasingly being questioned. Moreover, if the IFIs' power hinges on their role as gatekeepers of funding, what happens to the power of the IFIs when developing countries can access credit independently from other sources without the need for gatekeepers to facilitate financial flows into their economies? Clearly, the answer to this question is that developing countries augment their space for autonomous decision-making and thus their power of contestation. In fact, home-grown ideas and policy paradigms find a more fertile ground to nurture policy-making the more independent of external funding this becomes. This simple answer has two immediate implications that have been less examined in the literature. One relates to the nature of power politics involving international organizations and developing countries as spaces of contestation and cooperation, and the other to the importance of context-dependent analysis in understanding different decision-making processes and political outcomes. For instance, in middle-income countries, where there is a highly politically mobilized civil society involved in the formulation of policies, the greater room for manoeuvre implies more contesting power on the part of local actors *vis-à-vis* externally driven paradigms. In contrast, in more international aid–dependent economies, policy ideas may be a much weaker contending element of power while the urgent need for funds may confer more power on the IFIs, as lenders dictating policies and compliance.

To explain the policy process through which the promotion of governance took place in Argentina, the tensions between political and technical understanding of institutional reform and the current dilemmas that the IFIs face in a changing political economy in the Latin American region, the remainder of this chapter elaborates an approach that combines – as little other research has done – theories of critical IPE, in this case Neo-Gramscian IPE (for instance, Cox 1986, 1987, 1989, 1993; Strange 1988, 1991; Gill 1995, 2000; Bieler and Morton 2001; Levy and Newell 2002; Bøas and McNeill 2004) and actor-oriented models of policy-making, in particular the literature of policy transfer and networks (Dolowitz and Marsh 1996, 2000; Dowding 1995, 2000; Evans and Davies 1999; Marsh and Smith 2000; Evans 2001; Stone 2001). The framework developed in this analysis seeks to compensate for the limitations of Neo-Gramscian theorists in IPE, so often focused on macro-level structures to explain developments in the global political economy, often neglecting empirical questions of dynamics, relationships and the channels of interaction among key actors and their material and non-material resources. As suggested in the following pages, policy change should be analysed in terms of policy processes, and policy processes as multiple spaces of contestation in which competing interests, incentives, material and ideological capabilities affect policy outcomes.

Equally, this study also attempts to compensate for the limitations of earlier writing in the public policy literature which overemphasized evidence and patterns in the adoption of public policies at the micro-level of government behaviour, assuming rational models in which ideas, policy models and institutions are transferred mimetically from one country to another. While this literature focused mainly on policy transfer in and between member countries of the OECD, it tended to overlook not only the interplay between multilateral institutions and developing countries, but also the nature of power relations and sources of power between actors (see James and Lodge 2003). Notwithstanding, models of transfer and networks have offered a straightforward framework that sheds light on processes and actors involved in policy change, enhancing the explanatory power of other perspectives on international and domestic policy-making. The combination of these strands of literature helps to contextualize conclusions about power dynamics and policy change in politically sensitive areas of reform in which external and local actors fluctuate between dynamics of tension and compromise.

Knowledge, funds and pro-reform networks

In order to legitimize new areas of involvement and policy-making within the IFIs, ideas on what constitutes good governance have been supported by research and the diffusion of knowledge which, in combination with funding, enhanced the reach and scope of IFIs' operations. Some scholars have claimed that research and knowledge management within the World Bank and the IMF became 'the visa required to cross funding's frontier' (Samoff 1992: 64; also Stone 2000; Momani 2007).

Mobilization of knowledge – in the form of ideas, research, analysis, normative understandings, policy and economic paradigms – has become a critical resource for the broadening consensus and legitimacy for new development issues. In addition to financial resources, knowledge-related activities help to create and reproduce consensual ideas over certain policy paradigms. But, as the analysis in this book suggests, knowledge production and diffusion involve policy processes in which contesting ideas shape the struggle over the implementation of paradigms. Policy ideas and knowledge-related activities are, in effect, considered as arenas for political engagement since local actors are not simply receptors of ideas and norms disseminated by the World Bank and the IMF.

The notion that knowledge creation, diffusion and implementation represent another source of power is central to the critical approaches in IPE to development assistance. From this perspective, it has been claimed that knowledge not only influences public debate, but also provides the ideological foundation for actors in pursuit of certain policy goals (Goldman 2005). Knowledge, together with financial resources, helps to construct the foundations of legitimacy for the involvement of the IFIs in certain reforms. More critically, it empowers – or disempowers – certain actors by supporting or legitimizing certain paradigms. Through the creation and support of certain policy ideas the IFIs 'frame' the ways in which major topics in development and development economics are conceptualized and packaged for policy implementation (Bøas and McNeill 2004). Knowledge is 'material for action' (Hentz 2004: 197). Furthermore, IFIs' financial weight and authority in development economics and development assistance confers unique capacity to combine knowledge and best practices with financial strategies in order to pursue policy reform in developing countries. How, then, does knowledge related to certain policy ideas percolate, or get into, the policy-making process? How does knowledge become materialized into policies and institutions? How do global paradigms and local ideas interact and affect policy outcomes?

As stated earlier, the analysis of ideas and knowledge as powerful factors in global politics has been widely covered in the field of IPE, but the contribution of such analyses suffers from the generalization and structural bias affecting IPE debates. Most critical contributions in IPE have not been accompanied by empirical cases that demonstrate the relative influence of different sources of power and power relations at a certain time and place. Moreover, some analyses in IPE tended to generalize knowledge as the embodiment of ideological representations

(Cox 1986; Gill 2000), creeds (Strange 1988: 123–127, 1991) or normative frameworks (Bøas and McNeill 2004: 213–214). This has been the
case in spite of arguments about the clash of rival ideas as the bases
of policy outcomes. So, how does the interplay between actors – and
'knowledges' – affect policy outcomes? More importantly, how do actors
construct *common grounds* based on which effective change occurs?

The empirical analysis offered in subsequent chapters shows that the
implementation of institutional reforms is a context-dependent process
and is highly political. Actors, political incentives and resources are critical factors shaping the path and depth of reform implementation. Thus,
borrowing Taylor's phrase, 'crafting consensus' with pro-reform local
actors is critical in ensuring that certain knowledge, in the form of policy ideas and development paradigms, is reproduced and reinforced on
the ground (Taylor 2004: 124). Rather than conveying funds and policy
paradigms, IFIs' officials need to develop a common ground 'by supplying not motivation but resources to *enable* the doers to do what they
were already self-motivated to do' (Ellerman 2001: 38, emphasis added).
In addressing these issues, this chapter puts forward three theoretical
arguments that structure the rest of the analysis. First, that the capacity
of the IFIs, in particular the World Bank, to produce and diffuse knowledge on what constitutes good economic policy (good governance) is
a powerful ontological instrument affecting the way people perceive
and think of economic development. Thus, production and diffusion of
knowledge has become a critical factor within the structure of power and
global scope of the IFIs, since it enhances their capacity to frame issues
and outline solutions. Second, that knowledge supports policy ideas
that are mutually reinforcing with financial capabilities. Yet 'knowledge
transferred' is not necessarily 'knowledge taken'. The implementation of
politically sensitive reforms in developing countries is intimately associated with the capacity of the IFIs to mobilize financial and knowledge
resources to articulate pro-reform networks with the local actors who
will steer these policies into the policy stream. Third, that the ability
of the IFIs to translate knowledge into instruments of policy reform
depends on their capacity to act as a 'broker', engaging with local actors
by compromising positions and developing common grounds for the
implementation of policies.

The choice of 'broker' in this study does not denote the 'neutral'
intervention of an impartial arbiter. Rather, 'broker' is here associated
with the idea that the IFIs may engage with local experts for the
amalgamation and compromise of knowledge(s) and policy positions,
empowering certain actors who can carry through a project. There is

an instrumental purpose in engaging with local experts: this is related to the ability to generate a broader consensus, ensuring that the norms and institutional practices supported by the IFIs are not only taken up by governments, but also implemented on the ground. While persuasion and transfer of normative ideas has been strongly emphasized by some accounts as important attributes in explaining how knowledge and policy paradigms translate into practice (for example, Finnemore 1996; Keck and Sikkink 1998; Barnett and Finnemore 1999), the instances of governance reform in Argentina suggest that persuasion and transfer by themselves do not make the difference. Surveillance and consensus cannot necessarily be taken as an expected consequence of the IFIs' knowledge agenda, but rather as the result of effective compromise between policy frameworks.

In response to some of the shortcomings identified in the literature of IPE, a key theoretical challenge in the development of this study is the inclusion of a critical understanding of knowledge as a powerful ideational resource without relegating it to a stand-alone or abstract explanatory factor. Knowledge represents a powerful resource in that it legitimizes normative frames around which development policy is oriented, and delegitimizes, at the same time, competing notions and policy approaches (Sending 2004: 59). Yet knowledge embodied in policy ideas is context-dependent and as such its significance can vary in the interplay between actors, incentives and contextual factors. The power of an international organization, from this perspective, is to be seen as a process, rather than as an attribute of a single actor.

To develop a research framework that addresses the matters discussed above we need to bridge critical theory in IPE and the micro-analysis of policy-making in developing countries. But, as we argued, overcoming the risk of generalization that somewhat restricts the scope of IPE power must be considered a relational concept. Likewise, to explore policy change, particularly in democratic societies, special attention needs to be given to accommodation and compromise amongst actors' interests, ideas and political agendas.

The framework developed in this chapter will help us to explore the extent to which policy ideas, both held by local actors and framed within the IFIs' development paradigm, do not exist in a political and ideological vacuum. Through the analysis of governance reforms in Argentina we show how ideas are taken up, contested or modified as they enter the political-economic and institutional circumstances in which actors interact. Likewise, local knowledge can argue against and thus challenge the authority and legitimacy of externally driven paradigms. This is even more the case as a country becomes less dependent on international funds to function. In a crisis context, such as that experienced in Argentina and other countries in the region in the late 1990s, new ideas emerged as part of a renewed game in the dynamics of national politics and as part of an ongoing process of governance reconstruction.

In addressing these issues, the concept of a policy network becomes an analytical device that helps to identify actors within the policy process as well as the properties that characterize relationships among the particular set of actors in specific issue areas. As a simple conceptual model, the notion of policy network serves as a 'corrective conceptual instrument', reminding us that policy processes are constructed by actors intentionally operating in a determined context, conveying different types of knowledge and policy ideas that substantiate the policy process and the different outcomes that emerge from it (Marsh and Smith 2000; Evans 2001).

Models of policy networks as developed within the literature of public policy are essentially descriptive, but their explanatory power rests on the fact that they address micro-relations amongst actors who convey a particular set of ideas. It concentrated on specific actors, sometimes portrayed as 'epistemic communities' (Haas 1992) or 'policy communities' (Stone 1996) involving specific policy areas. Essentially, policy network denotes a *relational* dynamic involving the interplay of different actors in their aim of achieving common ground for policy change. Yet it is important to draw attention, particularly for the understanding of the policy processes of governance reform in Argentina, to the point that the actors involved in networking may differ in interests and/or preferences as well as having incentives that may support or discourage the implementation of certain policies and norms. The importance of networking from this perspective is the emphasis on social relationships and ideas in shaping broader attitudes and common goals (see Marsh 1998; Evans 2001; McNeill 2004).

In the literature of Latin American political economy some scholars have developed the concept of 'policy transfer networks' as a sort of epistemic community that resembles the notion of 'transnational managerial class' developed in critical IPE analysis. Accordingly, policy transfer networks were explained in terms of technocratic experts, mostly trained economics graduates from US universities and even within the IFIs, who had extensive influence in the definition and implementation of neoliberal policies in countries like Chile, Argentina and Mexico (Teichman 2001). Such a group of experts were key actors in the diffusion of neoliberal ideas, including trade liberalization and state reform, into the policy stream (Sikkink 1991; Pastor and Wise 1998;

Domínguez 1997; Babb 2001). The analysis of policy transfer networks in the process of neoliberal reforms during the 1980s and 1990s in Latin America explained compliance and policy change as a process of globalization of economic expertise (Domínguez 1997; Teichman 2004). These conceptual, actor-led explanations for the emergence of neoliberal states in Latin America have been useful in depicting the actors and the ideas in play during the process of crisis resolution and policy change. Yet reform is explained as an expected consequence of a process of international diffusion of neoliberal ideas led, domestically, by technocrats that become important interlocutors for the external actors (Cox 1987: 254). Again, nothing is here discussed about spaces of contestation and the autonomy of local actors *vis-à-vis* international funding agencies. Ultimately, while structural analysis ignores the complex foundation of the political dynamics that develops on the ground, actor-oriented analysis in public policy brushes aside the complexities of policy-making when deferent ideas collide. Reacting to these caveats is thus in essence the task of this book.

Concurring with the public policy literature, this study suggests that the status and prestige of the members of a network and their superior professional training and expertise in regard to a particular problem 'is politically empowering and provides access to the political system' (Stone 1996: 88). Members of a network can create knowledge or act as gatekeepers of ideas that are diffused and applied to the policy stream and become institutionalized as regular patterns of social relations (Haas 1992: 27). The relevance of the network rests indeed on its capacity to mobilize policy ideas into a policy agenda and, more importantly, to influence the implementation of those ideas in certain policy areas. However, our analysis of governance reforms in Argentina and of the current political and economic trends in the region overrides some of the drawbacks identified above. First, the idea of a 'transfer' network pioneered in the literature of public policy implies a one-way process in which ideas flow uncontested from one source to another. Conceived this way, transfer assumes a voluntary or coercive process in which the ideas, policies and institutions within one political or social system are based upon the ideas, policies and institutions emanating from another political or social system which already has those programmes in operation.

Second, the descriptive term 'pro-reform' used in this study conceptualizes the meaning and the purpose of the concept in contrast to abstract definitions of networks as simply formal structure of elite-led organizations. The term 'pro-reform' suggests that the relationship between actors involved is tied not necessarily by reason of values and beliefs, but rather by the endorsement or promotion of particular policies or practices. Pro-reform networks are the manifestation of a group of actors, which in the case of Latin America's search for alternatives to neoliberal governance since the late 1990s involved social actors, academics and practitioners beyond the government, as well as, in cases, IFIs staff. These networks are emerging arrangements in pursuit of certain policies. From this perspective, networks are *ad hoc* phenomena set up at a specific time and with a specific intention. In countries where a politically vibrant civil society demands inclusive and responsive decision-making processes, local experts may engage in a pro-reform network with IFIs' officials for the development of a common understanding of a policy problem, its causes and its remedies. These networks may or may not share views and perspectives, but they may be willing to integrate or compromise on their positions moving towards a policy solution. In this context, pro-reform networks are often facilitated by 'brokers' who create or support policy networks bringing actors from diverse backgrounds together, even involving those who might have conflicting views of the world or contradictory interests (Sabatier 1993; Fernandez and Gould 1994). As a result, although they might not necessarily resolve conflicts of interest among different actors, pro-reform networks can work to institutionalize certain policy projects.

This said, rather than considering policy networks as acting as mere conveyor belts in the transfer of external agendas of development, the analyses in the subsequent chapters will refer to policy networks to explain complex dynamics in the knowledge–policy relation that are at the heart of policy negotiation between local and external actors. The reform networks are thus part and parcel of a process of amalgamation and compromise between different knowledge(s) and policy proposals. From the perspective of the IFIs, the inclusion of previously excluded local actors may be driven by new efforts to make the neoliberal projects of privatization, liberalization and deregulation truly dominant. Nevertheless, engaging with local actors in pro-reform networks also implies that the power and agency of local forces holding contesting ideas must be acknowledged. In some cases, local actors have managed not only to push their own agenda into the policy stream but also to transform the IFIs' agenda and modality of implementation. On occasions, this may even empower local actors to further their claims for more inclusive and responsive democratic governance.

The dilemmas for the IFIs in their engagement with these networks of local actors and their ideas are huge and often disappointing. In the empirical cases analysed in this book, the construction of governance models generated both challenges and resistance on the part of local actors, and thus 'good governance' as a political-economic project has been both contested and negotiated, for different reasons in different contexts, between local and external actors. In some cases the IFIs can lead reforms by acting as brokers, engaging and working on the basis of local proposals and ideas, or simply adopting a following 'business as usual' approach, seeking a limited consensus with key policy-makers and even by reproducing long-standing patterns of an elite democracy in developing countries. With this in mind, the following chapters concentrate on the policy dynamics in play in governance reforms, testing the micro-relations of power and the conditions under which the IFIs have had more or less influence in governance models.

A final note on brokers and conveyors of governance

The way in which the IFIs engage with local actors, as 'broker' or as mere conveyor of funds and ideas, is to a large extent defined by the way they perceive participation and ownership in policy definition and implementation. This perception is often shaped by different factors, often associated with the unequal power distribution in their governance structure which often secures that the main industrialized nations are more able to shape the mission and agendas of the IFIs than the borrowing countries. Another factor that affects the attitude of the staff towards formulation and implementation of policies in developing countries has been the thrust of the normative agenda and the 'corporate voice'. This corporate voice is well captured by the symbolic notion of the 'Knowledge Bank' that ultimately presented its staff with overriding paradigms that are often oblivious to the distinctiveness of local realities. Organizational structures and career path, as well as incentives on staff to disburse loans, are often identified as factors enhancing the tendency of the staff to take 'technical knowledge' as unquestionable truth and apply in one setting what worked in another (Wade 2007: 131).

In practice, two main patterns have distinguished how IFIs' staff pursue policy change on the ground: either they recognize the complexities of state–society politics as the motor of socio-economic reforms in developing countries, and therefore seek a more horizontal involvement, where local insights are part of the definition of the agenda; or they reproduce a more conservative style, vertical model of programme negotiation and implementation. The first dynamic characterizes the idea of engagement as 'broker', where global and local ideas amalgamate and compromise in reaching common ground. The second dynamic, in contrast, typifies engagement as 'conveyor' of financial resources and ideas on what constitute 'right policies', disregarding local expertise. These patterns distinguish IFIs amongst their own community as well as units within individual IFIs. Of course, in the face of highly mobilized political scenarios, the staff of an international institution may act pragmatically as a broker in an attempt to arrive at common ground for policy reform. From this perspective, in respect of their intervention, the engagement of IFIs' staff with local experts has a great deal of discretionary capacity that sometimes attempts against the 'best-practices trap' since they are not bound by Operational Directives for guidance on how to coordinate local knowledge and global (codified) knowledge. This is even the case regardless of new policies concerning the participation of local civil society that, in the case of the World Bank especially, resonate in the rhetoric of the IFIs since the mid-1990s (see World Bank 1996a). Participation remains simply as recommendations for staff acting in developing countries. Moreover, in the case of the World Bank, despite its corporate efforts to establish a 'Knowledge Bank', sharing knowledge within and outside is not a criterion for task managers' promotion or internal evaluation. As explored in the subsequent chapters, despite the development of a new corporate profile within the World Bank, which was in fact followed suit to different extents by other IFIs, innovation and adaptation has been very uneven across the institution, and staff predisposition to engage in new practices depends very much on the theoretical and practical inclinations of directors and managers on the ground. Politically contentious ideas for policy reform as well as innovative practices involving participation and institutionalization of local knowledge are linked to the personal background, criteria and orientation of task managers and the country team as well as to the political-economic context of the country in question.

The second factor affecting IFIs' staff engagement with local actors on the ground is related to the dilemma of how to advance governance reforms without contradicting their binding a-political mandate. In advancing judicial reform in Argentina, for example, the World Bank staff faced the difficult problem of either securing the adoption of loans by the government, overlooking locally based knowledge, or responding to local expertise by acknowledging its views. Judicial reform in this case was a highly politicized process and as such the political stance implicit in a reform programme supported by local actors gave rise to some unease on the part of the World Bank. Local actors' ideas conflicted with government incentives in the sector. In this case, the avowedly political nature of the local ideological stance conflicted with the Bank's a-political, technical understanding of reforms, and therefore with its definition and priorities in relation to governance.

The dynamics of the global marketplace and the balance of global economic power are changing, and in the process the power of the IFIs and the established rules are increasingly being questioned. The analysis presented here suggests that in the current political economy of developing countries, separating the notion of governance from its political connotation is not simply contradictory but can even be detrimental to democratic policy change. How local and external actors understand (good) governance can lead to conflictive or cooperative relationships. Certainly the foundations for sustainable democratic governance in developing countries will require the IFIs to avoid dealing with institutional arrangements as a technical goal to minimize transaction costs in their immediately relevant domain. Advancing governance requires paying broader attention to the empirical regularities that link specific institutional rules with the social and political realities in developing countries.

3
Complexities of Governance in Argentina's Political Economy

The IFIs have enjoyed almost uncontested power for over two decades since the early 1980s. Several factors contributed to that, in particular the financial needs of highly indebted countries. In a context in which most developing countries were struggling for financial survival, the power of the lender of last resort shaped the policy options at hand for borrowing governments. In many countries, especially in Latin America, the influence of the IFIs was exerted through technocratic networks involving officials of the IFIs, particularly the IMF, the World Bank and the IDB, and high-level government officials in developing countries. Through regular interaction over time these networks became the carriers of neoliberal ideas and thus shaped reform in a neoliberal direction.

In Latin America, crisis responses in the 1980s were shaped by the cautious transitions to democracy alongside simultaneous transitions to market-based economies. Despite democratization, state elites remained largely ring-fenced from civil pressures securing a swift adjustment to the global rule. However, democracy's disappointments have delegitimized politics and politicians and led to governance fatigue and a loss of faith in elite-led policy-making. Consequently, current pressures for alternatives to the neoliberal governance, everywhere in Latin America, is as much about the search to revitalize democracy and re-embed the democratic state socially as it is about new models of development and growth (Grugel 2009). These arguments are particularly relevant for a country like Argentina, where a strong base of local experts and civil actors have been politically active and have tried to mediate the relationships between the government and the IFIs, from the policy definition stages to negotiation and implementation on the ground.

This chapter thus concentrates on the political-economic context that underpinned the rise and fall of neoliberalism in Argentina in the 1990s, analysing actors, incentives and the competing ideas that confronted local actors and the IFIs during the neoliberal decade and in the aftermath. Despite there being seemingly less room for dissent from 'the global rule' during the 1990s in the heyday of the Washington Consensus, by the end of the decade neoliberal reforms began to be seriously questioned. Poor economic results and a top-down way of advancing policy reform by the government and by the IFIs created the conditions that led, in December 2001, to a massive economic, political and institutional crisis. The crisis not only confirmed the failure of neoliberalism to deliver stable and equitable growth, but more broadly a generalized rejection of the neoliberal model of governance. While a decade of neoliberalism had subordinated important decisions about the national economy to the interests of external forces the Argentine crisis opened a new space for re-defining priorities and re-balancing power in favour of sovereign decision-making. The chapter concentrates on the contextual factors that led to changing relationships between the IFIs and the Argentine actors in the search for stable governance.

The analysis follows in four sections. The first section analyses the years of neoliberal rule in Argentina. It explores the political, economic and institutional transformation during the ten years of Menem's administration (1989–1999) and the subsequent shorter term of De la Rúa until his resignation in the wake of the 2001 crisis. The analysis focuses on the twin pillars of neoliberal governance and the weakening of the rule of law that allowed discretionary government interventions to secure unpopular reforms and the leniency of the IFIs supporting those reforms. The second section explores the nature and depth of the crisis at the end of the decade and its culmination in December 2001. It is argued that this was a crisis of governance and thus we explore the main dilemmas for post-crisis governance reconstruction. The third section describes the characteristics of local actors involved in policy formulation for governance reforms. These actors were key players in the battle for alternative ways of approaching governance, contesting the technical definition that drove the IFIs' agendas. The chapter concludes with a brief discussion of the patterns to be analysed in depth in the next three chapters concerning the dilemmas of the IFIs in their promotion of governance in developing countries.

Neoliberal governance in Argentina

The fluctuating political economy of Argentina from 1980s onwards shaped the fluctuating relationships of the country with IFIs such as the World Bank, the IMF and the IDB. Argentina's growth patterns were repeatedly followed by deep depressions undermining the political, social and economic fabric of the nation by 2001.

The spread of liberal economic ideas into Latin America after the early 1980s marked the shift to a greater dependence on markets and a subsequent retreat of the state from the economic and social life. This trend was embraced by most of the countries that were on the edge of financial survival after severe debt crisis (Fitzgerald and Thorp 2005: 12). This was also a turning point for previous political and economic nationalistic projects developed throughout the mid-1940s to the late 1960s. The introduction of market reforms that took place alongside democratization and the two transitions gradually came to be seen as reinforcing a US- and IFIs-led global tendency. In fact, the 1980s represented a rising moment for the hegemony of these actors as 'rule-makers', globally and within Latin America (Grugel *et al.* 2008).

The end of import-substituting industrialization with its strong focus on the domestic market and a 'developmental state' proved economically erratic and politically unsustainable. By the 1970s one economy after the other showed the complexity of the protectionist tariffs and the loss of industrial competitiveness that restricted market expansion domestically and internationally. Latin America's alternative approach was in disgrace and social uprising soon succumbed to authoritarian governments. The severity of political repression was paradoxically contrasted with a new embrace in economic liberalization. However, the desertion of import substitution in favour of liberalism in most countries in the region was erratically managed and at the cost of uncontrollable external debt. In turn, the debt crisis and the shameful consequences of almost a decade of military dictatorships left Latin American governments in a weak bargaining position and thus prompted them to discard the idea that Latin America could offer an alternative development paradigm.

The debt crisis in the 1980s meant that the IMF and other multilateral donors were brought in the hope that their stabilization programmes would quickly restore some sort of coherence. Given credit rationing at the time, it became apparent, to Latin American countries especially, that in order to stabilize their economies and to participate in the international economy after severe debt crises, the financial assistance and support of the IFIs was key. In this context, multilateral financial agencies enjoyed influential power as lenders of last resort, being able to condition the disbursement of scarce funds upon the adoption of certain policies (Stallings 1992). From the mid-1980s the transformation of the state apparatus in many developing countries involved a disciplined compliance with policies and conditionalities set by the IMF, the World Bank and foreign creditors. The adjustment programmes that followed engineered a new orthodoxy around the privatization of public enterprises and export promotion, echoing the new precepts of the 'Washington Consensus' (Williamson 1990). The Consensus embraced in turn a political-economic model of governance that initially considered the state as the main problem besetting the 'naturally efficient' movement of the economy, and thus sought a new path from state-led development projects to open economies. Neoliberal governance was a new political-economic project that re-balanced the relationship between state, markets and society in Latin America. As a consequence, these changes severely weakened the actors at the core of the old national project – mainly the organized labour, domestic business, public sector employment and above all the role of the state as the motor of the economy (Oxhorn 1998). Furthermore, these developments contributed to a continuous dismantling of society's capacity to organize autonomously and to articulate contestation (Oxhorn and Ducatenzeiler 1998).

In the early 1980s, Argentina faced serious macroeconomic instability and an acute fiscal deficit, aggravated by a seemingly unsustainable debt problem that reached almost 100 per cent of GDP in 1989 (World Bank 2000b: ii). After eight years of military rule between 1976 and 1983, the challenge for the new democracy led by President Raul Alfonsín (1983–1989) of the Union Cívica Radical Party (UCR) was to strengthen the rule of law and to restore the economy to the international market. At the same time, the administration had to enter into negotiations with external creditors for a workable restructuring of the foreign debt, contracted largely during the period of military rule. Alfonsín's government had to respond politically and economically. From the political point of view, the government focused on law reform as a safeguard for human rights. On the economic front, Alfonsín initiated limited structural reforms in an attempt to end hyperinflation (Acuña 1995).

Despite some radical reforms, Alfonsín's administration could not, however, win the necessary support from key economic players to carry out the process of transformation, in particular from labour unions closely identified with the opposition party's political platform – the

Partido Justicialista, known as the Peronist Party – or from the private sector and business groups that questioned the heterodox foundations of the economic plan (Acuña and Smith 1994). Increasingly, Alfonsín's presidency became politically debilitated as poor outcomes and increasing opposition undermined political-economic stability. In turn, the fragility of the domestic scenario was aggravated by the loss of external support (Damill and Frenkel 1993: 62). Assistance from the IFIs to Argentina was irregular and subject to the government's reform commitments during that period. In the end, after arduous negotiations with the IFIs, the course of the Argentine political economy discouraged the IMF and the World Bank from assisting Alfonsín's final stabilization effort. With the emergence of a new hyperinflation crisis and erratic attempts to rally the socio-political support to combat it, the economic and political bases of Alfonsín's government succumbed, and the president was forced to resign five months before the end of his government's mandate (Bambaci *et al.* 2002: 80).

A pragmatic arrangement with the Peronist candidate consolidated the power of Carlos Menem, who took office as the new president of Argentina on 8 July 1989. The political and economic context in which Menem took office led to further consolidation of a strong presidential style of governance. While the Peronist Party capitalized on its opponent's failure, once in office it acted in a dutifully 'orthodox reformer' way undertaking sweeping macroeconomic policies and structural adjustment in tune with the exigencies of the IFIs. The IFIs, which had adopted a cautious approach towards assistance in the light of Alfonsín's economic and political plans, adopted a new lending strategy supporting Argentina's market-oriented reforms (World Bank 1997a).

Carlos Menem governed for two consecutive terms, 1989–1995 and 1995–1999, after successfully driving through a constitutional amendment in 1994, allowing him to run for re-election. In the midst of the political and economic turmoil surrounding the resignation of President Alfonsín in 1989, the abrupt change of government put the incoming Peronist government in a strong position to conduct far-reaching economic and political reforms and, in the process, regain the trust of international markets. This strategy was possible because the Peronist Party was able to win broad political support not only from the historically supportive working class but also from the reform-minded business actors and export-oriented industry (Palermo and Novaro 1996: 149, 169; Tussie and Tuozzo 2002: 28). Moreover, the politically dramatic exit of Alfonsín's administration also left an ideological vacuum, soon capitalized upon by the new administration of Carlos Menem. As argued by Palermo and Novaro, 'the sense of urgency and the fear of a new political and social chaos (that still echoed the years of military regime) prevailed over the public opinion creating a propitious context for fast and far-reaching decisions' (1996: 124). Similarly, Tedesco claims that 'Menem was able to structure a discourse around the idea of an *emergency* that needed drastic measures' in order to secure political and economic stability (2002: 474, italics in original; also O'Donnell 1994; Acuña 1995).

The crafting of a domestic base of receptivity and legitimacy was a necessary condition for reform. At the same time, achieving a 'seal of good conduct' from IFIs was needed in order to attract international private capital. In recognition of this, the government of Menem embarked on a broad agreement with the World Bank and the IMF to comply with the principles of the Washington Consensus (Tussie and Tuozzo 2002: 28). Menem initiated a shift to a market-oriented governance by reforming state institutions and the overall social and economic organization of the country. Three pieces of legislation were immediately sanctioned. In August 1989 the Congress passed the *State Reform Law* (Law No. 23.696). This law authorized the Executive to undertake 'partial or total privatization or liquidation of companies, corporations, establishments or productive properties totally or partially owned by the State, including as a prior requirement that they should have been declared subject to privatization by the Executive Branch, approval for which should in all cases be provided by a Congressional Law' (Ministerio de Economía 1993: 4). One month later, in September 1989, the *Economic Emergency Law* was passed (Law No. 23.697). This legislation declared public administration to be in a state of emergency and accordingly defined a plan and method for reducing public spending in order to achieve equilibrium in public finances. The State Reform and Economic Emergency laws granted power to the Executive to modify by presidential decree a number of critical aspects of economic and socio-political relations. These included (i) the suspension of state subsidies for industrial promotion; (ii) identical treatment for foreign and national investors; (iii) the modification of the Charter of the Central Bank; (iv) modifications to the taxation system; (v) downsizing of public administration by suspending contracts and the recruitment of new employees within the central administration, public enterprises and other state units (see Bambaci *et al.* 2002).

However, it was the adoption of the *Convertibility Law* in 1991, the third legislative pillar, that finally consolidated economic stabilization and the return of capital flows into the country's economy (Law

No. 23.928). After the launch of the Convertibility Plan in 1991, the Argentine economy underwent a significant transformation. The 'Convertibility Plan', introduced in 1991 by Domingo Cavallo, Menem's Minister of Economy, represented a turning point in economic and political reforms. It included a series of ground-breaking measures that were deliberately coincidental with policy developments sponsored by the IFIs under the framework of the Washington Consensus (Corrales 1997). The main feature of this programme, supported by the World Bank Group, the IDB and the IMF, was the establishment of a currency board arrangement. In addition, the new economic plan set the timetable for fiscal and tax reforms, privatization of state institutions, liberalization of trade and reform of the public sector. The Convertibility Plan successfully arrested hyperinflation by sustaining price stability, and set the conditions for a major surge of foreign capital. Macroeconomic stability together with the return of credit led to an immediate increase in consumption indexes and to a period of economic growth.

While the new normative structure was decisive in setting the framework upon which most reforms were based, the support of the IFIs was also critical in the pursuit of economic transformation during Menem's administration. The World Bank and the IMF, which had had a contentious relationship with the administration of Alfonsín, and had not approved any new loans between October 1988 and December 1990, resumed their lending strategies to Argentina in 1991. Moreover, in September 1989 the World Bank opened an office in Buenos Aires to provide economic advice to the government on loan and technical assistance for privatization and other macroeconomic and public sector reforms (World Bank 1996b: 8–10). This office became the sub-regional representation for Chile, Argentina and Uruguay as part of the decentralization process within the World Bank following the adoption of the Strategic Compact in 1997.

In sum, while opposition and economic turmoil paralysed the administration of Alfonsín, Menem's government managed to adjust to the domestic and international exigencies consistent with market-oriented reforms and to create good liaison with the IFIs. In contrast to the previous administration, the government of Carlos Menem managed to turn the critical economic situation into economic stability and international re-entry, and with it to build up political capital from different sectors of the social spectrum, thus securing solid bases of power accumulation which neutralized potential opposition to government political and economic plans (Palermo and Novaro 1996). Several factors contributed to this; in particular, the socio-economic conditions in which Menem took power, a growing understanding of an economy that had plummeted into uncontrolled hyperinflation and an immediate recovery of the economy and of international trust (Acuña 1995: 51–56). Furthermore, socio-political support was also handled by means of patronage and the use of public funds as the economy grew (Weyland 1998, 2002). Patronage and political clientelism, together with a high concentration of power in the Executive – identified by some scholars as 'neo-populist' – helped to advance controversial neoliberal reforms and top-down economic market orientation by controlling the opposition with compensatory programmes and clientelistic strategies (*ibid.*; also Corrales 1997; Gibson 1997; Schamis 1999: 239). In fact, at a high distributional cost and low public accountability, the style of Menem's administration strategically disarticulated forces opposed to the government's reform.

Another particularly important institutional instrument for pursuing the government agenda was the role of the Supreme Court. Article 117 of the National Constitution establishes that this federal organ has the power to review the constitutional legality of norms enacted by Congressional norm or Executive Decree. Menem's agenda needed the Supreme Court to support the administration's most contentious political and economic reforms, especially those linked to the privatization of services (Verbitsky 1993; Carrió and Garay 1996; Helmke 2003). As argued by Larkins, the experience of the previous government in relation to Court/Executive relations, particularly the fact that the judiciary was often able to frustrate government policies, might have led Menem to consider a strategy that 'corrals the independence of the courts and make them more receptive to his concerns' (1998: 427).

The increasing control of the Executive over the judiciary was strategically planned. Through the sanctioning of a new law, *Ley de Ampliación*, in April 1990, Menem increased the number of Supreme Court justices from five to nine. The national Constitutional charter ceded to the Executive the prerogative to designate Supreme Court candidates, with the approval of three quarters of the Senate, in which Peronist representatives held the majority of seats. Thus, only months after assuming power, Menem managed to reshape the composition of the Court by adding four new judges and impelling two of the sitting magistrates to resign. The increase in number of judges played an important role in the implementation of politically sensitive reforms.

Judicial power, in particular that of the Supreme Court, was a pivotal component for the government as this is the instrument that recognizes the constitutional legality of the policies adopted by the government.

In the two consecutive administrations of Menem the Argentine institutional relationship between the Executive and the Judicial Power was manifested in the latter's lack of independence and the former's need to ensure legitimizing procedures for key political reforms. As a result, the political/institutional dimension of Argentine market-oriented reforms was greatly affected by a consistent pattern of centralized leadership and by the frequent political interference of the Executive in judicial governance. The result was a government that managed to push forward its agenda without the Supreme Court overturning its decisions and, at the same time, a Supreme Court that developed strong corporate interests.

Despite the effects on the rule of law and the lack of transparency in the management of policy reform, the government agenda was coordinated with the strategies of the IFIs (Manzetti 2000). The adoption of neoliberal policies by the Argentine administration was applauded by the World Bank and the IMF, which provided funds and technical advice for the reform of the state (World Bank 1994: 7; Corbalan 2002: 85–89). The rhetoric of political abstinence of the IFIs ensured the apathy in their 'technical' assessment of the way reforms were undertaken on the ground. The government had even made use of external funds to further its own political agenda using IFIs' lending conditions as a tactic to justify the government's adoption of unpopular adjustment programmes (Casaburi *et al.* 2000: 512).

Between 1990 and 1994, the government of Argentina carried out aggressive privatization of state enterprises that affected the national airline, gas transportation and distribution, railways, power generation and distribution, telecommunications, postal service, and water and sewage systems. It also sold oil and gas extraction facilities, coal mines, petrochemical plants, steel mills and most public banks (Basualdo 2002). Alongside this process there was progressive deregulation of the economy, involving the liberalization of financial and foreign investment restrictions (*ibid.*). During the period of economic reforms, the state was rationalized in accordance with a specific understanding of the relationship between institutional arrangements and sound macroeconomic trade and investment policies. State spending on social welfare ceased when most social services, including the pension system, were sold to private hands (Bertranou *et al.* 2003). These reforms were carried out in accordance with a model of state that endorsed the technical, economicist and managerial view of neoliberal governance promoted by the IFIs. Their 'managerial stance' often ignored the way these reforms were carried out and the impact they had on democratic procedures in, sometimes, fragile democracies. From this perspective, governance-related reforms supported by the IFIs often widened the already highly centralized patterns of presidentialism and lack of accountability in many developing countries. Paradoxically, in other words, good governance not always served the purpose it was claimed to serve. Ultimately, the manipulation of the judiciary and the use of decrees to advance politically sensitive reforms in the case of Argentina was a manifestation of the hierarchical way of pursuing neoliberal governance reforms – and a contradiction in itself. As Tuozzo (2004: 178) suggests, the creation by decree of the National Public Ethics Office (*Oficina Nacional de Etica Publica* – ONEP) in 1997 (Decree 152/1997) and of the State Modernization Programme in 2001 (Decree 103/2001) highlight the fact that centralized practices in Argentina are hard to surmount. Just to further illustrate this point, for instance, while President Alfonsín issued 10 decrees, during his administration Menem enforced a total of 308, covering sensitive issues such as economic deregulation, privatization and tax collection (Ferreira Rubio and Goretti 1996). Yet while enabling market economies, 'good governance' ignored the political aspects of the reforms and the agenda supported by local experts and practitioners. Although IFIs-supported reforms were necessary to restore the fiscal capacity of the state and to promote economic growth, the 'depoliticized' agenda was negotiated by the Ministry of Finance and thus good governance reforms entailed the acceptance of a rather restricted notion of democracy that excludes the more encompassing social and economic dynamics previously in place in Argentina (Tuozzo 2004: 184).

These reforms were directly rewarded with lower inflation, renewed investor confidence and economic expansion – Argentina achieved 7.9 per cent annual GDP growth from 1991 to 1994. Politically, the economic success of the first years of the Menem administration ensured domestic support for new re-election plans in the presidential elections in 1995, and the achievement of an extra-parliamentary agreement known as the *Pacto de Olivos* signed with the former opposition leader Raúl Alfonsín in November 1993 (Acuña 1995: 125). The *Pacto de Olivos* assured the agreement of the opposition party's parliamentary representatives to Menem's plans to run for a second term by means of changing the Constitution. As a consequence, a major Constitutional reform was passed in 1994 to allow, for the first time, a president to run for a second term. In exchange, Menem agreed to create stronger control mechanisms over institutions to counterbalance the power of the Executive (Acuña 1995; Palermo and Novaro 1996: 399–414; Finkel 2004: 65).

That is, the *Pacto de Olivos* stipulated that the new constitution would 'ensure judicial independence by substantially modifying the method of designating judges so as to guarantee that *moral fitness* be the primary reason for their selection' (Lacana n/d quoted in Finkel 2004: 73, emphasis in original). In a context of partisan arrangements and lack of input from civil society, a National Judicial Council (*Consejo de la Magistratura*) was established. The Council was responsible for judicial selection and administration below the Court level, a privilege previously reserved to the Executive (Bill Chavez 2004: 476).

The reduction of presidential dominance over the judiciary was a consistent matter of discussion with the IFIs. In negotiations with the IMF for an Extended Funds Facility line of credit, the creation of the Council was included as a political conditionality in the Letter of Intent signed between the government and the IMF (see IMF 2004a). However, this demand was far less linked to enhancing democracy than to a technical approach that was concerned with access to information and efficiency in court management to reduce transaction costs and thus benefit investor's trust. From this perspective, little matter that despite the creation of the National Judicial Council the government still retained important prerogatives, for instance, in the selection of judges for the Supreme Court (see Chapter 4).

Despite the notably elite-led and highly 'presidentialist' model of governance – and its consequent weak rule of law – the progress of market reforms effectively made it easier for many actors, in particular the IFIs, to postpone discussions over quality of governance and the way in which economic and state reforms were affecting other aspects of the political and social life. Euphoria covered these aspects as Argentina experienced a strong average economic growth in the 1990s. For instance, the size of its economy expanded from US$141 billion in 1990 to US$282 billion in 1999 (World Bank 2000b: i). As argued by Manzetti, this outcome allowed Menem to enjoy the compliance (and misplaced optimism) of the IFIs and external creditors, despite increasing levels of corruption and the deterioration of democratic governance. According to Manzetti,

> during most of the 1990s, Menem's reform earned him high praise at home and abroad to the point that he was even invited to address the annual IMF/World Bank meeting in Washington as late as 1998, an honour granted to few heads of state from developing countries.
>
> (2002: 6)

In fact, one of the most striking paradoxes during Menem's administration is that while he presided over a period of unprecedented economic prosperity, and Argentina was a flagship country for the IFIs, the 'golden years' of downsizing the state were accompanied by rampant corruption. The far-reaching process of the privatization of state assets resulted in corrupt practices involving many top government officials and major international corporations like IBM, Citibank and the Spanish telecommunications company Telefónica (*ibid.*: 8; Chapter 5 in this book). Regardless of this evidence, President Menem was invited to be the keynote speaker at the Fall 1998 Joint Assembly of the IMF and the World Bank in Washington. This was the first time that a Latin American president had addressed the biennial meeting in Washington (La Nación 1998a, Economía: 3).

The lack of perception on the part of the IFIs regarding the negative consequences for governance as a result of the way market-oriented reforms were undertaken, led some local NGOs, such as *Poder Ciudadano, Centro de Estudios Legales y Sociales* (CELS) and *Asociación Conciencia*, to undertake campaigns denouncing the rising levels of corruption that were placing Argentina in the ranks of the most corrupt countries worldwide (Manzetti 2000). For instance, the 1998 Transparency International's Corruption Perception Index ranked Argentina in 61st position out of a total of 85 countries, indicating high levels of corruption in the country (see La Nación 1998b, Política: 16; Transparency International 2005). In this context, not only the government but also the IFIs involved in the process of institutional and economic transformation in Argentina from the late 1980s became the target of increasing public scrutiny.

Local actors concerned with issues of governance reform and anti-corruption found that there was no response to their claims that the IFIs acknowledge the linkage of social rights and the rule of law to economic development programmes. The positive effects of the Washington Consensus reforms helped reducing inflation, dismantling inefficient and patronage-ridden state enterprises and providing macroeconomic stability. However, it failed to bring further participation of broader constituencies to the formulation and implementation of politically sensitive reforms. Socially, the model also failed to deliver welfare. Rising levels of poverty and inequality defeated the positive outcomes of the reforms, not only in Argentina but across the region.

It is obviously difficult to generalize about the effects of neoliberal reforms and the consequences of economic and socio-political imbalances but in many Latin American countries increasing social and political polarization has been a result of both a distributive crisis and an intense popular dissatisfaction with the ways in which the resources of the state were being managed. This has contributed to deep and widespread rejection of neoliberalism as a development paradigm and the IFIs in general. In Argentina, the process of judicial reform, supported primarily by the World Bank, was particularly sensitive to social discontent as the process became a showcase for how tensions and contradiction between the technical approach of the World Bank and the political demands of the local actors alienated the latter from the World Bank, which was perceived as acting as a mere conveyor of funds and policy paradigms that did nothing to change the *status quo* (see Chapter 4). Ultimately, the fit between the IFIs' agendas and Argentina's priorities has been perceived less as a reflection of what Argentina really needed and more as the expression of a technical, a-political, economicist understanding of what was 'good' for an effective neoliberal governance. As long as growth was robust and capital market conditions were relatively favourable, the optimist projections of the World Bank and the IMF neglected the latent political and institutional crisis.

Crisis of neoliberalism

The health and fate of neoliberal governance started to change once the political-economic context in Argentina became progressively challenged by external financial crises. The Mexican crisis of 1994–1995 was in fact the first 'grey cloud', provoking capital outflows and high interest rates in Argentina, and thus depressing the economy. The exchange rate anchor and price stability as indicators of future of growth began to display its rigidities. The Mexican crisis affected investor confidence in emerging markets and meant that the Argentine government had no instruments through which to mediate the onset of crisis and the problem of capital flight (Gerchunoff and Llach 2003). This became apparent in 1998 when the effects of another external shock, in this case the crash of the Brazilian economy – Argentina's main trading partner – led to four years of recession and strong social reversal culminating at the end of 2001 in what was to be the deepest and most comprehensive crisis in Argentina's economic history.

As argued elsewhere, the social costs generated by the political economy of neoliberalism in the 1990s and the gradual loss of faith in market solutions to development are key to understanding why the crisis of 2001 led so definitively to a wholesale rejection of the policies of the 1990s (Grugel and Riggirozzi 2007: 92). Furthermore, the economic, social and political crises in Argentina confirmed the disappointing trend results in Latin America's market reforms not only in terms of growth and social equity but also in terms of the quality of democracy.

A new centre-left government, led by Fernando De la Rúa of the *Alianza por el Trabajo, la Justicia y la Educación* (Alliance for Work, Justice and Education), took office in 1999 amidst rising dissatisfaction with the economic slowdown, the decline in public services, rising poverty and deterioration in the rule of law. The *Alianza* promised reform and placed anti-corruption at the top of the new political agenda. From the outset of its campaign, the Alianza was advised by a think-tank, the *Instituto Programático de la Alianza*, which gathered together experts from the NGOs who had unsuccessfully pressed for anti-corruption policies during the Menem era. Although President De la Rúa was seen to be more receptive to opposition programmes to distance himself from the markedly presidentialist style of Menem, it was soon evident that the critical state of the economy placed De la Rúa in a major dilemma. Despite the need to re-affirm the rule of law his government also had to display political strength in the face of international investors who were quickly loosing confidence in Argentina's prospects. In this context, despite the efforts of local civil society organizations to put in place reforms upholding the rule of law, declining support and the inability of President De la Rúa to deal convincingly with economic urgencies led to the critical stalemate that resulted in the crisis of December 2001. Once in office, De la Rúa's administration was too weak to resist domestic vested interests and external pressures that kept pushing for the continuation of the neoliberal agenda. At the same time, strong pressure groups from the national industrial bases as well as civil society organizations with diverse motives kept clamouring for radical changes to the model.

Rather than bowing to changes, the administration opted to further preserve the *status quo* and decreed a tight budget constraint and fiscal disciplines for the provinces and the country in general. These policies brought about a political deadlock that combined with the deepening economic crisis became ungovernable. Indebtedness, in turn, precipitated the financial crisis as Argentina's public debt increased from 29 per cent of GDP by the end of 1993 to 38 per cent by 1998. Recession from the end of 1998 only worsened this scenario leading to a debt increase of 51 per cent by the end of 2001 (Escude 2002: 5; also Damill *et al.* 2005). These trends were reinforced by an increasingly and almost negligent IMF which kept pumping in money as a way of providing security for financial markets and local lenders fearful of a currency devaluation (Blustein 2005).

In addition to an unsustainable economic situation, the weak position of the Executive was further undermined by the resignation of Vice-President Carlos Alvarez in October 2000 following two major corruption scandals related to the appointment of salaried civil servants who drew salaries without doing any real work in the Senate and to the payment of bribes to opposition senators to guarantee the passage of a labour reform bill necessary for compliance with the exigencies of the IFIs. This was a major blow to an administration that had campaigned on the plank of anti-corruption and a turning point on the road to its downfall.

Even as the country entered the final phase, which was to lead to the crash of December 2001, the IMF continued its support for the failing regime providing loans although the country's economic difficulties were obvious and it was clear that an orthodox exit strategy would be extremely difficult, if not impossible, to reach. To illustrate the point, as the Argentine crisis deepened in 1999, the IMF supplied a loan of US$13.7 billion and arranged US$26 billion more from other sources at the end of 2000. As the crisis worsened, the IMF agreed another rescue package of US$8 billion in September 2001 (Akkerman and Teunissen 2001). It seemed at the time that the IMF was ready to lend almost any amount in order to avoid the collapse of a project so closely tied to the IMF image and receipts. The Argentine government, meanwhile, followed IMF recommendations, maintaining its monetary policy and tightening even further its fiscal policy. As it faced a severe financial deficit, the government announced a 'Zero Deficit Plan' in July 2001, a budget cut of 13 per cent in state workers' wages and pensions plus a fiscal commitment by the provinces and the reduction of transfers. Despite these moves, and the IMF's efforts to solve the unsolvable, the country's debt burden caused a collapse in investor confidence and the country's economic risk level soared.

Social unrest, labour protests and street demonstrations swiftly followed as the economic, social and political crisis rolled on. By 2001, the crisis was unstoppable and spread beyond the economy. Social opposition to the neoliberal project, and a debt situation that saw the worst default in the country's economic history left the country on the brink of rebellion and collapse. The devastating impact of the economic crisis and the country's dramatic increase in poverty, unemployment and inequality are set out in Figure 3.1 and Table 3.1.

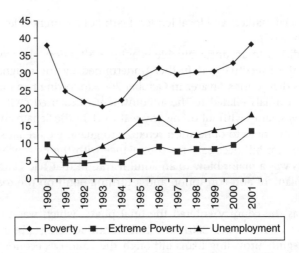

Figure 3.1 Poverty, Extreme Poverty and Unemployment in Argentina, 1990–2001

Source: INDEC – Encuesta Permanente de Hogares

The urgency of the crisis in Argentina was soon manifested in a highly volatile social situation and an institutional abyss. By early 2001 the economy experienced an accumulated loss of 20 per cent of GDP, a decrease of 30 per cent in consumption and 54 per cent in investment, which vastly affected the industrial production. It was also caught up by an unstable exchange and inflation rates that led to a critical loss of capital, equivalent to 7.6 per cent of GDP, that flew the country and seriously affected international reserves by 55 per cent that year. Levels of unemployment reached 23.3 per cent; poverty levels ascended to 50 per cent and extreme poverty to over 25 per cent of the population (Ministerio de Economía 2005). Another urgent problem was related to 'monetary anarchy', as 14 money denominations were circulating in 11 different provinces in parallel to the peso. In this chaotic scenario, lack of international financial support for both public and private sectors magnified not only the crisis but also the country's degree of isolation. In these circumstances, Argentina's state lost its capacity to regulate, mediate and resolve basic social conflicts, and this has led to a serious deterioration of the government agencies to exercise social cohesion leading to widespread delegitimized institutions and total crisis of governance.

Table 3.1 Changes in Income Distribution in Urban Argentina, 1990–2002

Year	1990	1992	1994	1996	1998	1999	2000	2001	May 2002	October 2002
Per capita household income (in 1999 pesos)										
Overall	240.3	292.7	302.8	270.4	294.8	280.6	275.7	253.3	189.7	176.8
Per capita income by decile										
1st decile (lowest)	38.3	45.6	43.2	28.1	31.7	30.4	26.3	17.1	9.0	16.1
5th decile	153.4	181.1	188.1	158.1	167.3	164.2	155.1	136.3	97.9	95.8
10th decile	825.4	1004.7	1060.7	992.3	1114.2	1028.2	1041.9	993.8	769.9	705.3
Relative measures										
Top 20 per cent share	50.7	51.0	51.6	53.7	54.8	53.8	55.1	56.8	58.2	57.2
Bottom 20 per cent share	4.6	4.5	4.2	3.6	3.5	3.5	3.2	2.6	2.1	2.8
Gini coefficient	0.454	0.456	0.467	0.493	0.504	0.494	0.510	0.530	0.551	0.532
Top/bottom 20 per cent ratio	11.0	11.3	12.3	14.9	15.7	15.4	17.2	21.8	27.7	20.4

Sources: World Bank (2003); INDEC Encuesta Permanente de Hogares (several years).

The worsening crisis came to a head in 2001. Large-scale demonstrations by citizens questioning the legitimacy of the existing representative institutions also criticized the strong connection, intellectual and monetary, between the ruling elite and the IFIs. A massive popular demonstration in December called for new institutional and societal arrangements. The popular slogan 'Out with all of them' (*Que se vayan todos*) seen in successive public demonstrations alluded to both parliamentary and judicial representatives (Dinerstein 2003). These popular demands were powerful enough to force the resignation first of the Minister of Economics, Domingo Cavallo, and then of the President, Fernando De la Rúa, on 19 and 20 December 2001.

A decade of neoliberal reforms had undermined both the incipient consolidation of democracy and the social welfare. Neoliberal governance in Argentina failed to provide welfare and equity, sometimes in the face of opposition from vested interests. Furthermore, the rapid process of impoverishment through the 1990s undermined faith in neoliberalism and unfettered market-led development – outside the relatively small group attached to the government – and it is key to understanding why the crisis of 2001 led so definitively to a wholesale rejection of the policies of the 1990s.

Contending ideas and the attempt to change governance in Argentina

The immediate impact of a decade of neoliberal reforms in Latin America's nascent democracies was extremely negative. Whether this was because neoliberalism leads inevitably to growth but fails to reduce poverty or whether it did so in the context of weak institutions and fragile linkages to the global market is an ongoing debate. The Washington Consensus reforms impacted negatively in many areas of governance. Institutionally, the lack of transparency, accountability and independence enhanced the power of the Executive, fostering non-consultative procedures of decision-making. Politically, the distance between the government and society grew as the deepening of neoliberalism increasingly meant reduced access to, and the exercise of, citizenship and rights (Grugel 2009).

In Argentina, democracy nevertheless proved resilient, even surviving three failed presidential attempts in less than two weeks that culminated in the establishment of a parliament-based 'emergency government' headed by Peronist leader Eduardo Duhalde in January 2002. Immediately after taking office, Duhalde recognized that crisis resolution was not simply a matter of 'getting the policies right' but rather one of acknowledging the need to restore the legitimacy of, and trust in, the political system. The government had to reconstruct the linkages between the state and the civil society. In addition to its obvious socio-economic aspects, the crisis was a crisis of public confidence in the political class. Crafting a domestic base of receptivity and legitimacy for new reforms was not only a necessary condition but an urgent one. The discredit of the neoliberal policies and lack of credibility in the IFIs as their chief promoters pointed to a new overview of policy and policy-making that would fit the new reality. This in turn meant, as analysed in detail in the subsequent chapters, that those actors that were discredited, disempowered and/or ignored were called back for the reconstruction of an alternative model of governance.

The crisis of neoliberalism in Argentina, therefore, opened a new spectrum of policy responses in the search for an alternative paradigm of development and governance. Rethinking governance called for a new link between the model of development and the integration of a fractured social structure, bringing in those who were out the circuits of the neoliberal capitalism (Munck 2003: 504). This presented an opportunity for alternative and hitherto ignored proposals for reforms supported by local actors with strong incentives to modify the model of governance.

In terms of policy formulation, participation of civil society and local experts in policy definition was first systematically curtailed in Latin America by the rule of the military regime (1976–1983) and subsequently by eroding the dynamics of elite-led decision-making processes in the years of neoliberal governance. Almost a decade of social censorship left intermediary groups without a voice and silenced local experts. A resilient civil society found its voice again in most countries immediately after the return to democracy in the early to mid-1980s. Social activists concentrated mainly in response to human rights claims. The return of democracy brought back the social impetus for transparent and responsive democratic institutions. In many countries, the articulation of civil society organizations and expert groups was encouraged by the involvement of an external agent, the United States Agency for International Development (USAID), in a programme to strengthen the rule of law (Blair and Hansen 1994; USAID 2002). In fact, USAID was the first external agency to work within the area of governance in Latin America. Its Rule of Law Programme was an attempt to support the re-democratization process in the region from the mid-1980s. In the case of Argentina, the Rule of Law Programme targeted judicial independence, court administration and judicial and legal education, and the creation of alternative dispute resolution mechanisms (*ibid.*). The Programme started in 1991 but was ended in 1995 after negative assessments showed limited political will to achieve reform. As a USAID report describes, 'inadequate incentives to overcome internal differences within the Court' and 'the lack of political will among judges of the Supreme Court and the Executive inhibited initial efforts to strengthen the rule of law' (USAID 2002: 34). Notwithstanding, the engagement of an international organization with civil society actors strengthened the lobbying capacity of the local experts and set a precedent for working with other external agencies. These civil society organizations opposed many governance reforms implemented during the 1990s and even networked with reformist factions within the World Bank to carry out reforms that were opposed by the government. Yet, the extent to which their activities made an impact was highly curtailed by elitist dynamics of decision-making.

Among these local civil society organizations, involved initially in the USAID initiative, was *Poder Ciudadano*, a non-profit organization that represented the national chapter of Transparency International in Argentina. *Poder Ciudadano* successfully pioneered a number of transparency actions, including lobbying for the adoption of a parliamentary bill that facilitated more access to public information (*Ley de Acceso a la Información Pública*) as well as for other policies that improved the accountability of public funds. Some of these campaigns succeeded in reforming the infrastructure of political parties, reforming election laws and creating an information database of all representatives in government.

The case of *Poder Ciudadano* is emblematic in the development of anti-corruption policies in Argentina and in the networking with valid interlocutors within the World Bank to advance its anti-corruption proposals on the ground. Established at the end of 1989 by a group of scholars and practitioners concerned with the protection of civil right, *Poder Ciudadano* evolved as a policy-oriented organization promoting collective action and networking with the aim of strengthening citizenship and citizen rights. Its long list of achievements in the establishment of anti-corruption policies since the early 1990s includes watchdog activities, advocacy and campaigns for transparency in public administration and information disclosure on norms and public funds and databases on policy-makers and financial assets (see Poder Ciudadano 2005). This national NGO has worked continuously with international organizations. Not only has it collaborated closely with Transparency International as the national chapter of that organization, but it has also developed flexible collaborative links with the WBI, coordinating training activities on anti-corruption and judicial reform programmes oriented to policy-makers and civil society in Argentina and other developing countries. Personal exchange and close links between Moreno Ocampo, the founder of *Poder Ciudadano*, and Daniel Kaufmann, Director of the Governance Division of the WBI, have been frequently recognized by various participants (Daniel Kaufmann, interview with author, 25 February 2002).

In recent years other NGOs traditionally concerned with human rights advocacy and watchdog campaigns focused their activities towards a more proactive engagement in analytical and policy recommendations concerning transparency policies and the reform of the judicial system. Some of these NGOs are the Civil Rights Association (*Asociación por los Derechos Civiles* – ADC); the Centre for Legal and Social Studies (*Centro de Estudios Legales y Sociales* – CELS); the Environment and Natural Resources Foundation (*Fundación Ambiente y Recursos Naturales* – FARN); the Institute of Comparative Studies in Criminal and Social Sciences (*Instituto de Estudios Comparados en Ciencias Penales y Sociales* – INECIP); the Users and Consumers Union (Unión de Usuarios y Consumidores) and the Centre for the Implementation of Public Policies promoting Equity and Growth (*Centro de Implementación de Políticas Públicas para la Equidad y el Crecimiento* – CIPPEC). A number of scholars and practitioners in these NGOs developed a common framework of the conceptualization and understanding of anti-corruption policies. Intellectually, most of these social actors were formed in the same universities, predominantly the Universidad de Buenos Aires in Argentina and Yale University in the US. In their practice, most of them were founders and/or participants in the advocacy work of *Poder Ciudadano*. As described by a former member of *Poder Ciudadano*, 'they resemble a peer group similar to an epistemic community' (Marcela Santos, interview with author, 17 December 2003).

Although these organizations had little influence on the agenda-setting and planning of judicial reform programmes during Menem's administration, they developed as a referential body, capitalizing on their practical and analytical expertise in the areas of rule of law and anti-corruption, mostly aided by the work of USAID. The impact of their work was mainly *indirect*, campaigning for greater transparency and accountability of government officials. In their work, they also developed effective networking activities with World Bank units, in particular the WBI and the PREM, which were the most open to local knowledge among the World Bank units, for the design and enforcement of anti-corruption policies in Argentina and other Latin American countries (see Chapter 5).

While a community evolved among NGOs and experts in the area of anti-corruption, a second community of civil organizations, mostly business-oriented or legal think-tanks, evolved by reason of their focus on judicial topics. These business-oriented and legal think-tanks developed mainly as consultants and advisers to private and public agents. Thus, in contrast to the NGOs involved in anti-corruption, the work of these organizations aimed at *directly* influencing policy formulation rather than at campaigning for greater civic awareness and participation. Some experts within this second 'epistemic community' rather moved across from private to public practice, some representatives having been recruited as civil servants within the Ministry of Justice. Their main focus of expertise has been the functioning and efficiency of the judicial system. Some relevant organizations within this group are the Forum for the Study of Justice Administration (*Foro de Estudios sobre Administración y Justicia* – FORES); the Libra Foundation (*Fundación Libra*); the Latin American Economic Research Foundation (*Fundación de Investigación Económica Latinoamericana* – FIEL); the Business Development Institute (*Instituto para el Desarrollo Empresario en la Argentina* – IDEA); and ARGENJUS, a consortium formed by representatives of NGOs, think-tanks, experts and consultants, and educational institutions, most of whom are members of the above-listed organizations and work on issues connected with the justice system.

These organizations have played a major role in the generation of diagnostic sector studies and academic work for the last 30 years. Informally, there have been important and fluid linkages between these organizations and policy-makers within the judiciary; some of their ideas have percolated into policy streams since they endorsed, or at least did not conflict with, government and World Bank perspectives on governance. In particular, experts in these organizations were called upon to participate in joint sector assessment supported by the World Bank's Legal Department in the initial stages of its intervention in 1993 and 1995. These linkages, however, were adversely affected when disagreement on priorities and approach led to conflicts between local actors, the government and the World Bank country team. As claimed by Tuozzo, although 'there seems to be plenty of agreement on diagnoses, agreement between different bodies in the judiciary about possible routes of action has proved to be far more difficult to achieve' (2004: 190). This tension between national experts and the World Banks Legal Department reflects the major question of how the Bank engages in judicial reform within a framework of non-interference in the political affairs of its borrowing members as required by its Charter (World Bank 1992). This was even more so since 'home-grown' consensual knowledge for judicial reform, articulated by experts from legal and business think-tanks and from the Ministry of Justice, was considered by the Executive and the Supreme Court to challenge the *status quo*.

Jodi Finkel, in her analysis of the judicial reform and electoral incentives in the case of Argentina, poses a relevant question that reflects the dilemma faced in the political-economic context of Argentina in the 1990s: 'why would a ruling party agree to institutional reforms that limit their own political power?' (2004: 56). Her assumption is that 'political leaders prefer to minimize constraints upon their exercise of power, ruling parties should not be expected to deliberately enact reforms that increase the judiciary's potential to limit government authority' (*ibid*.: 59). Yet the way judicial reform succeeded in reaching the government's agenda was by negotiating a 'technical' initiative on judicial reform presented by the World Bank's Legal Department that did not include the more 'political' aspects claimed by the local experts (see Chapter 4). The World Bank's interest in legal and judicial reform was in effect not related to the political aspects of the system, but rather to the technical ones linked to conditions that facilitate a sound investment climate (Dakolias 1995: 167–168). Ignoring issues of transparency and politicization of the judiciary that certainly affected the provision of justice in general and the quality of democratic governance in particular, the problem of the Argentine legal system was defined throughout the World Bank's report on the legal and judicial sector in Argentina merely as a technical and inefficient system that increased the costs of commercial transactions and hampered the development of a market mechanism based on contractual obligations (World Bank 2001b). These views were echoed by the IMF, which also claimed that widespread tax evasion and non-compliance were a consequence of the ineffectiveness of a judicial system that encourages such behaviour (IMF 2004a: 30). In this context, the World Bank's a-political stance made the Argentine government seek a less contentious ally, namely the World Bank's Legal Department and its programme, rather than proposals put forward at the local level and accordingly, allied with the World Bank, setting aside the domestically advanced proposals. However, as explored in the next chapter, the interplay of power politics between these actors decided the ill-shaped and ill-implemented reforms that ended in resistance from and conflict with local actors and subsequently in the cancellation of another World Bank judicial reform project. Moreover, the quality of judicial reform became an inescapable concern in the reconstruction of post-crisis governance in Argentina.

Finkel's question can also be applied to the case of anti-corruption: what are the incentives for a government to embrace anti-corruption policies that could scrutinize its own administration? However, in this case the initial political and institutional settings were significantly different from the political setting that shaped the path of judicial reform. Anti-corruption was placed on the agenda by the new President Fernando De la Rúa of the centre-left coalition *Alianza*, who succeeded Menem after the general election in October 1999. Those organizations that participated in the strengthening of the Rule of Law Programme led by USAID found a new opportunity as they were called upon by the government to set, together with the WBI and the World Bank's PREM, an anti-corruption programme leading to the establishment of the Anti-Corruption Office in Argentina.

In contrast to the judicial reform programme, the task manager from the World Bank involved in this case was Lynne Hammergren, an official from the PREM network who was a former leader in USAID's Rule of Law Programme. Both the PREM and the WBI were more willing to engage with local actors through institutionalized exchange of knowledge and funding for programme design and implementation. Also, in terms of reform outreach, a key difference between judicial reform and anti-corruption was related to the nature of these programmes; that is, in the case of judicial reform the issue at stake was the reform of a long-established state institution, while in the case of anti-corruption reform did not demand the modification of an established institution, but the establishment of a new one in order to set up new policies. Therefore, the implementation of anti-corruption policies was enhanced by the deliberations of experts rather than limited by corporate interests. From this perspective, while knowledge and policy became contending grounds in the case of judicial reform, in the case of anti-corruption policies the engagement of World Bank managers and local actors both articulated and compromised thus on positions facilitating policy change (see Chapter 5).

Ultimately, what these two cases of governance reforms suggest is that the role of World Bank units crafting judicial reform and anti-corruption programmes varied depending on the extent to which the World Bank sought either to *transfer* or to *broker* financial resources, best practices and expertise to foster the implementation of policies on the ground. While dominant theories in IPE suggest that the power of the IFIs as providers of market discipline and practices helped the spread of neoliberal reforms in the region, what these theories do not say is how, and the extent to which, local actors outside the government take, contest, modify or reject the policy ideas implicit in IFIs transfer of funds and knowledge. This is even more critical when analysing the relationship between ideas, actors and policy reforms in the aftermath of the 2001 crisis. As explained in Chapter 6, several Argentina's actors articulated proposals that pushed for a paradigm change in stark contrast to the neoliberal understanding of the IFIs.

The focus on project level in the cases of judicial reform and anti-corruption developed in the next two chapters illustrates the importance of analysing the context in which reforms are undertaken, and the interplay between actors and ideas involving international institutions. This focus also illustrates the interplay between actors and ideas in another way: prior to the crisis local policy-makers and IFIs conceived governance as a technical matter and sought to implement programmes that chose to ignore the political implications. But the principal tenets of neoliberal governance were called into question as the widening gap between political and economic participation affected a great majority of citizens. In fact, the economic and political crisis that affected most countries in Latin America at the turn of the century showed that democratic governance was a highly political matter, and massive popular demonstrations demanded an end to elite politics. In some cases demands called for an overhaul of the entire political class and a change in the political-economic paradigm. As explained in Chapter 7, these protests signalled the end of neoliberal governance as it stood, and in turn a regional call for an alternative mode of making politics. This situation spread from Argentina to other countries. As Salman noted in respect of the protests in Bolivia, 'people lost all confidence in democracy as a possible mechanism to reverse the persistent socio-economic division because the polity's attitude was simply one of keeping the electorate out of the sort of decisions that decisively affect it' (Salman 2004: 7, quoted in Grugel 2009). This situation also represented a new stage in the divergence between local actors and IFIs over what constitutes good governance. As such, public scrutiny also turned to the IFIs and their involvement in governance reforms.

Conclusion

The mainstream paradigm of the 1980s and 1990s, framed as the Washington Consensus, largely reflected the diffusion of the IFIs' ideas and an international order in which most developing countries, in particular Latin America, were fertile ground for those ideas when supported by international funding. The neoliberal paradigm that accompanied the funding programmes of the IFIs was thus not simply a set of ideas about development but also a powerful tool for 'norm diffusion' and a means of embedding those ideas in developing countries. Neoliberal governance in developing countries was thus the result of this prescription.

In public policy literature and in much IPE scholarship there is substantial evidence that points to the close connivance between local elites and external actors in the implementation of development paradigms that made paradigm diffusion a less top-down imposition. Both IFIs' staff as donors and local actors as recipients of funds and knowledge have incentives that affect the prospects of the reform. Furthermore, in the absence of binding operational guidance on the agendas of the IFIs on how to approach governance reforms, it may be that a decisive factor for donor officials is the need to reduce risk in loan approval, as this is a tangible criterion for staff performance evaluation. In this context, if local experts' proposals become 'highly political', task managers might be more inclined to act without local experts in the design and implementation of programmes since they may endanger the transfer of resources, and thus they prioritize their relationship with governments rather than local experts. Under this rationale securing agreement with key policy-makers rather than reaching agreement with local experts discourages linkages with local experts and practitioners, overlooking other sets of ideas, proposals or simply other communities of thought. This has been usual practice amongst the IFIs and the bases of technocratic networks with governments for which the adoption of 'a-political' reforms could give useful signals to private investors without changing the *status quo*. Whether government commitment results in further project implementation, however, is not an expected consequence of loan approval. The contrasting outcomes in the cases of judicial reform and anti-corruption in Argentina prove this point and show that materialization of policy change is a complex process that entails more than simply technocratic networking.

While focusing on this relationship between local and global actors, critical literature in IR and IPE has ignored the proliferation of influential local actors beyond government elites. The following chapters analyse how contesting ideas disseminated by less-formal social organizations in Latin America, like those presented in this chapter, have challenged and even changed the course of neoliberal governance. This was even more the case after the crisis of 2001–2002 in Argentina, where old lobbying and policy-oriented groups of experts together with a range of social movements, from piqueteros to neighbourhood organizations, swiftly brought in a new generation of political leaders that were not part of the regular 'transmission belt' as represented in technocratic policy networks that encouraged elite-led governance reforms during the 1990s.

4
Contesting Governance: Power and Politics in Judicial Reform in Argentina

This chapter discusses the contradictions between the a-political, financial missions of the IFIs and the intrinsically political nature of conditionality and more directly of governance. The case of judicial reform shows that governance reforms are less likely to be successfully implemented when the IFIs are reluctant or fail to engage in pro-reform networks. The failure to recognize local contestation and the importance of local actors in this reform area jeopardized the implementation of externally-led policy change since adverse power relations grew out of mistrust and competition. The present analysis of judicial reform in Argentina concludes that a project loan and its conditions may be agreed with government officials, but the process of reformation of policies and institutions is affected by the political, institutional and economic contexts in which actors' incentives, ideas and policy paradigms can either favour or inhibit policy change. In other words, policy change should be the result of consensual arrangements with local actors which legitimize a political-economic programme supported by the World Bank, and where these actors are participants in the progress of the project implementation.

The analysis is organized into four sections. The first section resumes the discussion on governance and knowledge management and the implication of these aspects of development assistance for the way in which different operational units within the World Bank engaged in the promotion of good governance. The second section concentrates on the judicial sector and explores the principal demands that underpinned local efforts to reform prior to the involvement of the Bank's mission into this sensitive policy area. The third section analyses the rationale and role of the World Bank in the promotion of judicial reform in Argentina. It is argued that the staff of the Bank's Legal Department tended to reduce the goal of judicial reform to a logic of loan approval ensuring the government's agreement, rather than seeking a broader consensus with local experts who had been previously pushing for reforms in the sector. The fourth section of the chapter discusses the implications of the Bank's acting as a mere conveyor in the transfer of paradigms and best practices for the judicial reform programmes. It develops an argument towards the understanding of the relationship between knowledge, policy and pro-reform networks in the implementation of judicial reform. It is claimed that the World Bank's approach to judicial reform ultimately competed rather than cooperated with local knowledge and local paradigms and, consequently, its 'Model Court Project' (*Proyecto Juzgado Modelo* – PROJUM) failed in its goal of institutional reform. The chapter closes with some remarks on the role of the World Bank in judicial reform in Argentina and the different patterns of involvement followed by the PREM and the WBI in the case of anti-corruption.

Governance: The IFIs' (a)political dilemma

Legal and judicial reforms are one of six main themes of the World Bank's governance work, the other five being anti-corruption, civil service reform, decentralization, public financial management and tax policy administration. The new institutional economics paradigm supporting this agenda sees economic development as dependent on stable and predictable market transactions. Good governance reforms have developed within the discourse and practice of the IFIs as a response to the failure of the so-called 'first generation of reforms' that comprised the Washington Consensus, namely infrastructure projects and structural adjustment programmes. As governance became a focus of World Bank development strategy a growing number of its senior economists and staff in general contributed to a body of literature on the topic. Bank research projects and publications not only underlined the importance of good governance for development but also reinforced a globally standardized discourse on what 'good governance' means. The work of the Bank's Economic Research Group, in particular the WDR, was critical in this aim as it defined the approach and involvement of the World Bank in governance-related reforms (McNeill 2004: 110; Riggirozzi 2007). Paradigmatic among these are the *WDR 1997: The State in a Changing World*, outlining the agenda for action to improve the performance of governments; the *WDR*

2000/2001: Attacking Poverty, which develops the discussion on the importance of good governance and effective public sector institutions for poverty reduction and outlines procedures to improve the efficiency and effectiveness of those public institutions that contribute to a sound economic role of the state; the 2000 and 2002 World Bank reports, *Reforming Public Institutions and Strengthening Governance*, systematizing the work done by the World Bank on governance-related programmes and outlining the way forward in accordance with the new corporate strategies introduced in the Comprehensive Development Framework (CDF); and the *WDR 2002: Building Institutions for Markets*, which specifically defines 'good' governance as including 'the creation, protection and enforcement of property rights, without which the scope for market transactions is limited' in achieving the absence of corruption and judicial efficiency as important pillars in the development of market economies (World Bank 1997b, 2000a, 2001a: 99, 117–131). Similarly, the World Bank's publication *Reforming Public Institutions and Strengthening Governance* proposed a proactive role for the Bank fostering governance and institution-building in developing countries, placing specific emphasis on the promotion of judicial reform and anti-corruption programmes as main components on the new development agenda (World Bank 2002a).

It was increasingly accepted both within and outside the World Bank that development is impossible without effective institutions, or at the very least produces only sub-optimal outcomes (Burki and Perry 1998; Kapur 1998; Birdsall 2001). The new normative goals embraced in 'governance for development' led the World Bank to modify several of its norms and routines and to define new priorities in development assistance to complement the ongoing economic adjustment implemented by most developing countries. Externally, the credibility and legitimacy of the IFIs' governance agenda was reinforced by new theoretical debates within the academic community in the fields of political science and development economics. Some authors argue that the extent to which governance-related ideas have become part of development economics is associated with the fact that these ideas were supported and contested in both academia and policy domains (Bøas and McNeill 2004; Tuozzo 2004). Nobel Prize economist Douglass North and other supporters of the New Institutional Economics suggested that the nature and effectiveness of a country's institutions are critical to the development process because they set the environment within which an economy performs (North 1990; Harris and Hunter 1995; Landell Mills 2003). Implicit in this view is the idea that 'cost-effective' institutions set the 'rules of the game' for what constitutes good governance in developing countries.

The promotion of new norms of governance has changed the way the IFIs 'do their business' with the developing world as it represents a critical break with the IFIs' traditional economicist agenda. The goal of good governance has been approached differently by the different international institutions, albeit in a narrow and technical approach. More ambitious targets, however, were embraced by the World Bank and the IDB, while the IMF maintained a more conservative mandate. For instance, the multilateral banks promoted reforms in areas such as judicial and state reforms that arguably extend beyond the realm of purely economic policy. The IMF, loyal to its original mandate, defined good governance almost exclusively in terms of transparency-advancing programmes related to the institutionalization of mechanisms that open information on foreign reserves, central banks' transactions and banking systems (Germain 2004: 226). Although these are, undoubtedly, important pillars of governance since they limit the discretionary powers of policy-makers and bureaucrats, the IMFs' concern over good governance on these terms concentrated on coordinating measures that essentially provide information for investors. In general, the approach of the IFIs to governance has purposely evaded political and social concerns about the *distribution* of justice, for instance, or more broadly the *quality* of democracy. According to Trubek there are two reasons why distributional issues were downplayed. First, the rule of law simply creates a framework for efficient allocation of resources and does not itself have distributional consequences. Second, in robust neoliberal economic thought, distributional issues are generally downplayed (Trubek 2003).

Despite being carefully justified in terms of creating an institutional environment to enable private investment and overall a healthy market, the promotion of governance has not taken place without seriously challenging the mission and mandates of the IFIs (Santiso 2002; Marquette 2004). Moreover, far from being a-political exercises, governance reforms essentially touch on the nerve of state institutions and on the relations between state and society. It is hard to refute the argument that reforming the legal systems in any given society may affect the institutions governing the way economic, social and political rights and obligations are distributed, and therefore the opportunities people have to take part in political and socio-economic realms. Intentionally or not the promotion of governance reforms by the IFIs encompasses a contradiction between the technical and the political aspects in reform programmes that often backfires at the time of implementation, when 'ownership' of reforms becomes a matter of dispute and is seriously compromised if citizens see the reform agenda as resulting from external pressures. This has been the story of power relations in developing countries involving local and global actors in the reform of politically sensitive policies. Conditionality has often created a dilemma of ownership among local constituencies, and is a decisive element in the thrust of policy change.

These assertions were recognized by the World Bank's 2003 *Annual Review of Development Effectiveness*, which recommended that sufficient attention be paid to alternative perspectives in Bank intervention and to individual country circumstances (World Bank 2004a; also World Bank 2005: 8). This recommendation was not exclusively oriented to the World Bank but to the aid community in general. Unquestionably there are fundamental differences in how ideas and development practices were taken up within and across international institutions. Essentially, the challenge for the IFIs has been how to integrate global paradigms and policies with local expertise and home-based proposals for reform. The way the IFIs' managers face this dilemma affects the relationship of the IFIs to local actors as well as to the policy-making process and implementation outcomes. The remainder of this chapter considers these issues in the case of judicial reform in Argentina.

The politics of judicial reform in Argentina

Judicial reform efforts in Argentina did not begin in the 1990s with World Bank's intervention in this sector. A strong local knowledge base developed prior to the arrival of the World Bank with judicial reform proposals. The earliest attempts to reform the judicial system date back to the 1970s when, paradoxically at the time of military regime (1976–1983), FORES, the national legal think-tank, organized a seminal workshop to discuss the problems and prospects of judicial reform in Argentina with members of the judiciary and civil associations. Some proposals were drafted at the time, but political and institutional obstacles prevented any effective achievement of these programmes, and gained insufficient political support.

Internationally, among the first agencies to raise awareness of the need to support the rule of law and judicial reform in Latin America was USAID, which began legal system-strengthening activities in the early 1990s. The bilateral agency proposed a judicial reform under its *Rule of Law Programme* in Latin America, at the time when most countries in the region were experiencing a process of re-democratization. The Rule of Law Programme for Argentina aimed at capacity-building supporting a national judicial school initiative to meet the training needs of the Federal Court system. Also at stake was a change in procedures for the selection of court members through a merit-based scrutiny process; this proved unworkable inasmuch as the Executive essentially refused to recognize its validity – in other words, refused to surrender its prerogative of making political appointments to the bench (Blair and Hansen 1994: 37). As pointed out by a former USAID official, 'these initiatives did not go far as USAID's task managers encountered resistance within the national Supreme Court, the organ that approves reform projects together with the Executive' (Linn Hammergren, interview with author, 17 May 2004; also Hammergren 1998). Nor was national political leadership outside the court under President Carlos Menem fired with the importance of reforming the judiciary (Blair and Hansen 1994: 21). Resistance to any change in the *status quo* from the Executive and the judges of the Supreme Court was a key aspect of the political and institutional incentives that shaped the prospects of reform throughout the process. Any involvement of the IFIs in this sector had, therefore, to face this fact.

Argentina has a federal system of governance based on a constitutionally stated division of power, but is nevertheless strongly presidential. Historically, political alignments and processes determined an in-built tension in the Argentine system of governance: while constitutionally the independence of the judiciary is guaranteed, political manipulation of the Courts is a pattern reproduced by different socio-political arrangements in both military and democratic governments (Iaryczower *et al.* 2002). In fact, over the last half century, state institutions have been gripped by partisan politics, first between antagonistic political forces represented by Peronists and anti-Peronists, and since the mid-1990s by other forces that entered the electoral scene (Bambaci *et al.* 2002). The lack of checks and balances has been the cause as much as the consequence of heavily top-down-managed policy changes (O'Donnell 1999). Pastor and Wise have argued that at a high distributional cost and low public accountability, the strongly presidentialist and autocratic style of Menem's administration strategically bypassed legal rules in order to disable forces opposed to the government's reform agenda (Pastor and Wise 1998: 19). Argentina's Supreme Court was subject to powerful political manipulation especially after it was expanded from five to nine members by President Carlos Menem, who chose the four new members. As explained in the previous chapter, the new constitution of the Supreme Court secured an 'automatic majority', which consistently backed the interests of the administration (see Chapter 3).

Several public opinion polls confirmed the alarming deterioration of confidence in the judiciary and the rule of law in Argentina. According to Gallup, at the time of the democratic restoration in 1983, confidence in the judicial system was rated as 57 per cent; by 1991 the percentage had fallen to 26 and by 1993 to only 17 (quoted in Blair and Hansen 1994: 29). Another Gallup poll in 1994 showed that 72 per cent of respondents considered the judges 'too influenced by the government' and that 69 per cent believed that the decisions of the Supreme Court were either 'extremely politicized' or 'very politicized' (Larkins 1998: 429, emphasis in original; also Iaryczower *et al.* 2002: 3). This negative perception of the administration of justice in Argentina, and the lack of confidence in it to fight against political manoeuvring and corruption, strengthened demands from civil society organizations, local scholars and experts for a more transparent and responsive judicial system. In turn, even those business and economic actors who had benefited from the macroeconomic adjustment and market-oriented reforms undertaken by Menem's administration joined in claiming that the deterioration of the rule and predictability of laws were affecting the investment climate (Asselin 1996).

The inefficiency of the judicial system and the costs of malfunctioning state institutions, in particular the Supreme Court, to economic development were analysed by the national think-tank IDEA, a nongovernmental institution whose members were some of the most important corporate executive officers in the country. IDEA conducted a study that identified lack of independence and high levels of corruption as the main problems of the sector, caused by deficiencies in the system. This report was presented at IDEA's annual meeting in 1993 and discussed with government representatives and other representatives from the justice and business sectors. The concerns of the private sector were also echoed by another business-oriented think-tank, FIEL. In its report *Reform of Judicial Power in Argentina*, published in 1996, FIEL emphasized the importance of an efficient judiciary for economic development (FIEL 1996). The empirical evidence provided in FIEL's report was highly influential in key economic circles and legal think-tanks, like FORES, which articulated, in turn, a series of policy proposals and diagnostic work for reforming the sector based on the findings of the national think-tanks. These concerns were also consistent with other surveys and analyses provided by bilateral organizations and international NGOs, such as Transparency International, CASALS and the Canadian

Foundation for the Americas (FOCAL). Like USAID, these international agencies highlighted widespread corruption and political discretion in the manipulation of the Supreme Court appointments as serious factors affecting judicial efficiency (Moreno Ocampo 1993: 199; Manzetti 2000: 18; Buchanan 2001). For instance, the 1998 Transparency International's Corruption Perception Index positioned Argentina as one of the most corrupt countries in the world (see Transparency International 2005). Finally, the increasing appreciation of the costs of inefficient judiciaries for economic development was swiftly championed by the World Bank, the IMF and the IDB (Buscaglia and Dakolias 1996; IMF 2001; World Bank 2001b).

In this apparent urgent situation, President Menem's strategic response to increasing demands for transparency and accountability was pragmatic. As analysed in Chapter 3, although the constitutional amendment of 1994 ensured some institutional changes, these changes did not challenge the tight control of the Executive over state institutions. For instance, notwithstanding some institutional reforms, such as the creation of a National Judiciary Council, a Jury of Impeachment and the establishment of a National Office of Ethics, transparency and accountability did not go further than a cosmetic change. The setting up of these 'oversight' institutions never took off, held back by the lack of parliamentary agreement on issues like membership, regulatory policies, norms and procedures (Bill Chavez 2004: 477). The control of Parliament by Menem's Peronist Party, from 1989 until 1997, enabled the government to delay the taking off of these institutions that might have endangered the Executive's political manoeuvres over the Supreme Court (*ibid.*). It was not until the victory of the opposition party, the Alianza, in the parliamentary elections of 1997 that a window of opportunity opened for a new start in governance reforms. However, it was not until the end of the decade, nearly five years after the promulgation of Argentina's new constitution and when the country was on the eve of its most dramatic economic and political crisis, that the new oversight institutions finally began to function.

Ultimately, policy processes in the consolidation of neoliberalism in Argentina proved restrictive for divergent ideas. Local actors working on proposals for policy and institutional reform found no interlocutors among the decision-makers and thus only technical, a-political aspects related to certain regulations and the institutional *façade* were likely to percolate into the policy stream. In other words, when reform proposals were pro–*status quo* and did not change the internal balance of power that was grounded on a highly dependent judiciary, they were more likely to be supported by Menem's government. Likewise, proposals concerning politically sensitive goals related to the functioning of the system, access to justice, provincial governance and the decision-making process in the judiciary were excluded from the Executive's agenda. As pointed out succinctly by a local expert, the judges of the Supreme Court were reluctant to undertake reforms that would modify the *status quo*, and the Executive did not seek to discomfort an institutional branch so vital to the advancement of its political purposes (Bohmer 2004). Therefore, as stated by the Director of FORES, 'notwithstanding the work of local actors and the increasing demands from different sectors, opportunities for local experts and practitioners to influence policy formulation were often limited' (Horacio Chayer, interview with author, 1 December 2003).

In this context, the World Bank's Legal Department entered the national arena with its own judicial reform paradigm. As analysed in the next section, the World Bank staff soon recognized that unless the initiative for judicial reform was tailor-made to reduce it to a technical, economicist goal, loan negotiation and approval by the government would be seriously jeopardized. The dilemma faced by the World Bank staff in this case was whether to promote governance-related programmes on the basis of technical, managerial, a-political ideas of what constitutes good governance, an approach that after all was not at odds with the World Bank's a-political mandate, or whether to engage with local experts to compromise and amalgamate their respective positions utilizing joint expertise in the framing of policy reforms and their implementation. Incentives to advance a limited understanding of governance and thus of judicial reform as a managerial task were prioritized as such stances were expected to secure the approval of the government and thus the chances of disbursement were more likely. This is no minor issue, given the institutional culture that pervades the World Bank. As a World Bank Senior Public Sector Manager and task manager for Anti-corruption programmes in Argentina explained, 'country managers are rarely assessed and rewarded on the extent of and ways in which they engage with local experts, and their expertise, but rather according to funding disbursement for project targets' (Linn Hammergren, interview with author, 17 May 2004). This situation led the IFIs' task managers to act according to their pragmatic choice in most instances, securing approval for a judicial reform programme that neglected more politically sensitive issues in favour of the technical aspects of court management. Thus rather than engaging in networking with local experts on the ground, the World Bank's mission followed a less participative route acting as a mere conveyor of funds and policy ideas. This mission was undertaken even at the cost of enhancing undemocratic practices in the country (Hanlon and Pettifor 2000; Tuozzo 2004).

The World Bank as a conveyor of funds and paradigms

Several proposals, both home-based and externally supported projects, for the reform of the judicial system and the enhancement of the rule of law were discussed and elaborated during Menem's administration. However, the judicial reform was prompted only by the intervention of the World Bank in 1998. In fact, the initial World Bank involvement in the policy areas of judicial reform and anti-corruption was part of the sector assessment undertaken between 1993 and 1995. On this occasion the Ministry of Justice requested the World Bank's Legal Department to finance a comprehensive diagnostic study of the problems affecting delivery of justice in Argentina. As a result, the World Bank's *Judicial Sector Study* was carried out under the direction of Maria Dakolias, a Bank expert in the Legal Department. The team that conducted the Sector Study was composed of Argentine lawyers selected by the Ministry of Justice and international experts, contracted in the main by the World Bank, who had participated in other judicial reform undertakings supported by the Bank in the region. Unsurprisingly, the problems of the judiciary were identified as lack of independence, delays in trials and sentences, and widespread corruption. Court officers, including judges, personnel and government officials, were found to be at the root of the problem and identified as the main obstacle to change (World Bank 1998a: 3; World Bank 2001b: ix–xi).

Despite the highly political issues raised by the *Judicial Sector Study*, the World Bank's Legal Department progressively re-directed its support towards more technical, managerial aspects related to market efficiency in justice delivery, ignoring more controversial aspects related to the increasing politicization of the system, the lack of transparency and the discretion of the Executive in Court management, priorities that were, as an official of the Argentine Ministry of Justice noticed, highlighted by the local experts before and during the development of the World Bank's sector study (German Garavano, interview with author, 20 November 2003). The World Bank's limited perspective was later framed in a publication, the 1996 *Judicial Reform in Latin American Courts: The Experience in Argentina and Ecuador*. This document defined the main obstacles for a well-functioning judiciary in Argentina in line with the World Bank's a-political stance. Inefficiency in court management, process delays, resource allocation and institutional inertia were the main factors that were identified as hampering the judicial system. In this view, these factors hindered the predictability of enforcement of the rules, in particular those of property-right values and thus the transaction costs for economic activities (Buscaglia and Dakolias 1996).

In 1998 the World Bank's Legal Department had negotiated and approved its first lending programme in the sector, the PROJUM (PID 50713). This project entailed a US$5 million Learning and Innovation Loan aimed at identifying, establishing and evaluating conditions which would support the realization of judicial administrative reform and eventually form part of an overall legal reform programme to be replicated in other cases (World Bank 1998a). The PROJUM was launched as a pilot project for specific Federal Courts and its results were intended to be replicable in other courts. The project was highly technical in its approach, as it came clear from its three main components. The first component was 'court management', aimed at developing interchange activities between the different levels of the judiciary (Supreme Court, courts of appeal and trial judges) to enhance the efficiency of judicial administration and to reduce case backlog. A new case management system and a new record management system were identified for implementation. The reorganization of the judicial administration included actions coordinated by the Supreme Court and the individual judges involved in the project. According to the project document, 'judges spend much of their time on administrative matters, thus curtailing their ability to concentrate on substantive judicial matters' (World Bank 1998a: 5–6). Thus, PROJUM attempted to 'utilize the existing personnel in the most efficient manner' (*ibid.*: 6). The programme also considered reducing delays by incorporating a new computer system to enable the courts to develop more efficient case management and distribution among judges and records management. Particularly important was the efficient use of these practices in tracing tax-related cases (*ibid.*: 6–7). A second component included the development of a training and education policy for the judiciary. The training of judges and other court personnel in the areas most relevant to implementing successful model courts were expected to enhance personnel skills in new case management techniques (*ibid.*: Annex 2). The third component was the evaluation and dissemination of best practices through, for instance, seminars and workshops in order to reach the goal of further replication of project results in other Argentine courts.

According to a former Executive Director of PROJUM in Argentina, 'financially PROJUM has not represented a big project within the whole portfolio of the World Bank for the country but its prospects in terms of further replication made PROJUM a relevant case for the Bank's managers' (Virginia Simari, interview with author, 4 December 2003). PROJUM was designed as a pilot reform project for five Federal Courts in Argentina for further replication in another 12 Federal First Instance Courts throughout the country. The selected Courts were Federal Courts located in the provinces of Buenos Aires and Chaco dealing with civil, commercial and labour cases, and new Social Security Courts in Buenos Aires dealing with tax and social security cases (World Bank 1998a: 5). According to the most recent Executive Director of the project, 'PROJUM was expected to be used as a demonstration effect to further replicate a *model of court* in other countries of the region' (Moises Litchmajer, interview with author, 16 December 2003).

Paradoxically, the World Bank presented and negotiated closely with the Executive the Model Court project in 1998, the same year, but after the local experts had unsuccessfully presented an alternative project, the *National Plan for Judicial Reform (Plan Nacional de Reforma Judicial)*. The 1998 National Plan for Judicial Reform was a home-grown programme sketched out by local experts based on three main sources: (i) findings provided by the aforementioned national business-oriented think-tanks such as FIEL and IDEA; (ii) previous work of legal think-tanks like FORES; and (iii) contributions by local experts working in the Ministry of Justice. A first sector analysis report carried out by the World Bank's Legal Vice Presidency Unit in 1993 was also part of the background analysis that nourished the design of the National Plan, according to the participants (Horacio Lynch and Horacio Chayer, interviews with author, 25 November and 1 December 2003). Like the World Bank's PROJUM, the National Plan mainly addressed issues of judicial efficiency and management, but in contrast to the Bank's initiative the National Plan also proposed reforms on more political issues including access to justice and judicial inequality and transparency in court management. Special attention was given to the work of social and family courts and to judicial reform at the sub-national and provincial levels (Plan Nacional de Reforma Judicial 1998). In addition, it proposed the creation of a Centre of Judicial Policy and Management Supervision (*ibid.*: Chapter 3).

The National Plan was elaborated by experts within a group of legal and business-oriented think-tanks, local consultants and civil servants within the Ministry of Justice. It was presented to the national government by the Ministry of Justice, under the direction of its Minister Ricardo Gil Lavedra, in October 1998. Although the National Plan was approved by Menem's administration, the programme faced two institutional constraints that inhibited its further implementation. On the one hand, although the Ministry of Justice had the power to present bills and policy initiatives to the Parliament and the Executive, it had no power of implementation and enforcement. On the other hand, the lack of funding from the national government to support its implementation was consistent with an unwillingness to support and move forward a process that could change the *status quo* of the judiciary. This situation, in turn, created disincentives and competing objectives among local experts and the policy actors at the core of the decision process. These competing objectives became clear after the World Bank successfully negotiated its own judicial reform programme with the government.

In terms of policy dynamics, while the depoliticized judicial reform proposal advocated by the World Bank's Legal Unit enhanced the government's agenda and thus empowered the Executive, it disempowered the local experts and civil society organizations that endorsed contesting programmes of policy change in the sector. In fact, the political incentives of the government and the judiciary and the policy paradigm of the World Bank's Legal Department were not in conflict. Thus, the staff of the Bank's Legal Department were reluctant to engage with local experts in a process that might involve more compromise and amalgamation than Bank officials wished to concede. This was the case despite initial collaboration with local actors.

The alignment of the Bank's Legal Unit with the government's view was further confirmed in the management of the reform implementation. The National Plan had proposed that the executing agency of the project be located in an independent commission, comprising members designated by the Judicial Council and the Supreme Court, to carry out functions in coordination with an Advisory Committee (Plan Nacional de Reforma Judicial 1998: 121). This proposal was aimed at preventing further politicization in the implementation of judicial reform. However, the World Bank's PROJUM's Executing Unit was established under the wing of the Executive branch, in a coordinating commission which included representatives from the Supreme Court, the Ministry of Justice and the Chief of the Cabinet Office within the Executive branch (World Bank 1998a: 8). Once again, by granting the management of the reform to a Project Executing Unit led by the Supreme Court and the Executive, the World Bank enhanced their power over the local actors who supported a different view to that of the reform programme. Ultimately, the strong presence of the Executive in the management of the judicial reform programme subsumed the reform process into its own political agenda and to a logic of restricted participation and systematic disempowerment of the local actors. According to Horacio Lynch, director of a national law consultancy,

> The capacity of the Bank to allocate funding toward reforms, either via loans or via technical assistance and training, has been a critical element enhancing the influence of the World Bank policy ideas in the reform process. Furthermore, this capacity of funding its policy paradigms and ideas has *sterilized* local efforts.
>
> (Interview with author, 25 November 2003)

Ultimately, the involvement of the World Bank in judicial reform simply reinforced the leadership of the Executive and a system of governance that relied heavily on the president. Indivertibly or not, the Bank's involvement in judicial reform in Argentina had a collateral effect on the quality of democratic policy-making. That is, while the Bank was successful in triggering judicial transformations in Argentina's domestic agenda, the reforms it endorsed jeopardized broader participation, sidelining local experts' ideas, and encumbered, to a certain extent, the development of a more comprehensive reform related to access to justice, transparency and judicial independence. Ultimately, the process reinforced exclusionary practices in a democracy that was already questioned thus serving the cause of governance inadequately.

Despite the corporate changes operated within the World Bank towards the development of a 'Knowledge Bank' and the high-profile declarations of the importance of local knowledge and experience, the logic of the involvement of the World Bank's Legal Department in the implementation of judicial reform in Argentina revealed two fundamental contradictions. First, 'the simultaneous need for the policies adopted to fit within the strategic framework espoused by the Bank, and be freely chosen and owned by client governments' (Cammack 2004: 207). Second, contesting ideas supported by local experts were considered highly political and thus Bank task managers were more inclined to act without these actors and their expertise in the design and implementation of the reform programme. The 'depoliticized' approach to judicial reform pursued by the Legal Department provided the government with a less controversial ally, at the same time displaying encouraging signs to the private investors worried about the deterioration of the rule of law and the predictability of the investment climate. In the end, judicial reform in Argentina did little to change the *status quo* and the structure of incentives underpinning interference by the Executive in judicial norms and procedures. The Bank not only 'helped indirectly to expand distrust and fragmentation within the sector' but was itself 'caught up in a domestic conflict' in which particularistic tendencies and corporate interest in keeping the *status quo* intact were reinforced (Tuozzo 2004: 115).

In terms of policy outcomes, not only did this situation discourage linkages between local experts and policy-makers to discover common ground, but the involvement and influence of the World Bank in judicial reform did not help to close the gap between the local experts' proposals and the political tensions in the sector. From the start, the involvement of the World Bank was determined by a situation in which the main actors at the centre of the decision-making process, the judges of the Supreme Court, were reluctant to undertake reforms that would change governance aspects of the judiciary, and by an Executive that did not wish to discomfort an institutional branch so necessary for the advancement of political purposes. In a context in which the political class lacks incentives to reform, IFIs like the World Bank have competitive advantages to advance 'neutral' policy paradigms. Foremost because projects are tied to money, but more importantly because the Argentine government found in the World Bank's a-political stance, for instance, a less controversial programme than in one proposed at the local level. From this perspective, Bank practices discouraged linkages with contending groups, other sets of ideas and proposals. By championing a restricted paradigm, the World Bank promoted particular norms in defence of a particular project, in this case that of the government. The notion of reform was in fact sought as a process of hierarchically structured interstate consensus in which the state was reduced to a 'transmission belt' adjusting the domestic environment to the requirements of the global economy. But the results on the ground deviated in important ways from the intended model showing that creating new, or improving on existing, institutions is simply a matter of getting the government's assent. The clash of rival ideas affected the prospects of legitimacy, the construction of common *ground*, on which basis effective change occurs.

The Bank management defined the project's implementation period as three years, effective from May 1998 to November 2001. Despite the closing date, the project implementation was severely delayed, ending in 2006 with acknowledgably unsatisfactory results. The result was additional public debt, public discontent, protests and a negative evaluation within the Bank that led to the cancellation of a project, *Reform of Justice*, whose approval within the Bank was subject to the results of PROJUM (World Bank 2000b: 40). The failure of this project was strongly attributed, at the level of local experts, to the 'top-down' approach to policy formulation, negotiation and management sustained by the World Bank staff (Bohmer 2004). The project's design and negotiation reproduced patterns associated with a deeply embedded culture of loan approval and secrecy, which restricted the scope of participants in the policy process and inhibited the exchange with local experts who put forward contesting 'political' proposals.

The evidence of PROJUM and the cancellation of the project brought about a progressive loss of legitimacy and influence in the process of governance reform for the World Bank. Despite the Bank's rhetoric regarding participation, public accountability and transparency, it has played an ambiguous role in advancing these principles in governance reforms. The World Bank's Legal Department acted as a mere conveyor of funds and policy paradigms advancing a model of the judiciary and thus of the state the implementation of which affected policy practices on the ground. The Bank's initiatives were centered on the adoption of a model that enforced a specific technical and market-friendly perspective. As such, the reform overlooked other aspects of the democratic system of governance that were strongly proclaimed by local actors. By the end of 2001, Argentina had undergone a major economic and political crisis that had critical consequences for the national institutional setting and its system of governance (Peruzzotti 2001).

In October 1999, Fernando de la Rúa, the candidate for the centre-left coalition *Alianza*, won the presidential election with promises of revising the economic direction and ensuring transparency and democratic accountability. However, once in power the administration was unable to secure sustainable and equitable political and economic governance. As explained in Chapter 3, the country entered a critical recession in 1998 leading to a comprehensive economic and political crisis in 2001. This critical context, however, also opened a door to a more proactive incursion of local experts and their expertise into the policy process. The economic setback of 2001 soon confirmed the need for new institutional and societal arrangements. This was clearly evidenced in the popular slogan seen in successive public demonstrations, 'Out with all of them' (*Que se vayan todos*), alluding to parliamentary and judicial representatives (Dinerstein 2003). These popular demands were powerful enough to force the resignation first of the Minister of Economics, Domingo Cavallo, and then of the President, Fernando De la Rúa, in December 2001. The increasing loss of legitimacy of the political class and with it that of the IFIs that supported their governmental programmes meant that the involvement of the IFIs on the eve of the crisis and in post-crisis resolution, as Chapters 6 and 7 suggest, was not guaranteed unless they tailored their advice and aspirations to fit in with domestic politics and the economic agenda.

Judicial reform in the aftermath of the crisis of neoliberalism

The crisis in Argentina in 2001 was a manifestation of the failure of the established model of neoliberal governance and thus of the structure of policy-making supporting it. The political impact of the abrupt rise in poverty is hard to exaggerate and it was, in effect, the most obvious legacy of the failure of a decade of neoliberal reforms. The other legacy was the systematic failure of traditional institutions of the representative democracy both to meet the demands of an increasingly mobilized and frustrated society, and also to close the gap between the poor and the rich in a country where it had become alarmingly large (see Chapter 3: Figure 3.1 and Table 3.1). In mid-December the country defaulted on its external debt, and within two months the value of the peso had dropped more than a third and was to fall still further in the coming year. Between 2001 and 2002, presidents came and went in quick succession until a temporary Parliament-led government finally assumed some degree of institutional command in January 2002, and Eduardo Duhalde became interim president. Duhalde was elected as provisional president by a congressional commission. The challenges facing Duhalde were enormous.

The immediate post-crisis administration faced three main challenges: recovering the macroeconomic instruments to reactivate the economy; regaining political legitimacy; and achieving social peace (Grugel and Riggirozzi 2007). The government faced these challenges in strongly adverse initial conditions: an accumulated loss of 20 per cent of GDP; a decrease of 30 per cent in consumption and 54 per cent in investment; a decrease of 30 per cent in industrial production; unstable exchange and inflation rates; a critical loss of capital that fled the country in early 2001, equivalent to 7.6 per cent of that year's GDP; a loss of 55 per cent of international reserves; levels of unemployment that reached 23.3 per cent; poverty levels of over 50 per cent and extreme poverty levels of over 25 per cent of the population (Ministerio de Economía 2005; also Chapter 3 in this book). In addition, other pressing aspects were related to a monetary anarchy as 14 money denominations were circulating in 11 different provinces in parallel to the peso; a conflict-ridden social situation and an institutional abyss.

President Duhalde faced a critical point by acknowledging that economic reform alone would not get Argentina out of crisis. The government also needed to address the underlying political and institutional flaws that encouraged excess public sector borrowing, corruption, politicized judicial systems, and lack of transparency in government activities. In a highly mobilized society, any attempt at policy reform was under public scrutiny which now demanded a change in the traditional bottom-up models of policy decision-making. This extended to ongoing and new programmes negotiated with the IFIs. For the first time, for instance, the World Bank's action on judicial reform was publicly rejected and, as a senior official from the Ministry of Justice noted, PROJUM as a project was targeted by civil groups which, in a public demonstration, distributed pamphlets with the slogan *PROJUM es Corrupción* ('PROJUM is Corruption').

In order to stem the rising tide of contentious politics, the government launched a consensus-building initiative, the *Mesa de Diálogo*, in January 2002 with the support of the Catholic Church and the United Nations Development Programme (UNDP). Organized in thematic round tables, the *Mesa* encouraged inputs from a broad range of society-based actors for the ranks of labour, business, NGOs and unemployed workers who articulated in what became known as *piquetero movement*, as well as political parties and the IFIs' representatives. *Mesa de Diálogo* was a critical government-led initiative that helped to reconstruct the links between the political class and society, which now mediated the policy-making process. Important initiatives were discussed and outlined in the context of the *Mesa de Diálogo*. Amongst the most significant were the adoption of state policies of social inclusion (Grugel and Riggirozzi 2007: 96–97) and the revision of state reform projects. In this context, in the case of justice system, a *Discussion Panel on the Reform of the Judiciary* held regular meetings in the Ministry of Justice headquarters, gathering different NGOs, think-tanks and government representatives to discuss the current circumstances in the sector. Not only did the World Bank's Legal Department's task manager, Maria Dakolias, not participate, but the funds to carry out this initiative were provided by UNDP. According to the World Bank's task manager for judicial reform in the country, 'political circumstances and conflicting views about the reform excluded the Bank from the dialogue' (Maria Dakolias, interview with author, 18 May 2004). According to the president of ARGENJUS, the consortium of NGOs that coordinated *Mesa de Diálogo*, however, 'while rigidity inhibited further discussions and the participation of Dakolias' team, other World Bank representatives from the PREM, such as Linn Hammergren, task manager for anti-corruption programme in Argentina, were invited and attended discussions of *Mesa de Diálogo'* (Ramon Brenna, interview with author, 9 December 2003).

In general terms, the lack of recognition of the importance of social contestation in policy struggles and the absence of networking efforts to close the gap between the World Bank's 'best practices' and proposals based on local knowledge challenged the power of the Bank's Legal Department to implement its paradigm regarding judicial reform. Furthermore, the role of the Bank was discredited as its programme lost legitimacy, influence and position in the sector.

The PROJUM was fiercely questioned within the discussions of the *Mesa de Diálogo* and its continuation made conditional on a re-evaluation of outcomes and the goals for implementation within a broader programme designed and implemented by previously excluded local experts. In consequence, PROJUM's continuation was renegotiated and, in turn, subsumed within a new nationally based judicial reform programme, called the Integral Programme of Judicial Reform (*Programa Integral de Reforma Judicial* – PREJUD). The Integral Programme was drafted and implemented with the supervision of the Ministry of Justice in July 2000 (see Reforma Judicial 2004).

Néstor Kirchner, ex-governor of the Province of Santa Cruz, who was elected in May 2003 on a clearly anti-neoliberal/anti-Menem programme, was committed from the outset to the policies initiated by Duhalde. Economically, Kirchner consistently focused policy around rebuilding domestic industry, public works and public services. In a clear reversal of *Menemismo*, under Kirchner, the state undertook the role of monitoring and stimulating economic growth. Although he resisted re-nationalization, the government sought to renegotiate the terms under which foreign companies operate the public services privatized in the 1990s.

Politically and institutionally, Kirchner embarked on a radical programme based on the ongoing national proposals for judicial reform. Two main objectives were followed, one related to strengthening the judicial system, and the other to revoking the last remnants of the laws granting impunity to the perpetrators of crimes during Argentina's dark years of military dictatorship. These laws included the 1986 *Punto Final* (Full Stop) law, which set a 60-day deadline to file complaints for crimes committed during what was termed the 'war against subversion', and the 1987 *Obediencia Debida* (Due Obedience) law, which allowed hundreds of lower-ranking personnel to avoid prosecution under the claim that they were following orders. Congress sanctioned the annulment of these laws in August 2003, allowing the reopening of human rights cases against members of the police and military who took part in the 1976–1983 dictatorship. This was a major break with the past and an attempt to reconcile political with representative democracy (Peruzzotti 2001).

As for the goal of institutional strengthening, Kirchner also set in motion measures to strengthen the justice system. Soon after taking office, Kirchner called upon previously ignored civil society organizations and experts, some of who were involved in the aforementioned National Plan of Judicial Reform to help draft a decree to democratize the previously arbitrary selection of Supreme Court justices. Based on the pioneering report *A Court for Democracy*, Kirchner proposed concrete measures for a change in the selection process and the removal of judges of the Supreme Court, a reduction in the jurisdiction of the Supreme Court and other procedures leading to transparency and accountability (see ADC 2003). Both the substance of the proposal and the policy-making procedure based on the open participation of local experts addressed the long-standing conflict ignored by the World Bank's PROJUM. The proposal finally led to the presidential decree 222/03, in which the president of the nation self-limited his prerogatives in the designation of judges of the Supreme Court, and allowed major participation in the process of designation of such appointees. President Kirchner then established a new process that includes widely published announcements of judicial nominees' qualifications and a general profile for the consideration of civil organizations, the media and individuals who evaluate the proposed candidates. The curriculum of the nominee is made public on the website of the Ministry of Justice for public discussion. After three months, based on the results of the public scrutiny, the president can then present the nominee for the final consideration of the Argentine Senate. Equally radical, Kirchner pursued the removal of the Supreme Court members who were considered part of Menem's 'automatic majority'. By September 2005, either these judges were removed or they simply resigned. In 2006, Senator Cristina Fernandez de Kirchner, wife of President Néstor Kirchner and elected candidate for the presidential succession in December 2007, proposed a bill to reduce the number of Supreme Court judges back to five for parliamentary discussion.

It is important to note that despite the rapid introduction of crisis-resolving strategies, the institutionalization of a coherent and agreed-upon programme for governance is as yet uncertain. Institutionalization requires the generation of a social consensus about the 'rightness' of the policy mix, but the new balance of power among internal and external actors in the Argentine post-crisis polity is still evolving.

Contesting judicial reform

The former Chief Economist of the World Bank Joseph Stiglitz stated that the World Bank 'is in a good position to *scan globally* to identify good practices, and then it can play a brokerage role to facilitate a horizontal learning process between the developing countries facing certain problems and the countries with successful practice' (Stiglitz 2000: 12, emphasis in original). In other words, the (Knowledge) Bank can 'reinvent locally' if it acts as an 'intermediary' transferring *knowledge* about policies, administrative arrangements or institutions to be used in the development of policies, administrative arrangements and institutions elsewhere. This is reminiscent of what in the literature of public policy is referred to as 'policy transfer' and 'policy diffusion' (Dolowitz and Marsh 1996: 344). However, as it has been suggested in our analysis, whatever the leverage of the World Bank, both financially and in terms of knowledge and policy paradigms, grounding policy change in developing countries is not simply the consequence of one-way nuanced diffusion of ideas and policy paradigms. In other words, it would be misleading and unrealistic to expect World Bank knowledge and IFIs' policy paradigms in general to be codified and transferred from knowledge-producers to knowledge-users on the assumption that local actors are passive factors in the knowledge-policy process, especially in highly politicized democratic societies. On the contrary, local experts and practitioners can take, modify or reject a paradigm or policy idea. In this context, 'crafting consensus' with pro-reform local actors is critical to assure that certain policy ideas are reproduced and reinforced on the ground (Taylor 2004: 124). This is particularly so in countries like Argentina, where a strong basis of local actors in the sector has been critical in articulating reform proposals, even before the World Bank's mission introduced negotiations for reform with the government.

The capacity of the World Bank to produce and diffuse knowledge on what constitutes good economic policy and good governance is a critical factor within the structure of power and global scope of the World Bank. The power of knowledge can be understood as the capacity of the World Bank to frame issues and outline solutions for the developing world. However, the case of judicial reform in Argentina showed that despite the unquestionable capacity of the Bank to influence the way people perceive and think of economic development, production and diffusion of knowledge are not sufficient elements in themselves to ensure policy change on the ground. The implementation of policy and institutional reforms are context-dependent processes and thus highly political. Actors, political incentives and resources are critical factors in shaping the path and depth of their implementation.

In the case of the World Bank's PROJUM, a logic of loan approval prevailed as a rationale and thus it fixed on securing agreement with key policy-makers rather than on reaching agreement with local experts on priorities for project implementation. Furthermore, the Bank's approach to reform as a mere transfer of blueprints and best practices not only limited the opportunities of local experts to affect the agenda at the level of decision-making, but also nourished the power of the Executive in judicial decision-making. By empowering certain actors to carry out a Bank project, there is a choice to be made in disempowering other actors and their policy ideas, knowledge and proposals for reform. However, rather than improving the environment for reform by engaging with local actors in networking activities and enhancing the support and capacity to lead the reform, the World Bank in-country mission followed a restricted strategy that hampered the implementation of the reform and led to increasing discredit of the project and the World Bank's role in the area. The cost of its discredit was seen in the cancellation of a pipelined project for judicial reform that was waiting for approval upon the results of the PROJUM in World Bank's headquarters. Furthermore, the poor reputation of the World Bank's judicial reform left its managers apart from the new participatory initiatives, such as *Mesa de Diálogo*, organized in the aftermath of the crisis to debate the terms of post-crisis governance in Argentina.

Ultimately, this case shows that the capacity of the World Bank to translate knowledge into instruments of policy change is limited if the Bank is unable to act as a 'broker' engaging with local actors for the implementation of policies on the ground. In the case of judicial reform in Argentina the capacity of the World Bank management to act as a broker was limited by contextual factors, mainly the lack of incentives for reform among key policy-makers, the approach of the management team towards local experts and expertise, and so of competing policy paradigms. While not rejecting the possibility that the World Bank's team in Argentina might have had the genuine objective of carrying out an efficient judicial reform, what mattered most for the Bank's mission in this case was the consolidation of a preconceived project for the establishment of what the mission considered 'sound institutions'.

Within this rationale, the World Bank's Legal Department, by acting as a mere conveyor of funds and policy ideas, made the government the 'owner' of the neoliberal-like reform while remaining within the Bank's control. The result was deepening bad governance habits, despite good intentions.

The absence of linkages with local actors in this case showed that although the World Bank had some influence in the policy stream by persuading the government to adopt the World Bank's programme, the adverse relationship with key local experts weakened its capacity to act as an effective 'broker' and thus a competing rather than a cooperating dynamic ensnared the Bank in the intricateness of local politics. By overlooking the existing local expertise and experience involved in policy formulation for judicial reform prior to the arrival of the Bank in the country, the staff from the Legal Department followed a more coercive type of intervention that sought to 'reinvent locally' by 'transplanting' paradigms, policy models and best practices, which, in this case, did not materialize into policy change and new institutions.

As explained in the next chapter, the capacity to engage in pro-reform networks is, in turn, not only critical for the World Bank staff – or any other multilateral agency – to secure consensus, but also may in all likelihood mean the difference between a well-designed intervention that mobilizes critical support and a failed initiative that alienates crucial clients.

Conclusion

This chapter offered an empirical analysis of the role of the World Bank in the case of judicial reform in Argentina during the 1990s. The case of judicial reform in Argentina confirms that an effective combination of funding and knowledge management for the articulation of global/World Bank paradigms and local frameworks increases the capacity of the Bank's managers to implement institutional reform in politically sensitive areas. In this case, reform failed as participation and ownership became frustrated. The empirical analysis supporting this chapter thus shows that despite corporate changes introduced towards the development of a 'Knowledge Bank' and the high-profile declarations of the importance of local knowledge and experience, the logic of the World Bank involvement in the case of judicial reform in Argentina was led by a 'culture of approval' tradition by which task managers tend to secure loan approval to fit in with the strategic framework supported by the World Bank.

The Bank management followed a loan approval rationale that focused on securing agreement with key policy-makers rather than reaching agreement with local experts. In this case, the mission of the Bank discouraged linkages with local experts and practitioners, over-looking other sets of ideas and proposals that were considered politically contending and challenging to the *status quo*. True, government consent was an important instrument in setting the conditions for programme negotiation, yet the case of judicial reform in Argentina proved that the sustainability of its implementation is clearly context-dependent. The lack of involvement of local knowledge in the terms and objectives of the reform programme that was negotiated with the government not only silenced the debate, but also narrowed the basis of legitimacy for policy implementation. The result was the approval of a de-contextualized project that failed in its implementation goals and thus in its continuation.

The approach of the World Bank staff in this case reflects the technical against the political tension in the approach to good governance. In this case, the search for good governance assumed that there is only one form of institutional design. This is consistently seen in those a-political definitions of state that separates it from its historical development and thus promotes a model of state that can be replicated in one country after another. But state institutions, as well as the state–society nexus, take different forms within a national territorial space at a particular moment in time. The empirical analysis offered in this chapter for the case of judicial reform shows how the IFIs-restricted understanding of governance is subsumed into an uncontroversial characterization focusing on state institutions and functions. But it also shows that state institutions cannot be divorced from the social relations that legitimize them through support or undermine them via various forms of opposition. Ultimately, policy change requires a political process that involves amalgamation and compromises between power, ideas, legitimacy and consensus. These elements underpin the capacity of the IFIs to move forward political and institutional reforms in developing countries. As the analysis in this chapter suggests, the lack of recognition of the importance of social contestation in policy struggles and the absence of networking efforts to close the gap between World Bank's 'best practices' and local knowledge challenged the dominant position of the World Bank's Legal Department and created a societal response in which the Bank lost legitimacy, autonomy, influence and position in the area of judicial reform. In this case, the technical approach to governance and its implementation advanced by Bank officials not only widened distrust and fragmentation within the sector but led the Bank itself to get caught up in a domestic conflict reinforcing restricted notions of democratization and policy-making.

The next chapter concentrates on anti-corruption in Argentina in order to compare the extent to which a different approach to governance led the World Bank to act as a 'broker' engaging with local experts for the design of policies and their implementation. This empirical analysis supports the overall claim of this book that governance reforms are entrenched in complex policy processes in which the dominance of a particular actor or paradigm *vis-à-vis* other contending actors or ideas cannot be reinforced simply by coercive means, but rather by integrating contesting impulses into a broader consensus to implement policy change on the ground.

5
Governance as Political Engagement: Promoting Anti-Corruption Policies in Argentina

Anti-corruption has also been an important component of the normative framework of the IFIs. Since the mid- to late 1990s the IFIs devoted vast amount of funds to support new programmes oriented to achieve public sector accountability (Santiso 2006). As in the case of judicial reform, funding for anti-corruption became another milestone in the road to good governance and, in this case, the main understanding of it has been achieving fiscal credibility. Despite the wide-reaching and large-scale work carried out by the IFIs, there are a number of major critiques levelled against these institutions. Critics claim that the IFIs and the foreign aid in general have used anti-corruption as a tool to impose global standards of moral authority and thus punish governments in the developing world. Many of these critics have based their arguments on the fact that the IFIs have tended to focus on financial issues leaving un-addressed, for instance, the role of private contractors in the misuse of funds and delivery of goods and services. The same political constraints that held down the IFIs in their promotion of judicial reform have shaped their approach to anti-corruption. Nevertheless, as this chapter explores, grounding such an agenda in developing countries has brought new issues of implementation that affected the way IFIs' staff linked with the local actors. The nature of the anti-corruption programmes affects not only the formal institutions of accountability, like judicial courts or regulations, but also the capacity of citizens to hold their own governments accountable. The incursion of external agents in this area, paradoxically, offered a new platform for claimants and activists to leverage against their own governments.

This chapter concentrates on the role of the World Bank's PREM and the WBI in advancing anti-corruption policies in Argentina. It explores the linkages between local actors and staff from the World Bank and discusses how the capacity of the World Bank staff to arrive at common ground with local actors outside the government won their consent to implement policy change effectively. In practice, this meant that rather than transferring preconceived models, task managers instead relied largely on policy proposals, data and background knowledge offered by local experts.

Anti-corruption projects implemented in Argentina before the 2001 crisis were part of a narrow conception of governance that mainly targeted transparency and accountability in specific aspects of the decision-making process. However, as World Bank staff engaged and even relied on local knowledge and expertise, the extent to which those programmes involved local actors' concerns expanded and so did the cooperation between the external and the domestic actors. Moreover, unlike other projects of governance such as the judicial reform, in this case the involvement of the World Bank as a 'broker' helped to push the national agenda into the policy-making process and thus to change the *status quo* that had inhibited other institutional reforms. This empowered local actors to demand more inclusive and responsive democratic governance at the outbreak of the crisis of December 2001.

By specifically focusing on two anti-corruption programmes in which the Bank staff and local actors were able to establish mutual trust and networking, this chapter explains how the World Bank's PREM and the WBI were able to draw on both its financial and knowledge resources to build and consolidate 'pro-reform networks' with domestic actors leading to effective policy change. The chapter is divided into four sections. The first section concentrates on the World Bank's agenda for anti-corruption, resuming the discussion on Bank approaches to governance. The second section introduces the problem of corruption in the Argentine context and analyses the actors, approaches and incentives in play. The third section focuses on the involvement of the World Bank in anti-corruption programmes in Argentina. It explores policy outcomes in two specific projects: the Anti-Corruption Office Programme and the Crystal Initiative. The fourth section discusses the brokerage role of the World Bank, considering knowledge, power (and empowerment of actors) and networks in the light of the recognition that amalgamation and compromises between actors' approaches and interests shaped the implementation process of anti-corruption programmes. The conclusion resumes and expands the discussion of the technical versus political dilemma in the implementation of governance reforms in developing countries.

Anti-corruption within the 'Knowledge Bank': An attempt to avoid the 'best practices' trap

The fight against corruption has been a paradigmatic milestone associated with the presidency of James Wolfensohn in the Bank (see World Bank 1997c). In his 1996 Annual Meeting speech President Wolfensohn made the fight against the 'cancer of corruption' a pivotal aspect of sustainable development. This was a critical juncture for the World Bank's promotion of governance as it explicitly established the commitment of Wolfensohn to the promotion of anti-corruption strategies. As claimed by Marquette,

> In early 1996, Wolfensohn invited Transparency International to make a presentation to the Bank's vice-presidents. This meeting resulted in the creation of the Corruption Action Plan Working Group in mid-1996, which eventually drafted the landmark 1997 publication, Helping Countries Combat Corruption: The Role of the World Bank. This document sets the Bank's strategy regarding anti-corruption and continues to guide its evolution.
>
> (2001: 401)

Since its articulation within the rhetoric and operational agenda of the World Bank, 'fighting corruption' has evolved as a distinctive norm for development assistance. The 1997 report *Helping Countries Combat Corruption* provided the framework for the Bank to address anti-corruption programmes. It also identified ways in which the Bank could help countries to implement anti-corruption policies and suggested how the Bank should mainstream consideration of the issue in its work. In addition, the report discussed the ways in which the World Bank could contribute to international efforts to control corruption and examined the control of fraud and corruption within Bank-financed projects. The anti-corruption agenda evolved based on three main concerns: (i) whether Bank projects are likely to be affected by corruption during design or implementation; (ii) the extent to which the achievement of development objectives is compromised by corruption; (iii) the willingness of the government to act to control corruption if it threatens the effectiveness of Bank projects and/or economic and social development (World Bank 1997c: 4).

The analytical and operational work of the PREM and the WBI on issues of governance and anti-corruption was ground-breaking. Within the World Bank Group, the WBI's Governance, Regulation, and

Finance Division and the PREM developed a singular expertise in anti-corruption programmes which was reflected in funded projects as well as in knowledge-related activities for the Bank staff, civil society and policy-makers in developing countries. Incentive-creation and capacity-building was particularly developed as a 'fresh niche' in the WBI, according to the Director of its Governance, Regulation and Finance Division (Robert Kaufmann, interview with author, 25 February 2002). As for the PREM, it became the anchor at the interface between knowledge and finance operations within the Bank. As argued by Marquette, the PREM is a 'central clearinghouse' for anti-corruption work within and outside the Bank (Marquette 2001: 9). In 1997, a specific thematic group was also created within the PREM for the analysis and evaluation of anti-corruption programmes. This impetus drove anti-corruption strategies from the outset. According to a Bank official, the adoption of anti-corruption required the Bank staff to adapt to more comprehensive ways of approaching development economics and assistance efforts in developing countries (Sahr Kpundeh, interview with author, 19 May 2004). This claim was acknowledged in the World Bank's 1997 report by the statement that committed leadership and support from civil society are essential and thus 'the World Bank can help, but aid conditionality cannot substitute if political will is missing' (World Bank 1997c: 5). Furthermore, the 2004 review of progress in anti-corruption activities in World Bank assistance since 1997 acknowledged that

> In many countries where corruption is entrenched, governments lack either the will or the capability to mount effective anti-corruption programmes, [...] the Bank may choose to amplify citizens' voice and strengthen exit mechanisms.
>
> (World Bank 2004b: 52)

The recognition of local actors other than government officials – specifically civil society practitioners, experts, scholars, consultants, policy-makers and journalists – has been part and parcel of the anti-corruption programmes developed by the WBI and the PREM. Two main issues facilitated a more flexible approach to governance. First, these units are at the intersection between knowledge and funding (Riggirozzi 2007: 209–210). For instance, to integrate the knowledge content of Bank products into country circumstances, some units of the World Bank, in particular the PREM within the Public Sector Group and the WBI, developed activities aimed at drawing in local experts throughout the project cycle. Some of these activities were part of capacity-building programmes via taught programmes and training, such as seminars and in-country workshops, training and learning courses for policy-makers and civil society organizations. Other analytical work also involved country assessments, such as the Financial Accountability Assessment, the Institutional and Governance Review and governance indexes (WBI 2002). Furthermore, some of their staff brought with them the lessons of previous participation in the USAID Rule of Law Programme. This is, for instance, the case of Linn Hammergren, Senior Public Sector Manager for Latin America and Task Manager for Anti-Corruption Programmes in Argentina. Both the PREM and the WBI were strongly supported by President Wolfensohn as part of the institutional reconfiguration that led to the CDF and the Strategic Compact, including the emblematic Knowledge Bank.

The adoption of anti-corruption within the governance agenda came sometime after World Bank judicial reform programmes were already at the implementation stage in several developing countries, such as Venezuela, Bolivia and Ecuador. These programmes were caught in political tensions that jeopardized their implementation and thus the Bank's Legal Department was vehemently accused of advancing reforms as 'a template' that was replicated across countries, regardless of their political, economic and social characteristics (Human Rights First 2000). As analysed in the previous chapter, local actors considered the Bank efforts to be imposing a competing agenda designed 'to smooth the way for North American and Western European trade and investment in the region' rather than as a response to local priorities (Carothers 2001: 19). The programmes of judicial reform were often unsuited to local realities. In view of this, the WBI and the PREM officials targeted governance from a different perspective. As explained by a PREM Senior Public Sector Specialist, 'broadly, while judicial reform looked at the institutional bases of court management, anti-corruption initiatives focused on the micro-management of public expenditure, procurement, information disclosure and auditing. This emphasis placed the focus on incentives and thus working with the local actors proved critical for the achievement of anti-corruption reforms' (Richard Messick, interview with author, 17 May 2004).

Broadening the scope for action

The World Bank's governance agenda was carefully justified in economic terms and legitimized by a normative approach grounded on theoretical and evidence-based knowledge developed within its Development

Economics Research Group (DECRG), the operational unit involved in the promotion of new governance-related programmes and the WBI. Nonetheless, governance and its normative goals of promoting transparency, accountability and the rule of law in development countries were not formulated without controversy. The *WDR 2000/2001: Attacking Poverty* was evidence of not only the existing differences between an 'old guard and a new guard' within the Bank regarding new development paradigms, but also the fact that economic variables still defined the priorities and *modus operandi* of the Bank (Ritzen 2005: 113). The normative goals implicit in the new agenda of governance of the IFIs in general have not been accompanied by a critical discussion within the institutions about how to conceptualize their own operations and political implications of implementation for such politically sensitive changes in developing countries. In the case of the World Bank, Harrison argues that despite rhetoric it still lacks a 'theory of political action' (2005: 244–247). In other words, despite definitions, yet much about how to proceed with it was left to discretion of the missions operating on the ground. In some cases, as the analysis of the previous chapter suggests, the consequences for the modalities of promotion of governance goals have been, paradoxically, detrimental to the cause of quality of governance. In practice, in some circumstances the Bank staff approached reform as a process of *transfer* of blueprints and 'best practices' by negotiating funded projects with the government, overlooking local experts and expertise. In others, however, the Bank staff engaged with local expertise for the framing of the problem and the implementation of the solution.

Rethinking the implications of the knowledge/policy nexus for the implementation of governance-related reforms in terms of a theory of action provides new ground for further analysis of intervention by the World Bank in governance operations in developing countries. It also proposes a new approach in the analysis of how the Bank understands state, market and civil society relations. The cases of judicial reform and anti-corruption analysed in this book suggest that from the point of view of the World Bank staff the state is considered either as a complex relationship between the government (Executive and judiciary for instance) and local actors (civil society practitioners, local experts, academics, among others), or as a technical, a-political institutionalization of procedures and norms. Therefore, while in the first case reform is considered to be the result of a process of amalgamation and compromises between actors' interests and ideas, in the second policy change is expected to result from a (rational) decision-making process based on an efficient, cost–benefit choice. In other words, while the role of the Bank as a mere 'conveyor' of funds and knowledge or paradigms underestimates the importance of local knowledge, the process of norm-brokerage is critical in articulating global/World Bank and local knowledge to push through effective implementation of changes in politically sensitive areas of reform. The different approach to state and civil society among the Bank staff also reinforces the claim that the Bank is not a uniform institution. There are fundamental differences in approach in terms of an institutional lag resulting from the different adaptation of units and staff to new ideas and development practices. According to Weaver, 'judicial reform has been largely initiated by staff members with the previously marginalized Bank Legal Department'; moreover, she continues, 'the relation between PREM and the Legal Department's staff has often been quite strained' (2005: 42). In the case of Argentina's governance reforms, the lack of recognition of the political aspects in undertaking reforms in the judicial system, and the focus on institutional aspects of the reform had (unintended) effects on the implementation of policy change, and further empowered a government agenda that, paradoxically, sought to retain the *status quo*.

Moving away from the exclusive focus on the judiciary, the PREM and the WBI broadened their scope in terms of the actors involved. World Bank task managers and country officials within these units involved in programmes of modernization of the state and the promotion of transparency in the Latin America region acknowledged that a broader consensus on the reform agenda was needed. While judicial reform assumed that consensus at the highest level of government would suffice to make reform happen, reformers promoting anti-corruption within the Bank recognized the importance of including not only the government but also external actors such as the NGOs and the media as key drivers of anti-corruption reforms. Some units and staff within the Bank also recognized that demands for governance-related assistance might not be of interest to governments, given the political consequences that the enforcement of anti-corruption policies might bring. Thus, a different stance was taken by some task managers, which appealed to alternative interlocutors to foster policies that governments would not themselves apply.

In order to gain a broader consensus of local actors, staff from the WBI and the PREM promoted knowledge-related activities to strengthen the policy capacity of local actors in the formulation and implementation of policy and institutional reforms. Exchange of ideas and knowledge was undertaken through courses, training, workshops, exchange of experts and pilot programmes supported with grants or small loans. These activities were beyond formal consultation with civil society – an accepted procedure within the World Bank since the mid-1990s. Exchange of ideas and expertise helped to articulate World Bank and local knowledge and to put policy ideas into practice. In this context, the engagement of the World Bank in anti-corruption issues marked not only a turning point in terms of traditional areas of involvement and support in developing countries, but also the emergence of a new dynamic in terms of combining research and knowledge activities with funding instruments. The remaining sections analyse this experience and explore different patterns of involvement of the World Bank and the implications for the policy outcome in the case of anti-corruption policies in Argentina.

The problem of corruption in Argentina

One of the most striking Argentine paradoxes during Menem's administration was that while he presided over a period of unprecedented economic prosperity and a transformation of the state, this process was accompanied by increasing levels of corruption (Manzetti 2000). As explored in Chapter 3, the far-reaching process of privatization of state assets and market-oriented reforms, which established the country as a flagship for the IFIs, brought about corruption practices involving many top government officials and major international corporations like IBM, Citibank and the Spanish telecommunications company Telefónica (Verbitski 1993; Abeles *et al.* 2001). In turn, cases of corporate corruption gave the problem an international resonance that alerted investors considering further business in the country (Manzetti 2000). The IBM scandal that broke in 1996 was, in fact, one of many cases of corruption related to bribery and fraud involving the state. In the specific case of IBM, this involved a US$21 million bribe paid by IBM Argentina for a US$249 million contract with the state-owned Central Bank. Other cases of corruption involved contracts and procurement related to national services, such as the national pensions administration agency, misuse of public funds and embezzlement, and vote-buying scandals in the Senate as members of the Parliament were bribed to ensure the passage of controversial market-oriented reforms. By the end of Menem's administration, several corruption allegations included the prosecution of Menem and Cavallo for their alleged participation in the smuggling of arms to war zones (Croatia and Ecuador) in spite of international embargoes (Tedesco 2002: 474).

As in the case of judicial reform, anti-corruption proposals were articulated by local experts before the arrival of the World Bank mission in the country. Thus, in tandem with the growing awareness of the deterioration of the rule of law and the politicization of the judiciary, corruption in public administration soon became the focus of civil campaigns for transparency and accountability. Although there were limited opportunities to influence the policy making process and translate proposals into public policies during the ten years of the Menem administration, local experts and practitioners consistently worked on alternative policies of monitoring and increasing transparency and accountability and led civil campaigns to enhance public awareness of corruption. As analysed in Chapter 4, political interference in the administration of justice by the Executive neutralized the accountability functions of the courts and therefore created institutional incentives for encouraging corruption. Judicial investigation of corruption in this context was futile. Aware of the limitations of the judicial system as an oversight mechanism and that proposals for reform supported by the World Bank's Legal Department were oriented towards modernization of the system rather than towards tackling corruption in the country, a group of experts and practitioners from NGOs concentrated their efforts on alternative channels for the development of anti-corruption practices. Among these organizations, the campaigns of ADC, FARN and CELS were the most significant. These organizations were influenced to a great extent by the pioneering work of *Poder Ciudadano* and its campaigns on transparency and accountability in public administration from the late 1980s (Manzetti 2000).

The limited support from the World Bank's Legal Department on topics of anti-corruption led these organizations to seek external support from other units within the Bank that did acknowledge the importance of (local) knowledge for development and implementation of programmes, such as the WBI and the PREM. Local experts from organizations such as *Poder Ciudadano*, CELS and ADC noted that in contrast to the experience of the Bank's Legal Department in judicial reform, the WBI and the PREM were developing a rhetoric that put civil society and local knowledge at the centre of policy formulation and, more importantly, saw it as an indirect way of monitoring government policies and public services. This was most notably the case among some staff of the PREM who had been previously engaged with local actors as part of the USAID Rule of Law Programme in Argentina.

Internationally, in preparation for the 1998 Summit of the Americas, the US government launched a campaign through which the countries of the region would agree to observe public ethics and transparency in public administration (Acuña and Alonso 2003: 128–129). Additionally, this agenda was marked by three main international trends: (i) the establishment of the Convention Against Bribery of Foreign Public Officials in International Transactions of the OECD in 1996; (ii) the Inter-American Convention against Corruption (IACC), signed by 23 countries in March 1996 and ratified by Argentina in October 1997; (iii) the increasing international awareness of the impact of corruption on markets, led primarily by the World Bank, the IDB and (with a less proactive approach) other organizations such as the IMF.

While the international agenda of anti-corruption helped to amplify national NGOs' campaigns to propel the national agenda into the policy-making process, the government reacted pragmatically. While not fully committed to anti-corruption reforms since these could jeopardize members of Menem's administration, the presidential elections to be held in October 1999 placed the issue of curbing corruption under the spotlight of political campaigns. The lack of public support for Menem's presidential candidacy, which was launched despite an earlier Court decision claiming that running for a consecutive third term was unconstitutional, and the mounting corruption scandals led the government to respond to some trends that were, to some extent, unavoidable (also Helmke 2003). In this context, the Argentine Congress ratified the IACC through Law No. 24.759 and followed its recommendation by creating at the end of 1997 the ONEP. The ONEP was created by decree (Decree 152/97) and expected to (i) investigate public officials suspected of corruption, enforcing the requirements of the Inter-American Convention against Corruption at the national level; (ii) denounce to the judiciary those events that might constitute a crime; (iii) become a plaintiff in those trials where the Federal Treasury had been negatively affected; (iv) administer the sworn financial disclosures of government officials; (v) develop programmes to prevent corruption and promote transparency in public administration (Meagher 2002: 41). Although this initiative was seen as a first step towards transparent policy-making, the ONEP was part of the Interior Ministry, an institution that not only had been accused of arbitrary behaviour and corruption but was also under the direct authority of the Executive Branch. Predictably, the ONEP became an ineffective institution, created as it was as a strategic response to placate national and international concerns relating to the corruption scandals of the Menem administration. Despite the rhetoric, in practice this anti-corruption initiative showed no clear results. The ONEP lacked the authority to investigate cases. These reservations were supported by the fact that it was not until September 1999 that the Argentine Congress approved a Public Ethics Act (*Ley de Etica Pública*), which outlined the purpose and scope of the ONEP. Furthermore, two years after the creation of the Ethics Office, a Gallup poll surveying the perception of corruption in the country's public institutions showed that this public agency was considered by the public as one of the most corrupt institutions in the nation (Newsline 1999). Nonetheless, in December 1999 a window of opportunity opened as the change in presidential administration forced extensive consideration of the problem of corruption and the weak rule of law. Among local experts and practitioners there was tacit agreement that this was the time to move ahead with proposals and action plans that had been developed in the shadow of a decade of Menemist administration.

Local experts and contesting ideas: Promoting reform from within

Fernando De la Rúa took office in late 1999. He was the candidate of the winning electoral alliance, the '*Alianza*', formed by a traditional centre-left party, the Radical Civic Union and the Front for a Solidary Country (*Frente del País Solidario* – FREPASO), largely formed by dissidents from the Peronist Party. As corruption was a major political issue in the Argentine electoral campaign of 1999, once in power, the presidency of the 'Alianza' promised to eliminate corrupt practices and restore citizens' confidence in state institutions.

From the time it began to campaign, the Alianza was advised by a think-tank, the *Instituto Programático de la Alianza*, which gathered together experts from the NGOs who had been involved in the anti-corruption programme during the Menem era, who provided the background analysis and proposals to eventually form, with the support of the PREM and the WBI, the Anti-Corruption Office. While the experts and think-tanks making up the epistemic-like community in the area of judicial reform were not significantly involved in the design of anti-corruption policies, the experts who developed the field of anti-corruption in Argentina were less involved in judicial reform and more engaged in advocacy campaigns related to rule of law and human and civic rights rather than to public administration (also Chapter 3 in this volume). According to the former Director of the Monitoring Programme for Financing of Election Campaigns, one of the pioneering campaigns launched by *Poder Ciudadano* in 1999, 'the approach of NGOs and experts linked to anti-corruption campaigns brought to the forefront the relationship between money and politics, rather than mere institutional aspects of the system. This relationship was central to the democratic functioning of institutions' (Christian Gruenberg, interview with author, 15 February 2004). This approach underpinned the work of these organizations and gave this epistemic-like community a distinctive profile that differed from the approach to governance reforms adopted by the other community involved in judicial reform.

The fact that experts and practitioners from NGOs concerned with anti-corruption had a particular sense of 'belonging' since they were educated in similar institutions, such as the University of Buenos Aires in Argentina and the University of Yale in the US, helped in forming an emergent epistemic community. Their work, in the shadow of the Menemist administration, developed in the early 1990s from campaigning for civil rights and watchdog activities to more proactive proposals for policy reform in different areas of public administration. *Poder Ciudadano* acted as a platform for most of these actors and experts on anti-corruption. The set of knowledge they produced drew on their scientific research and, even more strongly, from their advocacy action. As part of *Poder Ciudadano* in some cases, and as independent consultants in others, local experts were involved in agenda-setting and the implementation of policies related to rule of law, transparency and accountability. They also interacted and participated in the design and dissemination of policy programmes and taught courses in collaboration with the WBI and the PREM in Latin American countries. Moreover, as explored further in the following section, in contrast to the experience of the experts in the policy area of judicial reform, the anti-corruption community capitalized on its work with the WBI and the PREM and, as explored in Chapter 6, in recent years they have turned their activities towards a more proactive engagement in governance reform in the post-crisis government of Néstor Kirchner.

The different approaches among local actors and organizations regarding governance were reflected in the proposals considered in the national discussion forum, the *Mesa de Diálogo*, organized by various actors following the economic and political crisis of 2001 (see Chapters 3 and 6). The evolution of judicial reform and anti-corruption reflected two discussions or paradigms that envisioned different definitions of problems and solutions in terms of how to approach institutional change. According to the Director of ADC, 'those involved in judicial reform emphasized efficiency and the administration of justice, while those involved in anti-corruption worked towards a different model of political and institutional structure' (Roberto Saba, interview with author, 18 December 2003). As indicated by the Director of CELS, 'the difference between those actors that concentrate merely on judicial reform and those that understand the problem as a broader crisis of corruption and impunity is a difference between reforming institutions or transforming them by means of establishing a new way of making policy' (Victor Abramovich, interview with author, 18 June 2004).

This idea of 'a new way of making policy' supported by local experts and practitioners advanced the national agenda of anti-corruption in Argentina and shaped the relationship between knowledge and policy implementation. As corruption was associated emblematically with the presidency of Carlos Menem, the new administration of Fernando De la Rúa made this issue central to its policy platform. Once in office in December 1999, Ricardo Gil Lavedra, De la Rúa's Minister of Justice, called in local anti-corruption experts to draft the anti-corruption policies to re-equip and enforce the work of National Office of Public Ethics, which had been discredited for lacking the power to investigate cases in its short life during Menem's administration. Two specific measures were proposed: (i) to review financial disclosure forms in search of potential conflicts of interest on the part of the newly appointed Ministers, Secretaries of State and other members of the Executive Branch; (ii) to draft an access to information bill. These proposals were institutionalized in the Anti-corruption Office in 2000. One of the first tasks of the Anti-corruption Office's Department for Transparency Policies was, in effect, to redesign the financial disclosure system inherited from the ONEP to monitor effectively the progress of the assets of public officials as well as to detect possible cases of conflict of interest (De Michele 2004: 9).

As analysed in the next section, the involvement of the World Bank in funding and knowledge-related activities was critical for the development of functions and recruitment to the Anti-Corruption Office. As argued, some Bank officers became more adept at facilitating and coordinating local knowledge producers, activists and decision-makers in order to put ideas into practice. In the case of anti-corruption in Argentina, the Bank staff from the PREM and the WBI created a policy window by brokering global and local knowledge for the formulation and implementation of policies. As the analysis suggests, this practice has had important policy implications since it was aimed at developing or strengthening local actors' expertise to develop the bases for further policy-making within the newly established Anti-Corruption Office.

The World Bank and the politics of anti-corruption in Argentina

Anti-corruption programmes supported by the World Bank were introduced in Argentina in late 1999, on the eve of a change in presidential administration. In 2000 the Public Sector Group in collaboration with the WBI and the Evaluation Department released the *Anti-corruption Diagnostic for Argentina* (World Bank 2000c). This report offered an overview based on research done in late 1999. Drafted immediately before the change of national government, the report was very critical of the anti-corruption measures implemented during Menem's administration and recommended conditions to overcome the political factors that affected investor confidence. The report called for the enforcement of transparency in public administration and the strengthening of the supervision of institutions that lacked a clear mandate and functions. The World Bank categorically stated that

> While ONEP during its existence in the Secretariat of the Presidency also received and forwarded complaints, neither it, nor the Ombudsman, whatever their other achievements, were reported to have accomplished much in this area. In short, the diffusion of responsibilities for administrative investigations among a variety of agencies, none of which had been adequately equipped for the job, only encouraged a dilution of accountability and a tendency for cases to be lost in the system.
>
> (*ibid.*: 12)

The World Bank's Country Assistance Strategy (CAS) for Argentina for the fiscal years 2001–2004 took some of this advice and explicitly required the new administration of De la Rúa to implement efforts to reduce 'waste and corruption' and to improve the business environment by reforming the judiciary (World Bank 2000b: 22–24). Following these recommendations De la Rúa initiated a series of initiatives, which included (i) enforcing the provisions of the Inter-American Convention Against Corruption (Law No. 24.759); (ii) the adoption of new regulations to increase the transparency, efficiency and equity of contracting procedures; (iii) the disclosure of information relative to public administration (the Crystal Government Initiative); (iv) an Anti-Corruption Office agreement with a number of local NGOs to perform monitoring activities over public declarations. The government also agreed with the World Bank on the initiation of a research programme to diagnose the incidence of corruption in the public sector (World Bank 2000b: iv).

Having experienced the crisis of rampant corruption, the new president was forced to give a rapid and satisfactory response not only to his constituency but also to donors and external investors. The change in government and the general perception of 'bad governance' not only provided opportunities for local experts and NGOs to influence a new way of approaching policy-making and anti-corruption programmes, but also opened the way for some World Bank staff to fill the normative vacuum. However, the task managers of the Bank involved in the promotion of good governance faced two dilemmas: either they became involved in the promotion of governance-related programmes on the basis of preconceived ideas of what constituted good policies and good reforms, or the Bank staff engaged with knowledge and local expertise for the framing of both the problem and the solution. The experience of judicial reform had demonstrated that the lack of compromise with local experts for the design and implementation of policy reform was a formula that led to truncated results. Development assistance in this case was reduced to a process in which knowledge (in the form of codified best practices) was considered by the Bank staff as a commodity to be 'transferred' from the donor agency to a receiving country. Moreover, although the Bank mission obtained government approval and secured loan disbursement, lack of consensus and support from local experts delegitimized the bases for the implementation of Bank-supported judicial reform. Evidence showed that the transfer of knowledge, and even the commitment on the part of government agencies to accept that knowledge, was insufficient to assure success in the implementation of policies on the ground. Putting local knowledge 'in the driver's seat' was a critical lesson for the Bank staff in terms of materializing policy ideas into new institutions. This was especially so in a country with a strong national knowledge base.

This recognition led to a different mode of involvement by the PREM and the WBI in the field, and to a different dynamic between knowledge and compliance in the implementation of anti-corruption policies. In the case of judicial reform, the World Bank's manager and country actors were unable to set a pro-reform network for the definition and implementation of projects in the sector. In this case, the rationale of loan approval led the World Bank's Legal Department to support the government agenda rather than the consensual knowledge articulated by experts from legal and business think-tanks and from the Ministry of

Justice. As explained in Chapter 4, the PROJUM's management did not seek to amalgamate and compromise the Legal Department's paradigms and normative approach to policy change with local actors' approaches and interests. Thus, the fate of judicial reform in Argentina was sealed by competition and mistrust that worked against an effective articulation of knowledge and funding for policy change. In contrast, in the case of anti-corruption neither the Bank staff nor the local actors saw each other's proposals as exclusionist options or conflicting paradigms.

On these bases, some officials within the Bank, in particular from the PREM and the WBI, strongly involved in governance topics recognized that when a given paradigm enjoys local consent and does not rely on explicit forms of persuasion or coercive indoctrination in the process of loan negotiation, it is more likely to gain political legitimacy for the implementation of paradigms. In order to enhance bases of local legitimacy, a process of amalgamation of local and World Bank ideas is needed, and therefore of compromises among paradigms or collective images that World Bank and local groups form individually regarding certain issues. But the change in incentives towards cooperation and exchange was recognized not only among the World Bank staff but also among local actors. Local experts reappraised the role of the World Bank in governance goals. That is, local experts and practitioners concerned with anti-corruption realized that the Bank is not an uniform institution and acknowledged that particular units and managers within the Bank were more inclined to combine knowledge and funds in pursuing policy and institutional reforms. Engaging in networking activities with World Bank managers, and participating in World Bank–sponsored knowledge activities could then be a vehicle to maximize their opportunities of visibility, legitimization and influence in public policy. Ultimately, synergies for mutual learning between the World Bank staff and the local actors were based on a mutual need to improve anti-corruption policies at the local level. At the same time, for the World Bank, and in particular for the PREM and the WBI, amalgamation with local experts and expertise enhanced cumulative knowledge, and set the parameters for the type of beliefs, ideas and world perceptions in the promotion of anti-corruption and governance programmes in general.

In this context, two projects were supported by the PREM and the WBI in Argentina: an Institutional Development Facility (IDF) Grant approved in June 1999 to support the establishment of the Anti-Corruption Office; and the Crystal Government Initiative, a technical assistance project aimed at enhancing transparency in public administration by making available online all the information concerning the public use of funds. This included not only statistics on the amount of money devoted to different government programmes, but information on the process through which these funds were administered. The Crystal Initiative was a component within a Bank-sponsored US$30,000,000 Modernisation of the State Programme. As assessed by Smulovitz and Peruzzotti, these initiatives were pioneering instruments that promoted new forms of social accountability, developing as vertical, non-partisan mechanisms of civic control of public management and policy-makers based on the proposals of civil society organizations (2000). These initiatives also capitalized on the innovation and progress of information and communication technology for public administration. In turn, the support of the World Bank's PREM and the WBI for the establishment of the Anti-Corruption Office and the portal-based Crystal Government Initiative helped to develop a system to monitor civil servants, policy-makers, politicians and party candidates, and at the same time this opened new institutional channels through which to denounce illegal actions in policy affairs. These policies not only nurtured the cause of good governance but also helped to reduce the democratic deficit related to the lack of checks and balances in state institutions (*ibid.*).

Although the local office gave new impetus to the involvement of civil society in Bank operations, consultation processes were particularly focused on issues of social programming such as maternal and child health, and nutrition and education. The formulation of judicial reform and anti-corruption projects within the local office's activities was marginal. In November 1998, the then Resident Representative Patricio Millán and the NGO Liaison Officer Sandra Cesilini agreed with a consultative group, the NGO-Working Group formed that year for the monitoring of World Bank general policies and activities, to discuss on an 'informal' basis the Bank's programme agenda for the country based on the (already approved) CAS for Argentina. The discussions were held in the Latin American Faculty of Social Sciences (FLACSO) in Argentina. This was the first time that such a meeting between the World Bank and the civil society had taken place in Argentina. The discussions were based on policy notes extracted from contents of the CAS since some parts, mostly those related to structural adjustment and institutional reform, remained 'confidential' (Senderowitsch and Cesilini 2000: 46). A further round of consultation was conducted between March and June 2000 for the development of a new CAS. Background material was *produced* and *provided* by the Bank to academics and representatives from NGOs based on the World Bank's Economic and Social Work and other operational documents.

Notwithstanding the relevance of these events supported by the World Bank's Resident Office, civil society participation differed from the exchange seen in the case of the PREM and the WBI for anti-corruption policies. That is, while the Resident Office fostered consultation and discussions with local beneficiaries and representatives of civil society organizations, the PREM and the WBI emphasized joint design and implementation of reform projects with local experts.

The Anti-Corruption Office Programme

The Anti-Corruption Office Programme is a World Bank IDF grant of US$410.000. It was approved in June 1999 for the purpose of institutional strengthening. The Anti-Corruption Office of Argentina was created by law No. 25.233 to enforce the provisions of the Inter-American Convention Against Corruption. The institutional design of the office reflected the basic structure of the Convention, which established pre-emptive as well as punitive policies (De Michele 2001). The main task of the Anti-Corruption Office was to replace the old ONEP, created in 1997 by the Menem administration (Decree 152/1997). The new institution was created to enforce the unfulfilled promises of its predecessor and thus to investigate suspected cases of corruption among public officials, as well as to develop anti-corruption policies (Ministerio de Justicia 2001). The Anti-Corruption Office's jurisdiction was designed to oversee actors and agencies managing public funds, such as the Executive, ministries and secretariats, public corporations and public or private institutions. Linn Hammergren, task manager from the PREM, supervised the Bank's IDF grant for the creation of this anti-corruption body. Disbursements of the grant were conditioned on the adoption of concrete and detailed plans aimed at institutional strengthening by the government of Argentina. The total disbursement was scheduled for two years, but an extension was granted till October 2003.

In an attempt to show independence and transparency in its undertakings, the Anti-Corruption Office capitalized on the work of non-party-affiliated experts, most of them from *Poder Ciudadano*, for the institutionalization of policies and procedures such as norms regarding public disclosure of assets (Manzetti 2002). Moreover, *Poder Ciudadano* was also the source of most of the members who created and later staffed the Anti-Corruption Office. For instance, Roberto de Michele, former President of *Poder Ciudadano*, was crucial in the establishment of the Anti-Corruption Office and was the Director of the Department of

Transparency Policies; similarly, Roberto Saba, *Poder Ciudadano*'s former Executive Director, and Néstor Baragli the current senior analyst in the Anti-Corruption Office's Department of Transparency Policies, participated in the design of anti-corruption policies. This circumstance was a major element in the shaping of the relationship with the World Bank staff for anti-corruption policies in the country.

As local experts and practitioners were the predominant actors in the sector, and given that their motivation was based less on ideological or partisan ideologies than on civic rights, the World Bank task managers faced fewer constraints in involving this local expertise in the formulation of anti-corruption policies for Argentina. Design, negotiation and implementation of policies have had as interlocutors policy-makers that have no partisan affiliation but rather were recruited to occupy positions within the Anti-Corruption Office based on their experience and previous participation in NGO campaigns and watchdog activities, in particular in *Poder Ciudadano*. In contrast to the judicial sector, actions taken in the area of anti-corruption were part of a generalized political will led by local experts and their knowledge rather than by a logic of corporate interests. The Prevention and Transparency Policies Department of the Anti-Corruption Office made important improvements in terms of the transparency of the sworn statement of new government representatives. It also brought in several cases of suspected corruption during Menem's administration. Some of the most important policies implemented by local experts with the support of the World Bank were the implementation of Internet-based financial disclosure forms; diagnosis of corruption in the National Public Administration; the evaluation of financial disclosure forms (illicit enrichment and conflicts of interest); legislation on lobby, whistle-blower protection, public procurement and access to public information; assets recovery research and corruption evaluations; and the implementation of IACC at sub-national levels.

The anti-corruption drive in Argentina has a fair way to go and the institutional mechanisms of enforcement need further strengthening, particularly at the provincial level; significant progress has nevertheless been made in the institutionalization of control and prevention and to a lesser extent in the sanctioning of corruption. The Anti-Corruption Office allows any citizen to make a claim of corruption to the Office for Investigation. If supported by preliminary evidence, the claim proceeds to the courts (Oficina AntiCorrupción 2001). In 2000 alone, the Office filed 180 such cases (Risley 2003: 8, footnote 23). As reported by De Michele, the level of compliance with new anti-corruption mechanisms such as the financial disclosure system was 89 per cent in the period January–June 2003. Likewise, De Michele reported that 481 cases were analysed and preventive measures were taken to avoid potential conflicts of interest in certain situations (2004: 11–12; also Oficina AntiCorrupción 2003).

The Crystal Initiative (*Iniciativa Cristal*)

The Crystal Government Initiative is a component of an encompassing programme for the modernization of the state supported by the World Bank's Public Sector Group within the PREM. It is aimed at enhancing transparency in the use of public funds. Crystal Government is a portal managed by the National Office for Information Technologies (*Oficina Nacional de Tecnología de la Información* – ONTI), based in the Chief Office of the Cabinet under the Secretary of Public Administration. It is aimed at disclosing and disseminating information concerning the use of public funds in Argentina. It was launched in early 2000 to fulfil the mandate of the September 1999 Fiscal Responsibility Law (No. 25.152), which required that the state make available to its citizens information related to the administration of public funds regarding, for instance, the execution of budgets, purchase orders and public contracts, and staff financial and employment data (Razzotti 2003).

The Crystal Project was financed with resources from the Undersecretary of Public Administration (20 per cent) and a World Bank loan (80 per cent) supporting the National Plan for the Modernisation of the State (Loan No. 4423-AR). This programme was managed by Ronald Myers, Senior Public Sector Specialist from the PREM. The Modernisation of the State Programme was, in fact, the result of a re-assignment of funds after a proposal by the government to re-direct the remaining funds from a previous project, the *Year 2000 Technical Assistance Project*. *Year 2000* was negotiated in 1998 to assist the government to contain the disruption in the country's social and economic infrastructure as a consequence of possible central government systems' failures in processing data properly after 31 December 1999 (World Bank 1998b: 4). The restructuring of this project facilitated the creation of Crystal.

The Crystal Initiative has been part of new innovative assistance within non-lending strategies promoted by the Bank within the e-government scheme. The portal includes information on execution of budgets; purchase orders and public contracts; payment orders submitted to the National Treasury; financial and employment data on permanent and contracted staff and those working for projects financed by multilateral organizations; account of the public debt; tax and customs obligations of Argentine companies and individuals and regulations governing the provision of public services (Panzardi *et al.* 2002). The Crystal portal is organized into three thematic areas: (i) 'The State within Reach of All', which publishes information related to the distribution of funds between the national government and provinces; (ii) 'Goals and Results', which gathers information on all national policies, management-related issues and allocation of public funds; (iii) 'Accountability and Representatives', which gathers information related to the fight against corruption (Radics 2001).

The Crystal project observed public information disclosure that the IFIs demanded. Despite some limitations in terms of results, this particular 'e-government' project was presented as a flagship project by the World Bank's PREM in its promotion of anti-corruption measures. The Crystal Initiative contributed with elements that support the empowerment of citizens with information that allows them to monitor their political representatives more effectively. Of course, the project was at times limited by the lack of sustained political commitment to expand its reach and scope. An additional contextual problem was related to the 'digital gap' and access to the Internet to monitor and hold accountable government information provided in the Crystal portal (Axel Radics, interview with author, 1 December 2007). Nevertheless, Crystal is recognized as one major step in terms of public access to information on public sector management. In effect, this e-application has become part of a new governmental procedure to increase access to information and to fight corruption. This procedure has also reinforced the work of local experts and practitioners who previously worked on public information law in Argentina. As ultimately recognized by many local experts, the Bank supported policies and proposals that could not otherwise have been implemented if reliant on public funds, while at the same time it enhanced its paradigm of good governance and efficiency in public administration. Online disclosure of government information is not in itself enough to combat corruption, but the case of Crystal set an important precedent in the institutionalization of procedures that enhance transparency in the Argentine state and public policy-making. Crystal represented a window of opportunity for the strengthening of citizens' access to information and control of national policy practices and for local expertise leading anti-corruption policies, in this case promoted by the Anti-Corruption Office in Argentina.

Brokering knowledge, funds and reform networks

To analyse the role of the IFIs in politically sensitive reforms, such as anti-corruption, and to assess the ways and extent to which they act as an effective 'norm-broker' in the articulation of pro-reform networks or simply as a conveyor of funds and external paradigms, there are three elements to consider: the context in which the IFIs' staff operated in the field; the extent to which the financial and non-financial instruments promoted favoured joint efforts with local actors; and the policy implications of combining knowledge(s) and funds for engagement with local actors in pro-reform networks for the implementation of programmes.

Contextual considerations for the brokerage role of the World Bank in the case of anti-corruption in Argentina suggest that the initial political setting in terms of actors and proposals for reform in this policy area was significantly different from the political setting that shaped the path of judicial reform. A key difference was related to the nature of the reform programme. In the case of judicial reform the issue at stake was the reform of a long-established state institution. In contrast, the adoption of anti-corruption policies did not demand the modification of an established institution, but rather the identification and creation of policies that, once institutionalized, could serve as bases for further policy-making. Anti-corruption policies aimed at auditing public funds as well as at modifying and preventing the institutional incentives that allow the development of corrupt practices. As analysed in the previous chapter, the Argentine judicial system was shaped by a complex structure of social relations and divergent incentives and approaches that affected the prospects of the reform process. Although Argentina provided some of the most influential experts on judicial reform to other countries, reform in the domestic setting was affected by socio-political structures, conflicting systems of knowledge and a top-down model of intervention in which the World Bank subsumed local knowledge (and the participation of experts) to the disbursement of conditional funds as a means of transferring the Bank's frameworks. However, the implementation of anti-corruption policies in Argentina presented a different case; rather than conveying funds and policy paradigms, the Bank's managers from the PREM and officials from the WBI fostered common ground 'by supplying not *motivation* but perhaps resources to enable the doers to do what they were already self-motivated to do' (Ellerman 2001: 38). From this perspective, the PREM and the WBI created – rather than imposed their own requirements.

Thus, while in the case of judicial reform, linkages between local actors and the World Bank staff were erratic and inconsistent, in the case of anti-corruption, engagement with civil society organizations was a fundamental element in furthering anti-corruption policies. Together with local experts and NGOs, in particular *Poder Ciudadano*, the Public Sector Group within the PREM and the WBI designed operational tools and analytical work to put anti-corruption projects into practice. Furthermore, the World Bank's anti-corruption work in Argentina was mutually enhancing both for the informal 'epistemic community' and for the work of the PREM and the WBI. The latter, in particular, benefited from contributions and exchanges with national experts in the development and running of learning courses and training activities for other countries. Local experts were also involved as consultants for the PREM and the Institutional Integrity Department within the Bank.

In terms of empowering local expertise (and local experts), some actors emphasized that in the area of anti-corruption, World Bank–supported activities provided financial and non-financial resources facilitating the implementation of a national agenda that previously lacked support and interlocutors from the government. In this context, although 'the anti-corruption problem' might resound in the rhetoric of the IFIs, the setting of the agenda and implementation of policies in Argentina relied on networking with local actors' expertise. In order to create synergies and policy skills for reform management, working groups were formed involving the World Bank staff and members of relevant agencies to allow the exchange of information and experience and to identify specific problems. Rather than preconceived policies, the staff from the PREM and the WBI brought to the country data and toolkits as well as evidence-based knowledge and recommendations for public service reform. The local experts provided the experience, country-based knowledge and suggestions for public policy such as financial disclosure, monitoring and control of assets, and systems to prevent conflicts of interest. In the end, governance case became an area of political engagement enhancing at the same time the capacity of the local actors to hold the government accountable.

Conclusion

The micro-level analysis developed in the last two chapters for the cases of judicial reform and anti-corruption suggests that the power of the local actors and their policy stand must not be underestimated. The IFIs can have an important influence over the domestic policy of borrowers, particularly as in the 1980s and 1990s, when the external debt crisis forced several large debtor countries in Latin America to turn to the IMF and the World Bank for funds and technical advice. In such a context the IFIs were leading 'globalizers' (Woods 2006). Decades of interactions stemming from the debt crisis and subsequent adoption of neoliberal recipes in Latin America nurtured a regular policy dialogue that was fed by the rise of technocrats in powerful governmental positions and favoured a sharing of ideas between local officials and the IFIs. Commonality of outlook favoured 'transnational policy networks' and the internalization of neoliberalism as 'the only game in town' (Teichman 2001, 2007). International policy networks explain many of the convergent patterns in economic and political governance during the 1990s. Neoliberal principles assumed hegemony in policy-making circles in many Latin American countries, particularly in ministries of finance and planning, and from there exerted strong influence on policy-making. In this case the IFIs convey funds and policy ideas and the government acts as a 'transmission belt' (Cox 1987: 254).

True, there have been differences in the nature of these networks and the way their engagement affected policy change on the ground. The different mandate and institutional culture of the IFIs have long affected their approach to participation, ownership and policy engagement. Most of the literature in IPE tends to concentrate, however, on the networking patterns that develop from local officials (usually government and economic ministers) and the IFIs' staff. Less studied are the ways and extent to which IFIs can endorse popular claims and thus have an impact on the official agenda. This has possibly been the case since there have been fewer occasions when the IFIs supported civil society groups to pressurize a government to be more responsive and inclusive. However, in the case of anti-corruption policies in Argentina, for instance, the World Bank staff turned from government agencies towards civil society experts as champions of the Bank's normative agenda of good governance. While not explicitly targeting political aspects of preventing corruption, but rather improving transparency in public administration and the modernization of the state, World Bank's PREM and WBI's support for anti-corruption policies based on local expertise was seen to have the collateral effect of curbing administrative discretion and reducing bureaucratic corruption. Capitalizing on local knowledge also helped the Bank to broaden its bases of legitimacy to implement programmes not only in the national arena, but also in other countries. This nuanced approach also reflected an attempt to set aside long-established patterns of involvement reproducing a logic of 'one size fits all' formulas in favour of a locally owned approach entailing the active participation of local institutions, experts and civil society organizations.

In line with the analysis of judicial reform offered in the previous chapter, the empirical evidence developed in this chapter reinforced the argument that the IFIs' paradigms are not 'commodities' that can be simply codified and transferred on the assumption that local actors are passive receptors in the knowledge-policy process. In practice, the transfer of ideas in the case of judicial reform proved insufficient to assure success in policy implementation. Thus, the success of the World Bank in forging judicial reform and anti-corruption programmes has varied depending on the way and extent to which the Bank staff sought either to 'transfer' or to 'broker' financial resources, best practices and local expertise fostering the implementation of such policies. In other words, the leverage of the World Bank in advancing certain political-economic paradigms is to be seen not in the extent to which a policy programme is negotiated and approved by both government and World Bank officials, but rather by the success (or lack of it) with which those ideas are effectively implemented in institutions on the ground.

The findings presented in the implementation of governance-related reforms in Argentina provide new ground for rethinking the IFIs' governance operations in developing countries. While often the engagement of the IFIs with local actors tend to reinforce domestic technocratic approaches that echo (global) neoliberal agendas of development, it is also true – as the case of anti-corruption shows – that for external actors to have any impact on policy change in democratic contexts the consent of the government may not be enough. Rhetorical commitment to good governance has to combine with practical commitment to local actors' ideas and involvement in country's policy-making. It is therefore critical that the IFIs assist national campaigners to drive the national agenda forward through a more responsive and inclusive policy process. This conclusion is particularly relevant for middle-income countries, like Argentina, where local expertise regarding public policy is highly developed and where dependency on external funding varies over time. Beyond the analysis at the project level, broader questions thus arise from the present study about, on the one hand, the extent to which the role of the IFIs as brokers can improve democratic policy-making and, on the other, the extent to which they can help to overcome the difficulties and challenges of the policy implementation process in different contexts. On the other hand, particularly in the current context of political turmoil in Latin America, the pursuit of governance embodies latent tensions derived from open opposition to both the ideological project of governance supported by the IFIs and the top-down promotion of 'forms of state' compatible with their neoliberal project. The way the IFIs responded to these tensions is part of a new policy game *vis-à-vis* the local actors. The next chapter extends the discussion of power relations and governance reforms to the Argentine post-crisis resolution by asking three central questions: has governance become more political than technical in the new post-2001 crisis context; to what extent can the IFIs affect models of the state and development in a context in which political and economic crisis required a new beginning in terms of policy-making and legitimacy; and to what extent has the trend away from neoliberalism transformed power relationships between donor and recipient countries?

6
Governance after Neoliberalism in Argentina

The economic and political behaviour of national and international actors during crisis resolution reveals complex policy processes which challenge established elements of dominance as well as the intellectual basis on which that dominance is exercised. In the case of Argentina, the political and economic crisis that erupted in 2001 epitomized the general regional discontent with the neoliberal paradigm that had dominated for more than two decades through the financial and intellectual capabilities of the IFIs. In the Southern Cone especially, governments were seeking to break with the IFIs-sponsored rules, although not to replace them by autarchic governance projects. Response to crisis in Latin America has been closely related to new attempts to articulate alternatives to the Washington Consensus. This response to crisis left the IFIs with a major challenge as to how to approach the changing political scenario. The social and economic price of neoliberalism was deleterious and thus the reputation and legitimacy of the IFIs called to account.

This chapter concentrates on crisis resolution in Argentina and how a new space for dissention from global rules affected policy dynamics between local and external actors. The chapter argues that the current backlash within Latin America against both neoliberalism and the IFIs raised new questions as to whether the IFIs could continue to shape global rules in the established way. In the case of Argentina, for instance, governance reconstruction showed that the power of a particular actor or paradigm *vis-à-vis* other actors and paradigms was not reinforced simply by the dominance, materially and ideologically, of external lenders over borrowers, but rather by their capacity to integrate competing impulses into a consensual policy decision. This chapter looks at those patterns focusing on how local and external actors interacted in

Argentina's post-crisis resolution. In this case, notions of power, interests and policy outcomes were subsumed to a strong need to restore local legitimacy and trust in the reconstruction of alternative political and economic governance.

Three central questions are thus explored here: has governance become more political and less technical in the new context that resulted from the crisis of 2001; to what extent can the IFIs affect models of the state and development in a context in which political and economic crisis called for a new beginning in terms of policy-making and legitimacy; and to what extent has the trend away from neoliberalism transformed power relationships between donor and recipient countries? In answering these questions, the chapter is divided into four main sections. The first section explores the political-economic context leading to the crisis in Argentina in 2001. The second section analyses contending paradigms and policy dynamics involving the IFIs in crisis resolution, focusing on emerging power relations and the implications for policy change. The third section looks at how the post-crisis political economy changed the relationship between the country and the IFIs as it facilitated a re-balancing of power in favour of sovereign decision-making. The final section offers a discussion on the extent to which the IFIs can affect models of the state and development from outside and the ways and extent to which local actors are able to challenge top-down models of policy change.

Governance: Technical versus political

In the early 1980s Latin America turned its back on the tradition of political authoritarianism and economic populism, and firmly embarked on a new model of governance embracing democracy and free-market reform. High levels of regulation, state interventionism and tax management were key aspects of 'bad governance' that affected many economies in developing countries. In Latin America, in particular, thorough reforms were needed following a 'lost decade' when economic growth was limited and unpredictable and inefficient and corrupt institutions affected the participation of many developing countries in international financial flows. At the same time, the debt crisis that affected large economies in South America, such as Mexico, Argentina and Brazil, in the late 1970s and the consequent threat of default on their foreign debts rallied the governments of the industrialized countries and the international financial organizations to impose drastic macroeconomic adjustments on the debtor countries, which suddenly became pariahs in the international capital market. The weakness of the debt-ridden countries paved the way for the international financial community, delivering orthodox economic ideas crystallized in the Washington Consensus, to dismantle the state-led development policies of previous decades and to impose a technocratic and normative view of development economics. The infamy of dictatorships, the political consequences of which were now clear, and the severe debt crisis left Latin American governments in a weak bargaining position. It was no longer possible to uphold the idea that Latin America could offer a sustainable alternative to the global rule. This made the transmission of ideas easier than in the past and justified the acceptance of radical neoliberal reforms by even traditionally populist parties.

The decade of the 1980s, therefore, represented the ascendance of the hegemony of global rules within Latin America. The neoliberal model of governance endorsing the policies of the Washington Consensus was oriented to the opening up of the economies in the region to foreign capital, and to the *modernization* of state institutions to offer a capital-friendly environment and a 'positive relationship' between the state, the market and the civil society in developing countries. Conceptually linked to economic liberalism, the creation of effective institutions was seen as the counterweight to arbitrary state action. There was even a feeling of revelation, a sense that 'poor governance' retarded growth and particularly hurt the poor in developing countries and that the expertise of the IMF and the World Bank were crucial to reverse the situation.

To make the neoliberal reform programmes legitimate the governance agenda promoted by the IFIs in developing countries was defined as a technical project. Good governance, institutional reform and state-building became part of an ideological presumption that assumed the validity of technical solutions. The IFIs thus embarked on reforms aimed at improving state 'efficiency'. The main emphasis was on public service management, accountability, the rule of law, access to information and transparency, fiscal responsibility and a competitive labour market. These became 'the hallmarks of an *intelligent*, democratic state' (Rondinelli and Shabbir Cheema 2003: 23, emphasis added). This approach to governance assumes that (good governance) institutions can be externally influenced and embedded in the domestic arena despite the existence of societal pressures and demands as constituents of stable and legitimate institutional mechanisms.

The claim of the IFIs remains 'above politics', reproducing what Ferguson (1990) called 'development as an a-political machine', and is at variance with the dynamics of social relations that shape the process of implementation of the IFIs' projects in a given context. As the previous analysis of governance reforms in Argentina suggests, by conveying funds and policy ideas the IFIs can empower and legitimize certain actors while *disempowering* others. As a result, regardless of the technical and economic justification of governance and development, the involvement of the IFIs in this type of reform, intentionally or not, affects the political context in which local actors define and resolve their political interests and their capacity to push their proposals into the decision-making process.

In general, the problems of governance – and not only in developing countries – have a technical side related to economic management. Nevertheless, the political consequences of reforming, or creating, institutions affect the most intrinsic constitutionalism associated with political rights, obligations and procedures that give institutional form to the state (Gill 1995: 9). Technical assistance to a defective judiciary may bring some help, but if it is not independent from political manipulation, it will deliver only minor improvements. As explored in Chapter 4, in domestic contexts where the political power controls the judiciary, reforming technical aspects of the judiciary will not be enough to reverse the incentive to lose its prerogatives. For some officials within the multilateral agencies the political ground and the domestic political involvement has been an argument for strengthening state-capacity rather than a problem central to it. While the role of the IFIs in technical assistance is justified by mandate, their role in political bargaining has been more challenging and even left to the discretionary interventions of their staff that at times jeopardized open and participatory decision-making processes. Politically sensitive reforms might even involve a degree of 'quiet coercion or legislative trickery' that sometimes went unnoticed by the IFIs (Cook 2006).

The overall philosophy in the governance agenda promoted by the IFIs thus was that a strong system of checks and balances was not a necessary condition to economic success. This favoured the establishment of a strong presidentialist system of governance in some developing countries that in some instances even violated democratic practices in pursuit of the neoliberal agenda. For instance, in Argentina President Menem changed the law to revert to the use of presidential decrees to pass unpopular reforms, and advanced a major reform in the constitution of the Supreme Court to increase the number of judges from five to nine, 'packing' the Court with his own supporters. These reforms ensured support for his agenda which largely consisted of market-oriented reforms (see Chapter 3). In a similar case, although more extreme, Peru's President Alberto Fujimori went still further closing down Congress altogether in 1992 and manipulating the judicial system. In the meantime, the IFIs were certainly amenable to the political manoeuvring of technocrats using political means to secure neoliberal reforms. Yet as long as neoliberal reforms were in place, dubious practices were often overlooked by the a-political stance of the IFIs. The approach to governance promoted by the IFIs knowingly avoided conflict with governments that were dutifully perusing neoliberal reforms. In fact, one of the most striking paradoxes was that Menem's reform in Argentina earned him high praise abroad to the point that he was even invited to address the annual IMF/World Bank meeting in Washington as late as 1998, an honour granted to few heads of state from developing countries (Manzetti 2002: 6). Even though the rule of law was seriously damaged at home, the approach to judicial reform in Argentina was another example of turning a blind eye in the search for neoliberal governance (see Chapter 4). In practice, both the IFIs' staff and the government had incentives that affected the reform process. From this perspective, contesting ideas supported by local experts could be highly political and thus IFIs' managers might be more inclined to act without local experts in the design and implementation of programmes in order not to endanger the transfer of resources – and staff performance evaluation. In the absence of operational directives, task managers' incentives may rate the need to secure disbursement of loans to developing countries above the need to engage in a broad process of conciliation with local claims for participation and compromise on policy ideas. As such, local voices were often set aside and channels of communication and negotiation with the government were privileged. However, in a context where local actors are politically active and local experts are involved in policy formulation and campaigns, 'elite-led' governance projects are more difficult to advance. As illustrated in the politically sensitive case of judicial reform in Argentina, top-down implementation of governance reforms is not necessarily guaranteed by the financial and ideological power of the lender, but rather by the capacity of the latter to compromise and amalgamate the policy stands and work of local experts, activists and decision-makers involved in the area.

The different patterns of involvement of the World Bank in the promotion of governance indicate that within the IFIs both the normative agenda of development and the management of ideas as resources are still contending terrains. This technical versus political dilemma has also been the stuff of controversy in the international development community. Joseph Stiglitz, former World Bank Chief Economist from 1996 to 1999, for instance, has denounced the World Bank and the IMF especially as economic and ideological handmaiden of the international capital (Stiglitz 2002). Within the IFIs themselves criticism is buffered but yet acknowledged by some staff. Some units within the international organizations, such as the World Bank's PREM and the WBI, however, have acknowledged these contradictions, and in some cases have tried to find ways to formalize 'partnerships' with local actors thus acting like brokers (Chapter 5 in this book; also Bräutigam and Segarra 2007). Overall, however, there is still little attention given within the IFIs' project cycles as to how to deal with societal pressures and demands to place governance reforms within a broader political project of stable and legitimate institutional mechanisms. Despite efforts to advance reform by engaging with local actors in some cases, however, the general idea amongst civil society in Latin America is that the narrow, a-political and a-historical understanding of governance promoted by the IFIs has notably failed the democratic systems, even deepening power abuse and undemocratic practices in some parts of the region. In the end, after more than two decades of neoliberal reforms neither the market economy nor the democracy succeeded in providing inclusive and responsive economic governance in Latin America.

It was this disenchantment that, together with the economic difficulties experienced in the region, led to forceful questioning of the local and global authority by the end of the 1990s. The crisis that erupted in Argentina in December 2001 was a manifestation of the limits of evasive, ambiguous and overall a-political definitions of governance and the disappointments of neoliberal reforms. In this context, the debate on effective and sustainable development was reopened, and with it the question of how to articulate the role of the state in a more inclusive development project. Rethinking sustainable governance spurred the need to integrate a fractured social structure composed of those who were integrated into the circuits of the neoliberal capitalism and those who were outside it (Munck 2003: 504). The Argentine crisis crystallized this debate and triggered the search for an alternative model capable of redefining the rules of the game to involve the relation between states and market and civil society. This is the very political dilemma facing Latin America today. Although discussions of 'a turn to the left' in the region have sometimes been exaggerated, some governments are experimenting much more overtly with nationalist policies and are trying to re-invigorate their domestic legitimacy through changes in the style of politics and occasionally with new experiments in welfare.

Promoting governance in a changing political economy

The financial and political crisis that affected Latin American countries at the end of the century marked a point of inflection for both the ideology of the Washington Consensus promoted by the IFIs and the way it was implemented. The crisis of neoliberalism fostered a noticeable degree of political and ideological renewal. The intensity of the crisis brought to the forefront an aspect of authority and legitimacy that had been hitherto ignored in the pursuit of good governance by the IFIs.

Like some East Asian economies, Argentina was once heralded as emblematic of the new liberal global political economy only to collapse shortly after in deep financial and social crisis. According to its national statistic index, INDEC, poverty rose alarmingly, jumping from 38.3 per cent in October 2001 to 57.5 per cent a year later. The number of people living in extreme poverty reached 27 per cent in 2002, more than double the figure of just 12 months earlier (see INDEC at http://www.indec.gov.ar). The impact of Argentina's crash, therefore, went far beyond the domestic environment: it was also seen as a challenge to the reigning ideology of globalization promoted by the IFIs. As in countries like Thailand and Malaysia, where crisis led to a reversion of earlier economic strategies in the direction of 'anti-IMF' expansionary policies (Thirkell-White 2005), in Argentina widespread criticism linked the failure of the orthodox programmes to the role of the IMF and the World Bank during the 1980s and 1990s, when these organizations had been seen as the main instrument for the imposition of market-oriented reforms.

Throughout the 1990s, financial support gave the World Bank and the IMF leverage to guide Argentine policy-makers as they increasingly adopted the IFIs' liberal conservative economic agenda. Government shifts towards market-oriented reform opened the way for 'rewards' based on increased access to financial flows. This dynamic defined the character of domestic choices that oriented the economy towards the reduction of fiscal deficits, liberalization of trade and orthodox control over exchange rate regimes. In 1991 the Convertibility Plan pegged the national currency to the dollar in a clear manifestation of the country's neoliberal economic agenda. As analysed in Chapter 3, Convertibility did away with 'undesirable' policies associated with past

economic failures, such as fiscal deficits, devaluations and state economic intervention, at the same time establishing a framework for
the state's involvement in the country's economy. Convertibility was
thought to be the solution to long-standing problems as it eliminated
the possibility of inflationary financing of fiscal deficits. But it also
limited the role of the Central Bank as lender of last resort and thus
the sovereign capacity of the state to make decisions about monetary
policy. The Plan was accompanied by reforms aimed at strengthening
the financial sector and opening the economy to international capital markets. Tax reform and the privatization of public enterprises
were designed to create a more efficient public sector, while trade liberalization brought about reduction of tariffs and the elimination of
import quotas. Convertibility provided instant credibility to the emerging neoliberal governance and the government was once again able to
raise capital through international financial markets.

But this approach did embrace a substantial contradiction: despite its
merits in containing hyperinflation and providing new grounds for stabilization, the rigidity of the currency board made it difficult to respond
to external shocks, recession and growing deficit (Damill *et al.* 2005).
Vulnerabilities to external shock became apparent after the Mexican
financial crisis in 1995. Although Argentina managed to escape the crisis
and secured growth in 1996, the growing fiscal deficits of the country's
provinces caused the federal government increasing concern. Imposing
austerity upon the provinces, however, met with determined political
resistance, and provincial debt rose to over US$23 billion by the end of
2001. In addition, the currency devaluation that resulted from the crisis
in neighbouring Brazil, Argentina's main trade partner, left the country
in a difficult position to adjust and, as a consequence, there was a rapid
fall into recession from the end of 1998. Increasing indebtedness precipitated the financial crisis as Argentina's public debt increased from
29 per cent of GDP by the end of 1993 to 38 per cent by 1998 and to
51 per cent by the end of 2001 (Escude 2002: 5).

By the end of the decade it was clear that Argentina's weak state
couldn't adequately perform tasks at the same time that perverse incentives to avoid crisis led the IMF and Wall Street to support Argentina's
disastrous debt habit. As the country entered the final downturn which
was to lead to the crash of December 2001, governance became less a
matter of sustaining institutions for development and more one dic-
tated by the need to sustain an inevitable financial collapse. In this
context, the IMF continued regardless, providing massive loans even
though the country's economic difficulties were apparent and it was

clear that an orthodox exit strategy would be extremely difficult, if not impossible. To illustrate this point, as the Argentine crisis deepened in 1999, the IMF supplied a loan of US$13.7 billion and arranged US$26 billion more from other sources at the end of 2000. As things worsened still further, the IMF agreed another rescue package of US$8 billion in September 2001 (Akkerman and Teunissen 2001). It seemed at the time that the IMF was ready to lend almost any amount in order to avoid the collapse of a project so closely associated with the IMF's image and its receipts. The Argentine government, meanwhile, followed IMF recommendations maintaining its monetary policy and tightening its fiscal policy still further. As previously analysed, even though the country was facing a severe financial deficit, the government announced a 'Zero Deficit Plan' in July 2001, entailing a budget cut of 13 per cent of state workers' wages and pensions plus the fiscal commitment of provinces and a reduction of transfers (see Chapter 3). Despite all this, and the IMF's effort to solve the unsolvable, the country's debt burden meant a collapse of investor confidence and a skyrocketing of the country's risk level.

The collapsed of such a fragile system was triggered by the decision of the IMF to withdraw its support in November 2001. In a desperate reaction to stop a massive wave of capital flight De la Rúa imposed restrictions on bank withdrawals and money transfers, a policy that became know as the '*Corralito*'. In response, a movement of the unemployed (*piqueteros*) rapidly emerged to oppose further cuts and to demand a re-nationalization of privatized companies and banks and the non-payment of the external debt (Svampa and Pereyra 2003). The middle classes and public sector employees joined in massive street protests. De la Rúa declared a state of siege and unleashed a wave of ferocious police repression which led to over 20 deaths. The overwhelming situation brought Argentina to the brink of chaos (see Figures 3.1 and 3.2 in Chapter 3). At the same time, an increasing level of indebtedness meant that the country was unable to comply with the international lenders and these exigencies in turn polarized domestic attitudes towards the IFIs in particular.

Remarkably, Argentina's democracy survived the crisis. After three failed presidential attempts, a Parliament-based 'emergency government' was constituted headed by Peronist leader Eduardo Duhalde in January 2002. The challenges ahead were huge. Regaining governing control was a tall order for the government, only achievable by re-integrating social actors into the formal channels of state-society networks. Thus, the re-definition of the rules of the game was driven by two main dynamics: on the one hand, a re-definition of the relationship between state and market; and on the other, the re-definition of the rules of engagement of state with society. These two pillars were fundamental to the reconstruction of post-crisis governance.

In addition to its obvious socio-economic aspects, the crisis was a crisis of public confidence in the political class as much as it was a crisis of the legitimacy of the policy-expertise that emanated from the IFIs. The failure of many top-down-led reforms promoted by the IMF and the World Bank acting as conveyors of funds and paradigms since the early 1990s suggested that reforms required a deeper commitment and support on the part of policy-makers and society for the reconstruction of post-crisis governance. Since the IFIs were seen as culprits, their involvement in post-crisis resolution was not guaranteed unless they tailored their advice and aspirations to fit in with domestic ideas and politics and the economic agenda, a requirement that might certainly be at odds with their narrowly defined, technocratic ideas and mandate (Woods 2006).

After neoliberalism, what?

As with other political processes, new paradigms of political and economic development emerged in the midst of a profound political-economic upheaval. The IFIs were, once again, trapped in the 'technical versus political' dilemma as two different stances crystallized between the local experts and the IFIs in the aftermath of the crisis. This was expressed as a debate between a strategy for recovery based on previously unthinkable nationalist-populist policies – sustained by political actors within the government of Duhalde and the Ministry of Economics; local socio-economic actors such as labour unions, industrialists and export-oriented manufacturers; and local experts and academics gathered in the so-called 'Fenix Group' working within the University of Buenos Aires – and a neoliberal stance supported by the IFIs and local orthodox economists, who proposed moving towards a complete 'dollarization' of the economy (Daniel Garcia Delgado, interview with author, 12 December 2005). The 'nationalistic' option insisted on the need to end Convertibility, to devalue and to foster an export strategy based on the local economic structure. Economically, the debate within government was between those who favoured an orthodox crisis response, emphasizing control over public expenditure, reform of the financial system, reduction in spending and taxes and the prevention of hyperinflation, and those who called for more heterodox policies, based on growth (Katz 2006; also Powell 2002). The orthodox lobby sought, above all, to regain the trust of foreign investors and the IMF. In contrast, the heterodox approach, based on a critique of the Menem decade, called for re-nationalization of productive assets and resources and efficient state regulation of the economy to foster growth and citizen welfare. Many documents produced by the *Central de Trabajadores Argentinos* (CTA) reflected these points (see also Schorr 2005). For the 'Fenix Group' in particular there was no trade-off between the re-activation of industry and investor confidence. These were rather complementary (see Plan Fenix 2001). In this, of course, they echoed a residual conviction in Argentina that only industrialization could provide the basis for stable development. Their programme gradually took on elements of an almost moral crusade. It was argued, for example, that neoliberalism had created institutional incentives for corruption through tax regulation and faith in the market which had allowed privatized companies to register massive profits while paying low wages, undermining the traditional employment structure of the country and, in the process, diminishing popular faith in the efficacy of the state (Lo Vuolo 2003: 141). Contrasting ideas advocated by neoliberal supporters, instead, called for the peso to be replaced with the US dollar at a fixed exchange rate and the elimination of the Central Bank as a body issuing currency, thereby reinforcing the model of the 1990s.

Because of the gravity of the crisis, the immediate post-crisis President, Eduardo Duhalde, was compelled first to address the governance dilemma since social unrest was challenging the prospects of financial stability. In the end, this response, perhaps more than anything else, shaped the nature of Argentina's post-crisis political economy. Duhalde's priority was to move towards social pacification and political stabilization, which became the pillars on which to build a new national development agenda. In the context of a highly mobilized society the government was obliged to balance the international investor's confidence, including the support of the IFIs, with domestic constituency confidence and legitimacy. The way President Duhalde solved this dilemma was by appealing to a new nationalistic rhetoric and a new approach to economic management, giving priority to the 'national-populist' option advocated intellectually by the experts in the Fenix Group, economically by the influential national industrial lobby led by Argentine Industrial Union (UIA), and politically by civil society groups that opposed to neoliberalism, in particular unemployed organizations, *piqueteros*. The alternative ideas held by these groups formed the basis for the new pro-reform network that pushed for an alternative model of growth and development in the aftermath of the crisis. To compensate for the low levels of legitimacy, the post-crisis government adopted a critical position towards the IFIs. Economically, this meant balancing the populist appeal of high government spending on social policies with the prudent fiscal and social management necessary to re-invigorate the economy and sustain growth while restoring the economy to a place in international capital flows. One of the first (and highly symbolic) decisions of the Duhalde government was therefore to abandon Convertibility and immediately to impose a moratorium on servicing the public debt, and to convert financial contracts to peso valuations. This controversial decision, called 'pesification', ultimately favoured debtors owing dollar debts but simultaneously undermined middle-class investors (Baldi-Delatte 2005). Despite controversial outcomes, the end of Convertibility and the debt default both echoed and calmed the critics who had rejected the neoliberal model.

In such a political-economic scenario, the IFIs faced pressure to reconsider their operational framework and programmes in the country. The dire situation in Argentina opened a window of opportunity for some flexibility in their operations, although this was far from a generalized shift in their policies. The way IFIs' staff engaged with local actors and compromised with local ideas and policy proposals in the aftermath of the Argentine crisis, however, diverged significantly. Together with the nature of their programmes, there was also a significant place for the role of ideas in the path taken by the IFIs. For instance, the operational approach adopted by the World Bank and the IDB involved not only reallocating funds from previous loans to finance social programmes but also effective interactions with groups of civil society at the country level to discuss further policy procedures. Soon after the crisis erupted, the World Bank reassessed its strategy for the country leading to a review of the existing portfolio and its CAS (see World Bank 2005, 2006). It also capitalized on its networking and mechanism of consultation with civil society and leaders at the national level (World Bank 2003, 2006). In November 2005, the World Bank's head of the Country Office, Axel van Trotsenburg, and other senior staff also met a range of social actors, such as labour union leaders, NGO representatives, business leaders and academics, to discuss priorities and insights for Argentina's development and where the Bank offers the most strategic support (*ibid.*; also Cesilini 2003). Likewise, the IDB, in particular its president at the time, Enrique Iglesias, played a central role not only in supporting social programmes but also in chairing the presentation of a 'nationalistic' economic plan prepared by the UIA in round-table discussions that gathered representatives from the World Bank, the IMF, the US government and the IDB in Washington D.C. in October 2001 (Jose Ignacio de Mendiguren, interview with author, 31 May 2006). The exchange of ideas through networking was also reflected in the participation of staff from the multilateral banks in consensus-building forums such as *Mesa de Diálogo*. As explained in detail later, this initiative was launched in early 2002 by the Argentine government with the support of the Catholic Church and UNDP to institute regular discussions with civil organizations to identify urgent solutions for the political, economic and social crisis.

In the case of the IMF, the nature of its operations and organizational culture makes it more difficult to depict the positions of the staff regarding their involvement in post-crisis resolution. As the IMF's ex-Western Hemisphere Chief Claudio Loser put it, 'by its level of vertical discipline and cohesion, the IMF can be compared to the old Communist, the Vatican or the army' and thus 'there is no room for dissenting ideas' (Loser, quoted in Tenembaum 2004: 44). In this context, engagement of the IMF staff with local experts was more difficult to achieve. Not only was the IMF seen as the body mainly responsible for the 2001 crisis but it also continued to, almost stubbornly, push for monetarism and structural reforms, in spite of strong local opposition and the lack of legitimacy and popular trust. Though there were initial attempts at negotiation, the government's nationalistic stance soon collided with IMF's orthodoxy. Governance priorities and the government's need to integrate the most contending political actions in the domestic field naturally reinforced its nationalistic position and thus the tensions between opposing paradigms *vis-à-vis* the IMF. However, the power of the IMF to impose political direction on the nationalistic Argentine government declined. By the end of 2002 the Argentine government could claim that it had quietened social protests, including the serious lootings that had happened just few months after the crisis erupted, and that it had made a good deal of economic progress, with dollars accumulating in the Central Bank's reserves, the peso holding steady at 3.5 per dollar and inflation under control. In this context, not only the IMF lost leverage but it also paid a high price for failing to recognize the new political reality.

The role of the IFIs in post-crisis governance

Not without difficulty, the attempt to establish an alternative model of political and economic governance went ahead and a new policy matrix evolved since 2002. The new government saw it as imperative to take control of the sources of production and to re-integrate social actors into the formal channels of state–society networks. As a first stage, Duhalde's government managed to put together a package in which social policies became part of an economic strategy of stabilization, seeking to halt pauperization and protest and to restore governability. The government endorsed the ideas and proposals discussed by local experts and policy actors. One of the most critical measures was to abandon Convertibility, which generated an important 'bounce back effect' in terms of exports and stimulated production of competitive tradable goods. The government also introduced a policy of price controls to encourage consumption and prevent inflation and a 20 per cent tax on export earnings from agricultural commodities and hydrocarbons, which served, in part, as the basis for emergency social programmes (Grugel and Riggirozzi 2007: 95–97).

This agenda became a source of particular tension between the government and the IMF. Moreover, the government maintained that the IMF had committed major errors in three policy areas which intensified the crisis. These areas related to the IMF diagnosis of the crisis and crisis resolution, its projections about an alternative economic plan in terms of stabilization and potential growth, and its policy prescriptions before and after December 2001 (Ministerio de Economía 2005). These tensions were translated into strained and prolonged negotiations with the IMF over a Stand-By Credit Arrangement for US$3 billion which was to be signed early in 2003. The IMF demanded that the country immediately suspend two main economic laws: the 'Economic Subversion Law' under which foreign bank executives were being investigated for aiding capital flight; and the 'Bankruptcy Law', which was viewed as being too debtor friendly. Financial support was also made conditional upon a programme of major macroeconomic adjustment that included control of monetary emission and, even more importantly, the signing of a new federal–provincial fiscal pact to commit the provinces to a 60 per cent reduction of their deficit and the removal from circulation of quasi-monies, which were issued by provincial governments to meet payments in the pre-crisis period (IMF 2004b).

Negotiating Argentine's readmission into the global financial community was an urgent task, and for this a deal with the IMF was critical. Duhalde took accordingly a pragmatic but firm line in the rounds of negotiations with the provinces, leading to the introduction of some adjustment policies. These policies not only allowed the government to claim compliance with IMF demands but also served to reconstruct federal authority and to impose a new institutional framework on national and sub-national governments. Given the long history of veto power by provincial governors and fiscal and monetary disobedience, the national government was keen to re-define state–provincial relations in ways that would strengthen presidential authority. It therefore presented a proposal to provincial governors for a basic understanding in which the national government committed to help finance the provinces in order to resume long-overdue payment of salaries and public service providers, while provincial governments committed to progressively reduce their deficit and to stop printing quasi-monies. This so-called *Pacto Federal* ('Federal Pact') was the first step in terms of consensus building for post-crisis institutional reconstruction (Alejandro Arlia, interview with author, 5 June 2006). Although triggered by IMF conditionality, the Federal Pact was the first post-crisis governance arrangement which reinforced state legitimacy in policy decision-making as well as a manager of resources. In fact, as international lines of credit were cut, most of the resources for the Federal Pact stemmed from the devaluation of the peso and the subsequent reactivation of national industry as it regained competitiveness in the international market.

Argentina's economic outlook, however, began to improve and with it its position in the international economy. A tentative recovery process began and space opened up for a new governance project as the political economy was led partly by targeted attempts to reduce dependence on external finance and partly by a favourable trend in international commodity prices. A dynamic export sector, aided by cautious manipulation of the exchange rate, provided the key to Argentina's spectacular recovery from the default and collapse of 2001 and allowed the government to re-balance its fiscal and current accounts. Venezuela's oil wealth was pivotal in the process. Over the last five years, there has been an agreement under which PDVSA, Venezuela's state oil company, sells fuel oil to Argentina and buys Argentine products (see Chapter 7). Moreover, in an attempt to diversify its sources of financing after the 2001 debt default, President Hugo Chávez has stepped in, offering strategic injections of capital to Venezuela's neighbours and buying Argentine bonds, thus freeing Argentina from the urgencies of external exigencies. In addition, new policies of aid for the region and cross-regional infrastructure and energy programmes point to what may be a serious attempt at regional cooperation on energy within South America. These initiatives also support rising pro-reform networks at the local level supporting financially and ideologically some of their initiatives and actions.

The Argentine government met IMF fiscal conditions over the course of 2002. Nevertheless, the IMF continued to adopt a hard line, refusing to conclude a deal and continuing to claim that more orthodox adjustment was needed (Cibils 2003). For instance, the IMF requested that Argentina obtain a higher fiscal surplus over GDP in 2003 and successive years; it also demanded a timeline for increases in the privatized utility rates that were frozen after the devaluation of the peso, and the renegotiation of the debt with private creditors under the supervision of the IMF (*ibid.*; also IMF 2004b). This 'tough' position of the IMF has been interpreted as a stance 'to set the record straight in the face of critics who considered it had been too lenient too long with the country' (Cline 2003: 36). But as the economy recovered, the power of the IMF as the lender of last resort decreased.

Eventually negotiations stalled. The IMF refused to give up on its demands for further reforms and the Argentine government rejected reaching an agreement at the expense of adopting unpopular policies like reducing social spending or raising taxes. The dispute over policies and approaches came to a halt when the Argentine government threatened a new default on a payment of about US$800 million to the World Bank in mid-November 2002 and of about US$800 million to the IDB early in 2003. This move established a new negotiating framework. The IMF came in with a US$6.78 billion package for Argentina to help it meet its immediate payments, not because it had become convinced by Argentina's strategy for recovery but because it could not afford another default or fear of contagion, given that, along with Turkey and Brazil, Argentina's debts accounted for more than 70 per cent of the Fund's outstanding credit. The January 2003 agreement, which the government wrested from the IMF, gave the economy breathing space and provided an apparent political victory – without the need to implement the policies the IMF requested.

As the Argentine economy continued to improve, the government not only regained fiscal authority but also began to win the confidence of key internal actors in economic and political decision-making. Local actors backed the policies that openly opposed the neoliberal stance of the IFIs and sustained a strong nationalistic rhetoric. At the same time, the bargaining power of the IMF was increasingly eroded. The shift to a more productive economy led to improvements in the terms of trade whilst devaluation, together with a competitive exchange rate, created trade and fiscal surpluses. All this served not only to induce growth but, more pertinently, to reduce the country's dependency on external sources of funding and to provide the government with the resources for a renegotiation of its relationship with external finance. As growth and output stabilized, a new dynamic between material resources and power relations was established. Domestically, the growing export sector created the basis for currency stabilization, making possible new social investments that helped to control the social situation. Internationally, the national political economy was now not constrained by dependency on external funding, and of course Venezuela's petrodollars were still visibly pouring in.

Regaining control of finance and macroeconomic instruments placed the Argentine economy in a strong position *vis-à-vis* the negotiations and conditions demanded by multilateral institutions and external creditors, reversing the trend of the last 15 years when donors had advised, and often forced, governments to reduce their direct engagement with the economy. When Néstor Kirchner took office, in May 2003, negotiations with the IMF for an enhanced loan agreement were in hand. Kirchner's administration, like its predecessor, put forward a rhetoric of nationalism that was accompanied by state policies to stimulate domestic demand before negotiating foreign debt payments. By November, the government made a critical move towards the re-nationalization of companies that were privatized during the 1990s, such as postal, water, electric and transport services. This was a key decision, and a proof of strength against the emblematic neoliberal policies implemented by the administration of Carlos Menem a decade earlier under his controversial agreement with the IMF and the World Bank. At the same time, it made clear that the government would not allow foreign creditors to dictate economic norms. This was also the approach taken by the government in dealing with international private creditors (Dhillon *et al.* 2006). By the end of 2005, the Argentine economy had grown since mid-2002 at a steady average of 9 per cent, a remarkable feat under any circumstances but, in the context of the collapse only four years earlier, an almost unbelievable one. Economic growth even allowed the government to go on to take a previously unthinkable decision to cancel its US$9.8 billion debt to the IFIs (5.5 per cent of GDP), making clear the extent to which the old paradigm of dependence on the IFIs no longer applied. The later decision by the Brazilian government to pay in full its remaining debt to the IMF, followed by Indonesia, Russia and Uruguay, suggests, moreover, that the IMF's neoliberal paradigm may be no longer applicable in a more general sense. In addition, alternative source of credit, with no economic policy conditionality attached, meant that a major instrument of Washington's influence in the region that helped to bring about neoliberal reforms was now challenged and even overruled. Unlike the crisis of the 1980s when Argentina, and Latin America in general, found itself in a weak bargaining position, over half a decade of post-crisis recovery since the end of 2002 reveals a different political scenario in which alternatives to the Washington Consensus are changing the political-economic map of the region and with it the power relations between domestic actors, the state and the IFIs.

The experience of Argentina's bargaining power with the IMF after 2002 is certainly unprecedented, not only in terms of how the balance of power shifted visibly and rapidly but also in terms of how clearly it reveals the contemporary operation of the international financial system. Not only has the IMF lost its political leadership in the country but some dichotomies between the IFIs became clear from their involvement in crisis resolution. Traditionally, a negative outcome with the IMF would have affected disbursements by the World Bank and other multilateral organizations such as the IDB and the UNDP. These institutions, however, continued to support important social programmes in the country contributing to social accord and complementing government spending, at the same time reinforcing the capacity of the state to conduct politics after crisis. The differences between the IMF and the multilateral development banks might be understood as merely conjectural, but willingly or unwillingly the World Bank and the IDB recognized the complexities of state–society politics as the motor of socio-economic reforms.

The World Bank and the IDB: Reinventing the Commons

There have been two main differences in the approach to post-crisis reconstruction by the multilateral banks compared to that of the IMF. First, in contrast to the vertical model of programme negotiation and implementation sought by the IMF in Argentina's post-crisis political economy, the World Bank and the IDB adopted a more pragmatic strategy of engagement. Second, and more fundamentally, in contrast to the general perception of the role of the IMF, the intervention of the multilateral banks has been seen by the general public as time-sensitive, targeting what really seemed relevant to Argentina's fundamental priorities of governance, chiefly social appeasement. Politically, the dilemma for the interim president was how to put in place economic measures to reactivate the economy without exacerbating social and political tensions. The stance of the new government against the neoliberal policies of the 1990s was a critical aspect in place in terms of social cohesion.

In this context of economic collapse, middle-class outrage and growing numbers of mobilized groups of poor people, post-crisis reconstruction demanded more than simply a policy readjustment or the replacement of 'bad' politicians with 'honest' ones (Munck 2003: 504). Recognizing this, Duhalde gave priority to stability, appealing to old ideas and to the residual legitimacy of the national development project which had been overturned in the 1980s. Duhalde's tentative policy response has come to be seen as a critical break with neoliberalism. In particular, it called for a proactive state both in the economy and in the delivery of social services and a new alliance between state, markets and civil society. Stability meant designing policies to combat social exclusion and the rising tide of contentious politics. This, however, could no longer be achieved simply through a new alliance with the trades unions, though they remained important. The flexibilization of the labour market during the 1990s generated a vast pool of low-paid workers 'disconnected from union activities and whose interests were not easily articulable with those of wage workers' (Villarreal 1987: 85 quoted in Levitsky 2003: 12). In other words, not only was the labour market now much more fragmented but social demands were less related to wages than in the past and more linked to basic concerns such as food, housing and jobs. In the context of rapidly rising poverty, new sites of social struggle had emerged – the *piqueteros*, neighbour assemblies and factory takeovers (*fábricas recuperadas*) – with which the state had no organic links. Yet these new organizations were increasingly serving as providers of an emergency social safety-net for people because they were able to solve immediate needs for food, shelter, clothing and primary health care in the face of the collapse of the state. In poor neighbourhoods new social organizations recruited the unemployed, social workers, teachers and low-skilled workers to create chains of solidarity around social practices that involved communal food, exchange of services and the set-up or the 'take over' of education centres (Juan C. Alderete, interview with author, 22 December 2005). Thousands of barter clubs based on non-official barter monies came into existence and abandoned factories even went into production as cooperatives (Pearson 2003; Petras 2004). The new social phenomenon of factory takeover and popular cooperative enterprises and assemblies emerged strongly throughout Argentina, Brazil, Uruguay and Venezuela. As a *piquetero* leader explained, 'the experience in other countries helped to draw lessons for the actions in Argentina. A critical element in the action of local actors in Argentina was the linkages with groups in Venezuela and Brazil, from who they received technical and financial support. This support grew despite market challenges and thousands of workers throughout the region were re-employed at cooperative-run businesses, which were closed down by bosses in the midst of the crisis and reopened by employees in its aftermath' (Juan C. Alderete, interview with author, 22 December 2005; also Buxton 2009 for an analysis on cooperatives in the case of Venezuela).

The government supported new social initiatives and committed to support new commercial agreements signed among various Latin American worker enterprises in areas such as tourism, wood and paper production, food production and processing, shoes and foot wear, plastics and transport (*ibid.*). The government put forward an agenda that compromised between the demands of popular movements and the pressures from national and international actors demanding economic stabilization and social pacification. In the words of Diana Tussie (2006: 11), 'the government faced the *realpolitik* dilemma of attempting to pacify powerful business interests and [its] electorates, seeking to maintain and consolidate the domestic constituencies of support to shore up [its] domestic popularity'. Duhalde quickly opted for the heterodox solution and thus aligned with local experts that supported the nationalistic ideas of the *Grupo Fénix* and the industrial union. Given the scale of social opposition to neoliberalism, it is doubtful, indeed, whether any other policy frame could have offered any chance of social peace.

Critical to the understanding of the role of the IFIs in this context is the very basic nature of the programmes they supported. The experience of the IFIs in post-crisis reconstruction in Argentina coincided with an exceptional context in the regional political economy. Since 2003, economic conditions in Latin America and the Caribbean have been very favourable. Several of Latin America's main export commodities have hit record highs feeding new markets, and countries like Brazil and Argentina managed not to overcome the urgent pressures of the post-crisis scenario. China's entry into the World Trade Organization (WTO) in 2001 – incidentally the same year Argentina collapsed economically and politically – improved the conditions of its market access and certainly contributed to boost the post-crisis recovery (see Figure 6.1).

The new torrent of capital in the global financial markets, together with discredit after disappointing records of the IFIs' intervention in development assistance in the region during the 1980s and 1990s, contributed towards the IFIs' declining loan portfolio. Their lending to middle-income countries slid down over the past decade, declining from about US$18 billion annually in the early 1990s to US$11 billion in

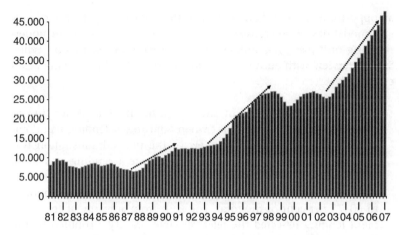

Figure 6.1 Argentina's Total Exports, 1981–2007 (in US$ million)
Source: INDEC Economía

2004. The buoyant commodity prices and brisk economic growth have also enabled some countries to make early repayments on their outstanding loans to the Bretton Woods Institutions (see Birdsall 2005). Finally, as argued in Chapter 7, in a context focus of renewed regionalism, some countries became not only more independent but certainly more vocal. The new financial and policy context in which the IFIs operate posed a challenge for the relevance and efficiency of multilateral financial institutions.

This meant that the IFIs were compelled to explore new venues to accommodate to the new regional reality and, even more critically, to more a country-based approach reflecting local political ideas. Retooling of their lending operations and softening some of the requirements and conditionalities thus became critical to remain significant in the region. Response amongst the IFIs varied. After much overlapping of credit lines and services the World Bank and the IDB turned to their origins resurfacing the importance of 'investment projects' which fostered social and infrastructure development and did not need a prior seal of approval from the IMF. In consequence, the multilateral banks responded by lining up a social agenda that left aside politically sensitive adjustment programmes – which are conditioned to on prior agreement with the IMF. The Argentine crisis thus represented a window of opportunity for developing countries to break free from the IMF and to engage in alternative arrangements – financially and politically – but it was also an opportunity for the World Bank and the IDB to revise their portfolios and modalities of engagement in the region 'and come to an understanding on those programmes which the Bank can settle on' (Felipe Saez, interview with author, 6 December 2007). The World Bank's CAS envisaged

> [...] an important shift in the composition of Bank lending as compared with the recent past when adjustment lending had dominated the programmes. The view of the new administration was that, in a post-crisis environment, investment lending was more in keeping with Argentina's development requirements, and it requested a programme in which investment lending would amount to 60–75 per cent of the total. The shift from adjustment to investment lending reflected the relatively low priority attributed by the Government to some of the structural reforms which the Bank considered important in order for the on-going recovery to be sustained. It was also consistent with the views of civil society expressed in CAS consultations that the structural reforms supported by the international community in the 1990s contributed to – or at least did little to prevent – the crisis of 2001–02.
>
> (World Bank 2006: 135)

Beyond voluntarism, the nature of the programmes managed by the IMF and the multilateral banks facilitated the extent to which the latter could re-direct their portfolios to attend to the social crisis in Argentina. The multilateral banks advance two types of projects, investment loans and development policy loans. Investment loans are made in support of economic and social development projects in a broad range of economic and social sectors, including infrastructure. Development policy loans, formerly known as adjustment loans, provide quick-disbursing finance to support countries' policy and institutional reforms. The latter had been the pillars of macroeconomic and governance reforms before the crisis and had been backed by previous agreements with the IMF, which acted as a 'seal of approval' in the negotiation of these loans between the banks and the government. According to the World Bank's Country Officer for Southern Cone, 'facing the political economy of the post-crisis, it was proposed that the Bank and the government search for common grounds on the bases of areas of agreement, compromising and amalgamating positions in those areas where the Bank could be involved, like investment in social protection, and leaving aside those conflictive areas like adjustment' (Felipe Saez, interview with author, 6 December

2007). This was a not insignificant result given that traditionally the World Bank would not move ahead without a previous agreement with the IMF. In the case of post-crisis Argentina, not only was there no agreement with the IMF but the firm nationalistic stance regarding the orientation of the economic plan that was in progress was in stark contrast to the policies supported by the IFIs in the 1990s. Although the multilateral banks did indeed recognize controversial aspects in the dialogue with local actors and in particular with the government in the post-crisis scenario, there was a tacit agreement by which the banks will advise but not condition their support to, for instance, more participation by the public sector in the reconstruction of the post-crisis political economy. In Argentina, certainly, there has been a move towards the strengthening of the role of the state in social and economic activities – even at the risk of high interventionism – however, this trend has not only not detracted the multilateral banks from supporting government-led policies but more importantly created new synergies between state, society and the multilateral banks for the reconstruction of important governance pillars, like the restoration of social safety nets. Moreover, there was a recognition within the World Bank, which was also observed by the IDB, that a new role for the multilateral banks could concentrate on investment in infrastructure and social policy. The redirection of the multilateral banks' portfolio as 'investment partners' was seen clearly in the World Bank's shift to 100 per cent investment lending, interrupting or at least pausing its intervention in the often-controversial adjustment programmes (see Figures 6.2–6.4).

Social lending, in effect, became the core of the Bank's response in 2002–2003. This trend consolidated in 2003, when the country started to show signs of steady recovery. In 2003, Bank lending

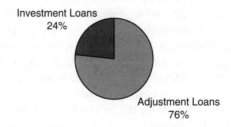

Figure 6.2 World Bank's Loan Portfolio for Argentina, 1998–2003 (US$7.8 billion)

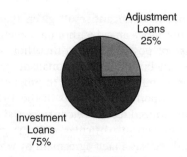

Figure 6.3 World Bank's Loan Portfolio for Argentina, 2004–2005 (US$2.0 billion)

Figure 6.4 World Bank's Loan Portfolio for Argentina, 2006–2009 (US$3.3 billion)

resumed first with a US$600 million investment loan in support of a government-sponsored workfare programme aimed at heads of households – the Unemployed Men and Women Heads of Households Programme (*Programa Jefas y Jefes de Hogares Desempleados*) (World Bank 2002b). Following upon that, the US$500 million Economic and Social Transition Structural Adjustment Loan marked a return to adjustment lending but this time in support of the government's recovery programme and without an active agreement with the IMF. The World Bank's role in post-crisis reconstruction has been 'pragmatic' avoiding involvement in controversial areas where the government is leading the restructuring, such as the energy sector (Felipe Saez, interview with author, 6 December 2007). Unlike the IMF, however, the World Bank and the IDB became aware that what are 'technical' problems for the IFIs could be highly political for the local actors. Finally, unlike the multilateral banks, the IMF has only adjustment programmes making it less flexible by nature and even less helpful for a country that has steadily increased its external reserves since 2003.

In Argentina, although financial assistance from the World Bank and the IDB was initially conditional on an agreement with the IMF, both institutions were soon aware that crisis and crisis resolution were not simply a matter of pursuing (and sanctioning) good or bad policies but rather of addressing the structural fractures that had jeopardized the neoliberal project of the 1990s. From this perspective, rather than acting within the traditional scheme of 'cross-conditionality', both the World Bank and the IDB quickly re-oriented their strategies towards support for crisis-driven socio-political programmes led by the Argentine government, local experts and other pressure groups (see, for instance, IDB 2004; World Bank 2006: 153). Consequently, while the IMF kept its focus on the functioning of the neoliberal project by demanding policies to reactivate the capitalist model of the 1990s, the World Bank and the IDB focused on the fissures and vulnerabilities of that project by working with government and civil society groups to establish social security and new forms of welfare and state–provincial relationships. In this way, rather than insisting on intensifying neoliberal reforms, the multilateral banks reoriented assigned funds to support the implementation of government-led social programmes. The World Bank pioneered this strategy by committing a loan of US$600 million in January 2003 (Loan Agreement No. 7157-AR) and, more recently, an extended US$350 million for the continuation of workfare programmes and expanding employment support activities, particularly education and training (Loan Agreement No. 32463-AR).

A significant turn in policy formulation and the decision-making process was also signalled by the fact that most of the policies supported by the multilateral development banks were born out of the recommendations of the new consensus-building initiative, the *Mesa de Diálogo*. Many proposals for social stabilization and state reform to temper the crisis were discussed in different forums sponsored by the *Mesa* – for instance, the reform of the judicial system (see Chapter 4; also Barnes 2005). The World Bank echoed these concerns and fostered networking activities, mediating between the community and the government by providing technical assistance for the implementation of programmes proposed by civil society organizations in concurrence with the government (World Bank 2005). Paradigmatic among this consultation process was a series of meetings between local actors and NGOs assembled in the NGO Working Group on the Bank in Argentina, and officials of the World Bank to discuss the role of the World Bank in crisis reconstruction in 2002 and 2003. These discussions helped to compromise positions and settle the grounds for cooperation attendant upon social and political priorities highlighted by the local actors. As part of this exercise, one of the most politically relevant and timely social programmes supported by the World Bank was the above-mentioned *Programa Jefas y Jefes de Hogares Desempleados*. This workfare programme started in April 2002, initially financed partly by a loan from the World Bank and partly by national income from export taxes. The plan was designed as an emergency plan to alleviate the impact of rising unemployment due to the worsening economic crisis (Galazo and Ravallion 2004). Another important programme that placated immediate social needs was a health plan, *Plan Remediar*, supported by the IDB, which organized the distribution of basic medicines to the poorest social groups. These and subsequent emergency plans were also an effective strategy in the control of social conflict as they were implemented in ways that brought the *piqueteros* organizations into national, provincial and municipal power circles. Social policies became a central mechanism for increasing state capacity and the political capital that empowered the post-crisis governments of Duhalde and his successor Kirchner, sometimes at the risk of reproducing old clientelistic politics (see Levitsky 2003, 2005).

For the multilateral development banks, the 'good governance doctrine' along with the neoliberal project since the mid-1990s suggested a different logic of support that now embraces a new 'state-centric' approach to governance and a different engagement pattern with local actors. This has been particularly relevant for a country like Argentina, where there is a strong base of local experts and civil organizations politically involved in the design of reform programmes both before and after the crisis. Moreover, as Argentina became less dependent on the IFIs for financial support, bargaining capacity in the negotiation of loan conditions and payments inclined in favour of the Argentine government. In view of this, staff from the World Bank and the IDB sought to adapt their programmes to the country context leaving aside traditional adjustment plans and focalizing their activities on infrastructure and safety net aspects. Intentionally or not, the World Bank and IDB staff reconsidered their relationship with local actors and their engagement on the ground. Rather than a top-down model of power imposition, the power of the multilateral banks to implement governance-related reforms has related to their capacity to engage with pro-reform local actors, articulating local and external expertise for the design and implementation of policy change. From this perspective, the institutional experience of the IFIs in crisis resolution in Argentina suggests that reaching social bases of legitimacy is a critical condition needed to carry through certain policies at the national level. The unpopular IMF policies proposals led not only to a loss of legitimacy but in turn to its disempowerment. This experience contrasted with that of the multilateral banks, which succeeded in adapting their interests and practices to the post-crisis political-economic reality in Argentina.

Ultimately, networking with local actors in the reconstruction of post-crisis governance in Argentina confirmed that despite the leverage of financial institutions the materialization of projects into new institutions and policies is a complex process in which the interplay between IFIs' staff and local actors can favour or inhibit policy change. State building and the construction of governance in Argentina, or any developing country, involves more than the transfer of 'good' values from external actors. How the IFIs adapt to (changing) domestic policy trends and ideas is critical to the way their promotion of governance forms and practices is taken by the local actors. This has been critical not only for advancing politically sensitive reforms, such as judicial reform and anti-corruption as explored in the previous chapters, but also for the current major challenge faced by the IFIs as they confront a new 'system of ideas' battling out in the region. Crises are always an opportunity for ideological contestation and accommodation of political and economic projects. In the case of current Latin America, as explored in the next chapter, the new repertoire of ideas and practices builds on the notion of the state as multi-faceted actor mediating the relationship between citizen and markets. In this context, it could be argued that the World Bank and the IDB acknowledged, even if pragmatically, the complex and dynamic relationships between government agents (the Executive, relevant ministries) and local actors (civil society practitioners, local experts, labour unions, academics) in the definition of policies. On the other hand, the IMF sought a technical, a-political institutionalization of procedures and norms in which the state was expected to act as a transmission belt for externally conceived paradigms. The IMF, thus, sought policy change on the basis of a (rational) decision-making process based on cost–benefit, uncontested adoption of the international norm. As a consequence, from an IMF perspective, negotiation of nationalistic policies and the re-insertion of the country into the international financial circuit were in constant tension. Moreover, the rigid outlook of the IMF in its approach to development and governance led the institution to act as a mere 'conveyor' of funds and policy paradigms, underestimating the importance of local power. A greater flexibility allowed the World Bank and the IDB to engage in the articulation of ideas and resources to push through effective implementation of reforms that were critical in the re-founding of the relationship between state and society and thus building the pillars of post-crisis governance. Of course, the extent to which this is evidence of a generalized shift in the World Bank's and the IDB's lending practices as a whole is still to be seen. However, the implications of new patterns of involvement by the multilateral banks in developing countries not only can help to restore the links between state and society but potentially can be a response to questions of the efficiency and relevance of multilateral lending institutions – as the debate in the Meltzer Commission showed – in a context where income from their investments and their lending in general has diminished (see Meltzer Report 2000; Woods 2006).

Certainly, the political and economic context in most Latin American countries has changed and forced the multilateral institutions to redefine their relationship with countries like Argentina, Brazil, Uruguay and Ecuador which have become gradually more independent and secured sustained positive balances in their fiscal and external accounts. These countries have even managed to sideline the relevance of the IFIs by writing off their debts to the IMF. Although not in a radical departure from the market economy, Latin America is moving towards greater regional integration and reducing dependence upon the institutions of the global economy. The presence of a regional alternative source of funding, mainly based on Venezuela's petrodollars, and tacit agreement among more realistic nationalistic governments throughout the region boosted the economic freedom of some Latin American economies that are now free from the IFIs-supported adjustment programmes and the conditions often attached to them.

In the present context of change in the political economy of Latin America, and in the developing countries in general, the relationship between the IFIs and local actors provide new grounds for a more profound discussion about how power relations develop in specific contexts in which local and international actors define and resolve (political) interests. What crisis resolution in Argentina demonstrated is that the reconstruction of the socio-political and institutional structures was possible even without obeying strictly the international norm. In this case, it was possible to re-establish some sovereign decision-making capacities and to build considerable autonomy together with the support of the multilateral development banks, which offered effective financing to palliate the socio-economic effects of the crisis contributing to governance stability. At the same time, the IFIs are visibly attempting to adapt to new circumstances and demands. Unlike the IMF, the World Bank and the IDB have found a new niche in which to develop a more targeted role in post-crisis middle-income countries. This has implications not only for domestic politics but also for the IFIs and how we understand their (power) relationships with local actors in the developing world.

Conclusion

The different patterns of involvement of the IFIs in politically sensitive reforms in the 1990s and after the political and economic crisis that erupted on the eve of the new millennium reveals that despite their technical approach to development – and to governance for development – the IFIs are not politically immune institutions. Efforts to advance a depoliticized agenda led not only to tensions between technical understandings of governance and the political reality and urgencies on the ground, but also to frictions and conflicts with the local actors. Implementing governance reforms produces a variety of effects on power relations in which local actors are not always the subject of co-optation or neutralization. The IFIs have often been able to influence both ideologically and politically the models of state and development adopted in developing countries. True, these models were often embraced in an attempt to consolidate the reigning neoliberal capitalist logic of global governance in the domestic arena. But the recent trend away from neoliberalism in many Latin American countries transformed power relationships between donor and recipient countries and facilitated a re-balancing of power in favour of sovereign decision-making in the latter.

By exploring the contending paradigms in the aftermath of Argentina's crisis and the policy dynamics involving the IFIs this chapter discussed issues of power, compliance and policy outcomes. The analysis of Argentina's governance reforms suggests that externally conceived paradigms are limited in terms of acceptance, legitimacy and success particularly in vibrant and politically informed polities. Local actors constitute a source of power that can enhance or limit the prospects of policy change. The crisis in Argentina in 2001 demonstrated that this is even more the case if formal democracy reinforces a logic of exclusion that is supported by top-down forms of intervention on the part of the IFIs. This is also true when what is technical for the IFIs becomes a political matter for local civil society.

The next chapter takes the lessons of the Argentine crisis and analyses, in a broader and comparative perspective, how the prevailing neoliberal model was discredited and eroded in Latin America, its consequences for the political economy of the region, and the role of the multilateral financial institutions therein. The chapter analyses how the emergence of new financial and epistemological schemes affected the role of the multilateral financial institutions. It embraces the general argument about the contextual character of power relations and the importance of the political reality of developing countries. It therefore extends the analysis of the IFIs into the contemporary period to discuss ideas, power relations and policy change in Latin America as a whole.

7
A Regional Platform for Alternative Governance: What Roles for the IFIs?

The impact of major international economic institutions such as the IMF, the World Bank and the WTO on developing countries is a recurrent question in the work of political scientists, economists, activists and practitioners. For the last two decades, a heated debate about these institutions has centred almost exclusively on their apparent lack of progress in fostering growth and sustainable development in the developing world. Questions were raised concerning the ways and extent to which these organizations improve or hinder the lives of the *poor* in developing countries. The mixed records of the IFIs' programmes on economic and social outcomes in the developing world were emphatically denounced (see Mosley *et al.* 1995; Easterly 2001; Stiglitz 2002; Vreeland 2003). The analyses developed in previous chapters pointed at these questions by featuring modalities of intervention of the IFIs in politically sensitive reforms related to governance. It was argued that when the IFIs' staff engage with local actors for the setting and implementation of development agendas the goal of 'good' governance is likely to be served according to local realities. In contrast, the imposition of best practices – of the perception of it – on the ground caught IFIs' staff in political deadlocks and struggles over meaning and practices with the local actors.

Most authors agree that despite successfully tackling problems of hyperinflation and economic stabilization, externally led neoliberal reforms impacted negatively on state–society relations and that it created vulnerabilities and insecurity particularly among low-income groups, which suffered the most from the costs of economic recession and high rates of unemployment. Latin America has been emblematic of these tensions between sovereign decisions, external exigencies and the local realities.

This study so far provided an analysis of empirical research on the impact of the IFIs on the relationship between local actors and the IFIs' missions in the implementation of politically sensitive reforms that altered political and economic governance structures on the ground. The findings are bound up with theories about power configurations that resulted from the involvement of IFIs' staff with local actors beyond the government circle. Local experts and their expertise have been in many cases a determinant factor shaping the approach to and the practices of development programmes in developing countries. By analysing the politics of governance reforms at micro and mezzo levels of relationships between external and local actors, and their knowledge and ideas, it was illustrated how in some cases politically sensitive reforms can create areas of conflict but sometimes also an arena for political engagement. The concerns picked up in this book explored how the contradictory nature of neoliberal governance as promoted by the IFIs has helped in some cases to achieve political and economic inclusion by engaging with networks of local actors for the implementation of policies, while in other cases the approach to governance reforms by IFIs' officials eroded and limited inclusion, participation and ownership of reforms. The implications in this last case often go beyond project performance, sometimes affecting the actual *quality* of democratic governance. As explored in the preceding chapters, internal dynamics of the institutions themselves and bureaucratic incentives within the international institutions affected the modalities of involvement of IFIs' staff with the broader civil society. Availability of funds often brings the risk of co-optation and discretionary use for political purposes that can negatively affect democratic processes. This is even worse if the mechanisms for civil society involvement in aid programmes are applied selectively by the staff of international organizations in their client countries. Although the IFIs have to some extent dealt with this matter and some measures have been put in place to secure a degree of openness, by and large these organizations remain secretive and the engagement of civil society has sometimes been reduced to a 'public relations' exercise, restricting consultation and discussions to documents already in negotiation with, or approved by, the local governments. Ambiguity and the lack of Operational Directives guiding staff practices on how to promote civil society participation and ownership have led to discretionary performance of loan negotiation and implementation. In short, while norms of good governance and the participation of civil society have been in place for some time within the IFIs, the degree of autonomy and discretion conferred on the staff affects how they interpret their environment and the terrain of domestic politics in developing countries.

However, as exposed throughout this book, in the context of changes in the political economy of many emerging markets and developing nations the re-accommodation of actors and resources means that despite the availability of funds and knowledge advanced by the IFIs, their normative and operational agendas are much challenged by a new direction in the struggle over meanings and policy goals in relation to governance reforms. This chapter takes the lessons from the Argentine crisis, in terms of the IFIs' relationships with local actors, and analyses in a broader and comparative perspective how the current neoliberal model became discredited and eroded in Latin America and the extent to which a new model of governance is taking shape. The analysis offered in this chapter explores the extent to which the current political and economic trends in Latin America transformed power relationships between donors and recipient countries. In the process, it explores what 'power' currently means in the relationship between the IFIs and developing countries and the book's implications for a broader analysis of the tensions between sovereign authority and externally driven demands.

The chapter argues that the current crisis of neoliberalism, and crisis management, has in fact created a new space for dissent from the global rules that became paradigmatic in terms of policy dynamics between local and external actors. This chapter analyses how a new ideological tide in Latin America, together with a change in global exchange terms, is currently challenging the authority and legitimacy of the IFIs to promote neoliberal governance. In so doing, it also explores the extent of such a normative and political discredit and its implications for the promotion and achievement of governance arrangements at different levels of authority – national and regional. The analysis explores the general argument about the contextual character of power relations and the importance of the political reality of developing countries.

The present analysis is structured in four sections. The first section explores the current re-definition of governance in Latin America, where the discredit of neoliberalism calls for a new start in terms of political and development models. It concentrates on the policy spectrum that emerged, in a variety of forms and responding to different realities, to contest the rule of neoliberalism. The second section turns to the challenges faced by the IFIs in the wake of alternative models of governance in a changing political economy. The third section analyses post-neoliberal governance as a regional response – although in different ways – to what development should mean, the role of the state and the participation of the IFIs in such projects. The final section discusses the factors that enhance the possibilities of governance as a new model of state activism and social/political inclusion post neoliberalism, and the challenges ahead for this model within the IPE.

Changes and dilemmas in current Latin American political economy

The previous chapters described how the overwhelming debt crisis during the 1980s and 1990s forced several debtor countries in Latin America to turn to the IFIs for funding and technical support. These two elements gave enormous leverage to the IFIs *vis-à-vis* the borrowing countries as they had the power to direct the re-insertion of these economies into the international capital flow and to act as 'gatekeepers' – a powerful role conferred by many private lenders who insisted that the IFIs approve government's economic policies before they extended loans to that nation. During that time the unequal distribution of power made developing countries less able to refuse a conditional agreement and, in this view, their financial dependency gave disproportionate power to the IFIs.

Good governance and sound economic policies were part of the IFIs' rhetoric in the promotion of sensitive market-oriented reforms that led to liberalization and deregulation of the economy in many developing countries. Yet, as discussed in Chapter 6, these policies proved ineffectual in securing sustainable growth at the same time worsening income distribution and the prospects for further democratization. Given the severe social and political inequality plaguing the region, the neoliberal prescription promoted by the IFIs gradually lost power – intellectually and materially. Increasing opposition among local actors called for new terms of social redistribution and state interventionism which in many countries led to a significant deviation from the models of governance promoted by the IFIs.

The financial and political crisis that affected Latin American countries at the end of the century, epitomized in the collapse of Argentina, marked a turning point for both the ideology of the Washington Consensus promoted by the IFIs and their tendency to treat it as unequivocal 'best-practice'. The perception that neoliberalism failed to deliver both economic growth and socially responsive democracy led to new calls in the search for more autonomous alternative pathways to development. This in turn became the rhetoric of an emergent nationalism that took place in one country after another in Latin America, in particular in the Southern Cone.

The regional political scenario now is thus very different from that of the 1990s and there are a range of elected incumbents not only critical of neoliberalism but willing to push for the adoption of alternative models of governance. This is so in the case of Chavez in Venezuela, Kirchner in Argentina, Vasquez in Uruguay, Morales in Bolivia, Lula in Brazil, Correa in Ecuador and Ortega in Nicaragua. For the last half a decade, these countries have embarked on a search for an alternative to neoliberalism and – despite the high level of 'personalism' and reliance on the leaders, often referred to as populism – the search for post-neoliberal projects has become an attempt to go beyond the 'Executive entourage'. In some cases intra-regional networks of civil society groups engaged in cooperatives and grass-roots enterprises compensating for welfare policies that weakened with a decade of neoliberalism in the region. Manifestations of crisis and the social coalitions pressing for an end to neoliberal governance vary within the region. In the two most extreme cases, Argentina and Bolivia, the crisis of neoliberalism was manifested by a tendency to national disintegration and a loss of control by ruling elites (Grugel and Riggirozzi 2009). Failure to construct social consensus over the direction of the economy affected the capacity of the governments to manage crisis. As argued in Chapter 6, the crisis of 2001 in Argentina reflected not only external vulnerability and the mismanagement of monetary policy but more generally a severe distrust in the political system. Likewise, in Brazil and to a lesser extent in Chile, popular dissatisfaction focused largely on the social and distributional costs of market economic reforms (Reinjfall 2009). In Brazil, discontent with the costs of economic modernization and external vulnerability led to the election of the country's first president from the leftist Worker's Party (Burges 2009). The most extreme anti-Washington Consensus politics are still developing in Venezuela, where a deep-rooted rejection of an elite capture of the state led to support for a model of 'Twenty First Century Socialism' (Buxton 2009). Despite these contextual differences, the undeniable search for alternative models of socio-economic governance in these countries became a platform for the reassertion of a new regional process that attempts to create new spheres of autonomy.

Crises are always an opportunity for the ideological contestation and accommodation of political and economic projects. In this case, the neoliberal transition has not been simply an economic project devoted to finding new avenues for capital accumulation and productivity growth. It has also, and primarily, been a political project aimed at restating the role of the state as an economic agent and the place where democracy is reproduced. In this sense, it has sought to reverse exclusionary patterns of neoliberal governance and to revive state–society relations within a more responsive political economy. New pro-reform networks involving local experts, opposition groups and (leftist) government are articulating alternative policies and a new rhetoric of autonomy and nationalism. These networks cut across the region and are part of a realignment of actors around leading national industrial policies in place of previously influential financial groups. Fuelling this process is the 'propitious' context in which Latin American contestants are defying the global rule – an international context that has reversed the long-standing unfair terms of exchange, prevalent since at least the mid-1940s. The extent to which a post-neoliberal project can be successful is a matter of ongoing debate. The fact that the Latin American region realigned its strategy to refocus on a more nationalistic course for development and governance is already a significant change, and is a challenge to the established global order.

What these experiences mean is that politically feasible and socially responsive governance under neoliberalism failed and that what post-neoliberal governance may look like is on the agenda for serious discussion for the first time in two decades. Of course the new spectrum of policy responses in Latin America cannot escape external constraints. The legacies of neoliberalism, in terms of market opening, external investment, export dependence and state retrenchment cannot be undone, and indeed many new leftist governments would not wish them to be undone. Paradoxically, what can be rescued from an ill-fated orthodoxy is a new understanding of globalization, less extreme than that held by neoliberal supporters to revise those claims that posit globalization as an enabling force (Weiss 2005). In effect, one of the striking characteristics of the 'new left' in Latin America is that rather than attempting to reproduce national autarchic models of the 1940s–1950s, post-crisis governance in the region is re-founding the mechanisms of social control and the leading role of the state in the economy, but in a context of open and competitive markets. The emerging 'open-markets nationalism' reconciles the centrality of the state in social life and its role as an economic agent, bringing together social spending and interventionism, export-led policies and a revival of regional integration as a platform for an alternative political economy. Again, while the re-accommodation of local actors and ideas have been crucial in the search for an alternative pathway to development and democracy, these dynamics are being facilitated by the emergence of 'alternative globalizers', in particular the dynamism of China and the petrodollars of Venezuela. Consequently, in contrast to the pressures on developing countries' policy choices during the 1980s and 1990s, the current process of globalization is far from diminishing the autonomy of national states, but actually fosters alternative projects that are part and parcel of a changing global political economy.

The crisis of neoliberalism across the region coincided with an increasing diffusion of financial and ideological power, epitomized by the emergence of Venezuela's participation in the region and China's role in the global political economy. China's robust economic expansion with double-digit growth for more than a quarter of a century and its trans-Pacific exchange crisis management and post-crisis recovery with Latin America have been a major factor in the economic recovery of the latter. Latin America represents an important source of energy resources, raw materials, commodities and market for Chinese manufactures. This has been particularly stimulated by the rising oil prices in the US since 2002–2003. Equally, trade between Latin America and China reached $50 billion in 2005, with China emerging as the region's third largest trading partner. According to ECLAC (2004: 184), Argentina's sales to China grew by 143.4 per cent, Brazil's by 79.9 per cent, Chile's by 58.5 per cent, Peru's by 13.1 per cent and Mexico's by 11.7 per cent. Between 2000 and 2004, Chinese exports to Latin America jumped by an annual rate of 42 per cent to US$21.668 billion, which was higher than the growth rates for exports to the rest of the world (2004: 184.).

Ideologically, the subsequent re-accommodation of actors and alliances in the 'historical backyard' of the US suggests a new opportunity to reassert alternative ideas. In contrast to the proverbial 'There Is No Alternative (TINA)', now promising alternatives not only emerge as possible options but chime with local demands for more responsive political-economic democracy which are being taken into account. The policy and economic understandings reached, for different reasons and in different circumstances, by China with Venezuela, Brazil and Argentina, for instance, suggest the emergence of a global order in which the countries of the South can forge new alliances based on a very different perception of the world.

This scenario presents many challenges for the role and participation of the IFIs in the politics of developing countries. One of the major problems of the development paradigm during the neoliberal reign was that free-market liberalism downplayed the role of the state and its complex place in society. Neither democracy nor the market nor the fight against corruption, poverty and inequality are possible where a state is weak. In the current Latin American scenario there is an urgent need to strengthen the quality in politics and in the institutional system. The persistent weakness and lack of credibility of political institutions demand additional efforts in order to conduct reforms in an environment of trust, legitimacy and ownership. Beyond clichés, these concepts confirm the importance of local knowledge in understanding the nature of the social constraints that any institutional reform must necessarily face.

Governance after neoliberalism can no longer offer one-size-fits-all solutions or a universal road to salvation. The IFIs' bias towards best practices has generated or deepened many social imbalances. A political dilemma, therefore, arises from the fact that neoliberal governance was predicated on the basis of certain power relations that tended to favour elite-led, pro-market projects and was thus reduced to arrangements between political-elite groups. The balance of forces in Latin America is changing, however, giving prominence to a political framework that is at variance with that adopted by the ruling classes for decades. In this context, the IFIs are trapped in a milieu where the demands for responsive governance have become strident, while their normative mandates are still wary of the status of their engagement in the politics of domestic realities in developing countries. The IFIs need to move towards reform and adapt their constitutive mandates and operational practices to the changing political-economic reality of their borrowers. Amalgamation of interests and positions of compromise between local actors and the IFIs will determine the extent to which the latter can retain an authoritative place in the definition of governance after neoliberalism.

Beyond neoliberal governance: Where do we go from here?

The adoption of the language of good governance, civil society participation and ownership within the World Bank and the IMF rhetoric has been regarded as part of an instrumental strategy of co-optation and neutralization of contesting forces. This strategy was a tool with which to tighten the grip of the IFIs on developing countries, locking out local alternatives to the neoliberal rule. As a technical project, good governance as defined by the IFIs carefully avoided raising questions about the politics of elitist democracies and, more generally, the politics of the dominant economic growth paradigm. Yet in many cases interaction with bureaucrats and often limited engagement with civil society organizations in formulation, negotiation and implementation of reform projects have possibly helped to create a false sense of 'ownership' in the cases where like-minded technocrats interacted with the IFIs. This was particularly the case of institutional reforms, including the state, which gradually shifted the domestic balance of power between internal and external actors as well as many formal channels of state–society networks. Of course, the progress of neoliberal governance and its consequences for domestic politics have not been uniform across Latin American countries; variances both across countries and across issue areas account for how neoliberalism evolved in developing countries. Nonetheless, economically and ideologically, there was a generalized trend founded on the rejection of the 'old statism' of the 1940s–1960s in Latin America and thus a turn to neoliberalism partly imposed but also as an outcome of the fairly traumatic political cleavages and struggles of the earlier populist/inward industrialization process.

   The constitution and reproduction of neoliberalism as a transnational hegemonic project involved processes where dominant actors – in the form of international organizations, regimes, states, classes – were able to generalize their interests and to organize compromises and consensus, in turn giving specific power configurations a certain stability and structure to certain practices in global governance (Görg and Brand 2006: 107). Yet, as current policy and ideological trends in Latin America and other developing countries demonstrate, the bases of power politics are dynamic and thus able to change with the fluctuations of power centres and resources. In other words, the bases for hegemony are not static and the chances of perpetuating the established order decline when the structure of power and authority is altered, either by a change in resource allocation or by a loss of legitimacy enforcing an 'universal' discourse. From this perspective we can explain how the current search for alternative and even more independent development models in most countries in Latin America became a possible and credible attempt to alter the established order. The emergence of new definitions of what governance in the region should be has been part of a new current in financial globalization that, rather than constraining, has been widening the region's capacity to engineer a new economy that re-defines the strictness of free-market systems that had ruled the region's political economy for more than two decades. This argument indicates, in contrast to many critical analyses in IPE, that the web of relations and strategies of different actors and their respective interests is not a passive reflection of powerful, unchallenged international institutions or global hegemonic powers. Admittedly, the IFIs have been a key component cementing neoliberalism in developing countries. Yet the current dynamics of the global marketplace and the balance of

global economic power are changing and so is the power and authority
of the IFIs to secure the implementation of global rules. For the past
few years a thriving literature within the field of Latin American political economy has attested to the ways new emerging 'leftists' projects
in Latin America are re-drawing the political and ideological map in
the region (Panizza 2005; Hershberg and Rosen 2006; Castañeda and
Morales 2008). A search for a more autonomous developmental model
is without doubt a reflection and an indicator of how the global balance of power is changing. The old 'rule makers' increasingly have to
share power with the 'emerging economies', which are not only expanding their markets but also helping to shape competing ideas about
development. Most new attempts are undertaken in countries fully integrated into the international financial markets. Furthermore, while their
exposure to the international arena largely constrained their choice of
political economy during the heyday of neoliberalism, the end of the
century is witnessing a wider margin for manoeuvre for policy-makers in
the international bargaining game. At the same time, it has freed politics
from externally-led ideological constraints. Multilateral financial institutions' discourse and practice were no longer the only possibility as
was the case in the context of previous crises resolution during the 1980s
and 1990s. The unique international context has thus never been better
for local actors in Latin America to take up new challenges contesting
the established rule. The global rule is no longer seen as a homogeneous
and omnipresent mantra and the external actors, such as the US and the
IFIs, are no longer in a position to undermine domestic experiments in
economic policies.

Equally important, if not paradoxical, is that the old dichotomy
between national developmentalism, which defined socio-economic
and political processes in the region between the late 1940s and the
1970s, and neoliberal globalization is today resolved, as nation-led
industrial models and macroeconomic stability become part and parcel
of the new political agenda of leftist leaders. Neoliberalism left a bitter
legacy; politically it was undermined by elitist and non-accountable
democracies and economically by unequal and exclusionary systems.
The lessons to be drawn from the experience are, as elucidated by
Hira,

> macroeconomic stability and export promotion, (fr. neoliberalism),
> *and* industrial promotion (fr. ISI) and attention to income inequality
> (through local value-added employment growth and access to educa-
> tion and health care) are not incompatible, rather they are a necessary

combination for development for the long-term benefit of the diverse groups of [Latin America].

(2007: 356)

At the present juncture, a partial and still unstable new political economy is taking shape. Attempts to modify neoliberalism is accompanied by bargaining processes with domestic and external actors to improve social welfare systems but within the context of globalized, open and privatized economies. This is a distinctive pattern throughout the region but its depth and pace is of course determined by the domestic context in which these policies are unfolding.

In the 1980s, economic crises beset the region and reduced the capacity of local actors to shape policy-making to compliance with externally led aid assistance. This was part of what was identified as the 'internationalization of the state' in a dominant neoliberal global political economy (Cox 1987). At present, in contrast, the capacity of the most powerful states, comprising the G8, to use the World Bank, the IMF and other multilateral agencies to 'internationalize' their standards is limited. Any attempts at imposition, or the perception that the IFIs act as a mere conveyor of paradigms and funding in seeking top-down dynamics of policy reform, noticeably alienate developing countries from the multilateral arena. The IFIs today are losing ground *vis-à-vis* economically and ideologically autonomous projects in countries like Argentina, Bolivia, Nicaragua and Venezuela. To a lesser extent Brazil and Chile are also freeing themselves from the IFIs' surveillance and in general from the rigidities of the global rule. This has particularly affected the IMF. Its lack of flexibility in the adjustment of its mandate to new circumstances and demands, compared to that of the multilateral development banks, put this international organization under severe pressure (see Chapter 6). Today the Fund is scarcely a crucial player in the region. As Wade argues,

> The Argentine and Russian debt defaults have shown the world that countries no longer ignore the Fund at their peril; they can ignore it, default and regain access to finance quite quickly.
>
> (2007: 130)

The crisis of confidence in IMF advice, in particular after the Argentine crisis, also affected its distinctive role as a 'clearance house' for other international economic institutions and private creditors to get involved in a country. The decreasing power and authority of the IMF has been visible in its weakened capacity to serve as a catalyst for negotiations with the Argentine post-crisis government and the international private creditors affected by domestic policies undertaken in the aftermath of the 2001–2002 crisis.

Having a more flexible mandate, the World Bank and the IDB have made some headway in shifting to project lending with less conditionality, incorporating the recipient countries' individual development goals and supporting local ownership through a more inclusive planning process. Changes within international economic organizations, however, are still a gloomy prospect. The adaptation of the multilateral development banks to post-crisis priorities in many countries in Latin America cannot yet be understood as a full commitment to comprehensively review the inner institutional and bureaucratic structures that limit their staff's incentives to engage with local actors, and their expertise, in borrowing countries. Even less is any acknowledgement of changes in the IFIs' governance structure and the voting power within their governing boards. However, the easing of the international financial market and the emergence of new sources of funding and ideas repositioned local actors in developing countries and they are now able to dispute the (perceived) trade-offs between honouring international obligations and compromising sovereign decisions.

It is now widely understood that development should not be a top-down, externally imposed technocratic process but rather an inclusive process of policy design, negotiation and implementation. This conclusion was not easily arrived at in the development community – it involved many disappointing experiences, inconsistencies within the IFIs and a record of unsuccessful development programmes. Furthermore, the contemporary shift in Latin America towards a re-evaluation of the role of the state in development goes far beyond the contemporary recommendations of the IFIs. The disillusionment with neoliberalism is not simply a difference in ideals. It represents a deeper frustration with the management of development throughout the twentieth century. What does this mean for governance as a new political-economic project?

The type of governance reforms promoted by multilateral organizations were biased towards a best-practice form which assumed it was possible to determine a set of appropriate institutional arrangements adaptable to any context. Convergence towards 'desirable' arrangements was almost an expected outcome and thus many IFIs' staff fell into the 'best-practice trap' (Rodrik 2008: 4). This trap, however, contained the seeds of self-destruction, particularly in middle-income countries where local experts and their expertise had equally strong incentives to carry out reforms and, more often than not, were already working on proposals or trying to influence the policy-making process before the IFIs' staff became involved in the area. The lack of networking with these actors led to conflicting relationships and tensions between technical and political understandings of governance, and eventually the IFIs-led project reached a dead end. The circumstances affecting the judicial reform in Argentina, as discussed in Chapter 4, are a case in point.

The broader point highlighted by these considerations is that there is no unique, non-context-specific way of achieving 'desirable institutional outcomes' – certainly not in a top-down manner promoted from the outside. Effective governance cannot map into unique institutional designs based on efficient 'functions'. As such it is futile for the IFIs to promote a-political, de-contextualized institutional rules in support of certain economic outcomes. Any search for alternatives to the Washington Consensus is nurtured by different social realities, legacies and commitments and faces many challenges that outweigh any mere technical approach to reform.

It is nevertheless important to be cautious about current efforts to move away from neoliberalism in Latin America. The consequences of crises and the extent of change and continuity in relation to developmental and government policies are varied and a fresh start is still an ongoing process. What the post-neoliberal model of state, society, governance and development will look like, and its impact on issues of inclusion, redistribution and political participation, is still very uncertain. What is certain, however, is that some sense of an alternative path to development is being outlined, and that this project is now a political rather than a technical one. Good governance now implies an embracing project that goes beyond institutional aspects such as judicial efficiency and modernization of the state. The quality of democracy and socio-political rights are at the core of the redefinition of governance in a post-neoliberal sense. Re-defining governance in Latin America is part of a new response to the consequences of the political developments and state reform processes which had been part of the neoliberal model since the 1980s. After a decade of quite indiscriminate state reforms during the structural adjustment years, the challenge presented to the state was not simply how to convert it into an efficient apparatus, but how to reconnect it with its society – a political rather than a technical question.

New rules of the game?

The current process of change, as we argued, does not mean an absolute rupture with the past. Rather, it is both enabled and constrained by the external dynamics of a globalized world economy. The intensification of political protests and social mobilization led by a variety of social movements was part of the growing resentment at what was increasingly considered a failed model of development, often constrained by the IFIs. Social demands from the organized movements of the unemployed in Argentina, an indigenous population demanding the (re)nationalization of natural resources in Bolivia, popular dissatisfaction with the social and distributional costs of competitiveness in Brazil and Chile and the Bolivarian revolution of Hugo Chavez in Venezuela represent as much a rejection of the elitist capture of the neoliberal state as a popular rejection of an externally imposed political economy of liberalization. The struggle for political legitimacy is thus a vital force in the reconstruction of governance in the region. In the most extreme cases, particularly the experience of 'institutional implosion' underlying the crisis of 2001 in Argentina and the so-called 'wars of water and gas' in Bolivia, generated a strong sense of empowerment for those social movements and political forces that allied against the alleged elite-led democracy. The emergence of new opposition movements in these cases was also supported by intellectual leaders and groups that contested the tenets of neoliberalism. Intellectual movements like *Grupo Fénix* in Argentina are backing those most immediately affected by helping to put across a political message that neoliberalism could be indeed reversed (see Chapter 6). In sum, the linkages between political mobilization and contesting ideas are embracing a new 'emancipatory potential' of local actors and their capacity to resist policy actions inimical to popular interests (Domingo 2009).

The socio-economic model that is leading the reconstruction of post-crisis governance in many countries is based, therefore, on the return of the state as a critical actor with the extraordinary capacity to rewrite the rules of the game and regain the command instruments of political economy. In the case of Argentina, as explained in the preceding chapters, this meant new economic policies, led by the devaluation of the peso and the consequent reactivation of national industry, helping the economy to regain competitiveness in the international market and the new government to raise income from exports. Other measures included the establishment of a tax on export earning, government-led price controls and targeted social spending. It was also based on the re-nationalization of services privatized during the decade of neoliberalism in many countries in the region as a significant and symbolic component on the road to a more autonomous governance model.

As argued in Chapter 6, many Latin American economies have, to different extents, managed to reverse their dependency on external financial flow in order to function – as they did in the 1990s – and rely on revenues from national resources and intra-regional financial and infrastructure projects. In some cases there has even been a process of 'de-borrowing', renegotiating and cancelling existing debt with the international financial institutions and private creditors without asking for any further loan and repaying the debt with national reserves. This tendency has been reinforced by intra-regional cooperation, not only at government level but also among emerging social groups such as worker leaders and campaigners. A number of bilateral and intra-regional agreements in the areas of finance, energy and trade were the result of inter-governmental agreements in an attempt to act as regional alternatives to the neoliberal order considered to reflect the interests of the major states, in particular the US, through the operational and knowledge agendas of the IFIs. What is even more striking, compared to crisis resolution in the past, is that national preferences to produce different political economies and responses to global/national crises also emerged from the articulation of new 'protagonists', like the above-mentioned unemployed movements or intellectual groups, that are drivers of some policies or at the very least an unavoidable pressure for the change in modalities of policy-making. For instance, new intra-regional cooperation in social enterprises such as cooperatives and the takeover of factories that closed down as a consequence of the crisis represent new social dynamics reinforcing home-grown projects of governance.

As a new and distinctive path away from the ruling neoliberal project of the 1980s and 1990s, recent policy processes related to crisis management and resolution in many developing countries show – more than ever – that the dominance of a particular actor or paradigm *vis-à-vis* other contending actors or ideas is not simply reinforced by coercive means, but rather by integrating contesting impulses into a broader consensus to implement policy change on the ground. Favourable international conditions and the mobilization of domestic actors in tandem facilitated a re-balancing of power in favour of sovereign decision-making, reversing the top-down model of policy-making that favoured the global norm over national needs.

In the observation of today's political processes in the international political economy, one matter that becomes clear is that the plurality of actors, levels of authority and diffusion of power resources are redefining the dynamics of governance. Interactions through negotiation and consensus building do not respond to a globalized, homogenous project but are now part of the complexity of political actions and the beliefs held by state and non-state actors, or domestic and multilateral actors.

These interactions also respond to a revitalized regionalism, at least in Latin America, driven by two sets of challenges: on the one hand, a generalized discontent with the policies of the Washington Consensus coupled with rising popular mobilization pushing for more alternative development projects; and on the other, the need to reconcile responsive domestic governance and the global rule. The outcomes of these forces are changes in the political style of decision-making processes; there are new models of growth and, sustaining all these changes, the re-accommodation of alliances among state and society actors as well as governmental and multilateral ones.

For the IFIs, the power to influence new governing practices is not simply a matter of persuading governments and their entourage of their financial and intellectual authority. How effective they are depends on how strongly they can persuade the new constituencies that became key in the post-crisis settlement. Many of these actors are the same, previously ignored by their governments and by the IFIs in their country missions. Although the IFIs' interests are embodied in political institutions in relation to their power resources – financially and in terms of knowledge production and diffusion – domestic actors from developing countries have now become central elements in the struggle for development autonomy. At the same time, the capacity of local actors to shape social power relations has been enhanced and transformed by the new governance processes that placed them at the core of the decision-making process – from the definition and formulation of policies to their negotiation and implementation.

Of course, any assessment of the processes of political, social and economic transformation taking place in Latin America can be only tentative. Nor does this analysis postulate that Latin America is in full-scale withdrawal from neoliberal policies. The emergence of alternative models of governance involving broader aspects of the political and economic life of Latin American countries is still a long way from being a coherent institutionalized project – and even further from being an equitable, long-term programme of development. But even in countries like Chile – often overemphasized and even misrepresented as a 'neoliberal miracle' – there is a huge social agenda of exclusion that is catching up with the triumphalist picture of neoliberalism. Both state-supported, export-oriented growth and rapid-response-targeted welfare spending have helped to relegitimize and reinstitutionalize governance in many countries facing the crisis of neoliberalism. A longer-term perspective, however, indicates that there are difficulties ahead. For instance, growth has been secured in many economies largely via the effect of soaring demand and commodity prices, effective and competitive policy schemes. Yet these trends are highly contingent on those of global markets. Furthermore, the easing of international conditions left more room for government interventionism, but this can create mistrust among foreign investors and some domestic businesses. Likewise, poverty, extreme poverty and employment still are far from resolution, and tackling these issues is a delicate task, balancing the 'distribution game' between business and labour. At the same time, although the economic recovery in many parts of the region, the re-insertion of the labour force into the market and the increase in social spending have created the basis for more responsive governance, they are also leading to inflationary pressures that risk, among other factors, balancing wage levels. On a more political front, there are questions about emerging tensions between the resemblance, though for different reasons, of the old technocratic political style characteristic of market-friendly governance and the new policy-making style which is greatly reliant on the figure of the president (see Castañeda and Morales 2008). Lastly, there is a large segment of 'losers in the crisis' affecting in particular the younger population that is widening the logic of growth with social fragmentation, thus creating vulnerabilities in the inclusive logic of an alternative model of governance (Grugel and Riggirozzi 2007: 101–102). These vulnerabilities are potentially the territory on which the multilateral lending institutions can interact with local actors and networks, creating the grounds for social programmes in support of a new sustainable and responsive governance.

As never before, the Latin American region is experiencing an interregnum, with the old model in a critical state but the emerging one still struggling to consolidate the hopes for responsive and inclusive governance. Underlying this situation is the emergence of a new balance of political and economic powers capable of changing the wider social organization that shaped the neoliberal governance. Thus, the relationship with the IFIs and their participation in the new project very much depends on their capacity to amalgamate and compromise with a wider range of actors and local knowledge producers, and in a new context that differs considerably from the one fostered by neoliberalism.

Alternative governance practices: Banking on autonomy

In recent decades, the IMF, the World Bank and the multilateral regional banks have largely controlled poorer countries' access to credit and development financing. Economically, these institutions allowed developing countries to avoid defaulting on their debt, provided funds in some difficult times and acted as 'enabler' to private creditors. Politically and institutionally, these funds supported the implementation of specific, market-friendly reforms in accordance with the IFIs' understanding of state efficiency and governance priorities.

The inauguration of the first Latin American *Banco del Sur* (Bank of the South) in early 2008 is a reflection of the search for autonomy not only in policy formulation and implementation but also in the institutionalization of an alternative financial architecture in response to the new regional political and economic trend. If it succeeds in terms of goals and achievements, such an institution could play a significant role in regional monetary policy and provide resources to secure sound balance-of-payments finance. A major distinction from established international financial institutions is that the *Banco del Sur* will not operate on the basis of conditional loans but intends to advance a more democratic decision-making process for its operations. The *Banco del Sur* not only institutionalizes *ad hoc* arrangements and lending but represents a new space for the rethinking and negotiating of alternative models for integration. Other initiatives such as the joint venture between Argentina's state-managed energy company, ENARSA (Energía Argentina) and Venezuela's oil company, PDVSA (Petróleo de Venezuela) and emerging arrangements for the supply of natural gas between Argentina, Brazil and Bolivia all point to new dynamics in a different direction from the logic of the 1990s.

These new institutions are part of a revitalized movement towards the construction of a new regionalism led by initiatives such as the Union of South American Nations (UNASUR) and the Bolivarian Alternative for the Americas (ALBA), which give new impetus, albeit one not without challenges, to already existing regional agreements such as the Community of Andean Nations (CAN) and the Southern Common Market (MERCOSUR). Moreover, it is still unclear how the new proposals will fit within the existing regional architecture and the extent to which new games of sub-regional leadership – especially involving Brazil, Argentina and Venezuela – will unfold. Nevertheless, the merits of the new regionalism rely on the renewed impetus for collective action, since it strengthens the capacity of individual states and local actors to challenge the hegemony of the neoliberal project that dominated the region for more than two decades. The establishment of alternative financial arrangements, such as the Bank of the South, thus represents the basis for a more comprehensive reformation of regional financial architecture so long dependent on the Washington-based institutions. In their more essential purposes, these initiatives herald a gradual substitute for the global, US-dominated institutions.

What these trends show is that Latin American countries are part and parcel of a changing international political economy. This is a critical moment at which the relationship between actors is affected at all levels of authority. Not only financial survival is no longer a pressing condition for these countries – and with it the power of external pressure from international financial institutions is in decline – but also many actors beyond the government circle are reaching central leadership in the search for political and economic autonomy. This is contributing to a process of political and ideological decentralization that is changing the nature of power relations among domestic and international actors. In this context, the success of new governance reforms depends not simply on the intrinsic and technical virtuosity of the IFIs' programmes, but more radically on the way different political 'logics' are resolved between the local actors and the IFIs. As Harrison pictured, to design governance reforms more effectively it would require a fuller political consideration of the country's – and even the regional – case (2005: 256).

This is a critical time in the Latin American search for more autonomous alternative strategies of political and economic governance. It is also a turning point in that the goal seems to be of balancing power as a *region* and not as a series of *individual responses* to the Washington Consensus and in particular to the US authority. This does not mean that the experiences and pace of change in the different countries are consistent. Rather the search for alternative models of governance differs among countries as do their social, political and economic realities. To speak of the emergence of a coherent anti-neoliberal model of governance in Latin America is to overstate the case. But, equally, we should not underestimate what unites most of these countries: a need to re-found the nation state and re-embed development through targeted state intervention, and a commitment to social justice. In fact, Latin America's search for economic development has always been shaped in one way or another by its responses to global rule and in particular to US dominance. But while the political and economic circumstances during the 1980s and the 1990s hindered any construction of regional power *vis-à-vis* the global rule, current circumstances in the political economy of post-crisis Latin America have opened a new window of opportunity.

The implications for the IFIs are still uncertain. However, many critics of these institutions, such as the former World Bank Chief Economist Joseph Stiglitz, have extended a warm welcome to alternative schemes that challenge the dominant position of the IFIs. As Stiglitz put it in his claim in support of the Bank of the South,

> One of the advantages of having a Bank of the South is that it would reflect the perspectives of those in the South (while in contrast IMF and World Bank conditions) hinder (regional) development effectiveness.
>
> (Stiglitz, quoted in McElhinny 2007a: 20)

The view that the IFIs are potentially experiencing more immediate financial competition from the Bank of the South as well as from the presence of other key powers in finance and trade suggests that not only is there a decrease in the material influence of these institutions but there is also a weakening of the symbolic and ideological force that underpinned their power in previous decades. In this scenario, the damage to their authority in the region becomes even more apparent.

Politically, the proliferation of intra-regional arrangements is evolving into a new organizational framework for state and civic activism. These arrangements in effect enhance the construction of new expressions of governance – at different levels of authority – after neoliberalism in Latin America. In this context, there have been some signs of adaptation by the IFIs to the new reality and demands of the regional political and economic spectrum. The case of Argentina showed the willingness of some units and staff from the multilateral development banks to broker deals with local actors, engaging in networking activities for the formulation and implementation of policy reforms (see Chapter 5). What the current regional context suggests, however, is that such efforts should be more encompassing and regular practice within the operational agenda of the IFIs if they are to be relevant participants in the reconstruction of more responsive and participatory governance in the region. In many ways, the IFIs are being called upon to adapt to their clients' political realities and avoid the 'best-practices' trap. This is a tall order for organizations that have often acted as mere conveyors of funds and knowledge, but a critical one if they are to remain relevant players in the region. Within the Americas, the general approach of the IFIs to governance projects has been chiefly guided, as seen in the previous chapters, by the need to achieve sound institutional responses to globalization. Following implementation criteria driven by the discretionary mechanisms of decision-making in project negotiation and implementation, the participation of local actors was often subsumed to a logic of top-down assistance, affecting not only the participation of local experts but the core of any democratic governance. Participatory mechanisms and networking activities with local actors beyond government officials have been used in a selective way and their application depended largely on the political sensitivity of the loans or on the ability to use the loans for electoral purposes; even at the cost of reinforcing embedded patterns of clientelistic relations in many areas. However, in some cases national experiences also revealed that the engagement of IFIs' officials in pro-reform networks with local actors for the incorporation of mechanisms of transparency, accountability and participation unleashed, at least to some extent, the nature of the IFIs' operations.

As many Latin American countries became less dependent on new money from the IFIs – either through their own resources or in the context of new regional agreements – the balance in terms of bargaining capacity in the negotiation of loan conditions and payments with international creditors also tilted in favour of Latin American governments. In this context, the IFIs' 'retooling' of their lending operations and the easing of some of their requirements and conditionalities became vital to their relevance in the region. This meant, especially for the World Bank and the IDB, exploring new avenues to accommodate a more country-based approach and to compromise with local political ideas (McElhinny 2007b). Recent debt cancellation in countries like Bolivia, measures to reduce interest rate for lending to middle-income countries and the re-orientation of their portfolios and committed funds to new programmes to respond to domestic priorities in developing countries – such as, as described in the previous chapter, those programmes that came about in consensus-building forums such as the *Mesa de Diálogo* in the aftermath of the crisis in Argentina – can all be seen as attempts to improve the competitive position of the IFIs in the face of growing financial and ideological alternatives.

The pressures on international organizations are escalating in unprecedented terms. Crisis in the international political economy has always been potentially cyclical. This time, however, discontent with the consequences of neoliberalism and its institutions cannot be interpreted simply as an 'isolated event of passing unhappiness, but [as] part of a long-term shift' (Hira 2004: 1). Growing recognition of this fact has propelled the IFIs towards an, albeit gradual, response. As was argued, cultural dynamics and bureaucratic processes within the IFIs dictate the way in which these organizations respond to norms. As suggested by Park,

an international organization may determine that its operations need to expand or be restricted on the basis that it is the right thing to do... Culture can explain how [international organizations] choose to respond in certain ways, but it cannot do so without explaining the environment within which the [organization] exists.

(2007: 538)

The World Bank and the IDB in particular are reconsidering political issues within their operations and approach to aid assistance, and also in their overall understanding of governance. As described in Chapters 5 and 6, room for new synergies are emerging as the multilateral development banks are concentrating on investment for social and infrastructure programmes that are vital for the reconstruction of the links between the state and society, reinforcing in turn the feasibility of a more responsive governance model. Changes in this direction are vital if the IFIs are to regain their legitimacy and authority in development assistance. Given the nature of their mandates and operational agendas, the task has been neither easy nor uniform across the multilateral lenders. For the IMF, in particular, readapting to a new reality in post-crisis, nationalistic Latin America presents a greater challenge. The IMF forfeited its leverage as the lender of last resort and 'financial supervisor', and the nature of the short-term orthodoxy that traditionally coloured its agenda is not easy to modify. In some cases the rigidity of the IMF stance led to critical disputes over policies and approaches that in the current political and economic context have disadvantaged its position. In such an institutional culture chances for lesson drawing are also reduced. As explored in Chapter 6, in the case of Argentina's post-crisis negotiations, the IMF refused to endorse nationalistic measures such as the regulation of utility companies and privatized enterprises, which were subject to a price freeze following the 'pesification' of the economy, the implementation of new taxes on trade and finance and other capital controls. The result was stalled negotiations and the eventual cancellation of all commitments to the Fund. This move was in many respects foundational in the relationship between developing countries and the international financial institutions and was also the catalyst for a new balance between sovereign decisions and external power as, in this case, the country freed itself from IMF tutelage. Naturally, the new spectrum of policy responses in Latin America cannot escape external constraints. The legacies of neoliberalism, in terms of market opening, external investment, export dependence and state cutbacks cannot be rescinded. Yet in Argentina, as in many other post-crisis emerging markets, the power of the international agencies in shaping borrowing countries' behaviour, policy choices and debates has been strikingly mediated by the new national and regional material capabilities and institutional forms that give prominence to the power of local actors creating focal point that re-defines the political-economic dynamics affecting them and the power relations involving external actors.

Re-defining governance in the era of regional profusion also means that the search for an alternative and more autonomous political economy demands the creation of norms and the generation of ideational harmony leading to a new balance between sovereign decisions yet integrated with the global economy. The involvement of the IFIs through networking with local actors beyond the government circle can directly weigh that balance in favour of a more inclusive economy and responsive democratic governance, recognizing and accommodating a wide range of actors. Compromising on policy positions and capitalizing on those areas of political engagement will certainly re-define the nature of power relations between the local actors and the international institutions. The outcome should be joint discursive and normative constructions to reverse the legacy or the temptations of elite-driven political and economic projects. There is, however, one important reservation to be made since current challenges and changes within the structure of social relations and power politics involving the IFIs and developing countries are not analogous across the developing world. The ongoing huge external debt in many developing countries and the disadvantageous terms of exchange still ensure enormous leverage for mainstream international financial institutions, and they continue to exert major pressure on the policy choices of such countries.

The calls for nationally led governance projects emerging from many Latin American countries, despite the many differences that can be identified across the region, have grown out of the unfulfilled promises of neoliberalism, as well as from the declining legitimacy and authority of the IFIs' promotion of certain rules and administrative processes related to state effectiveness and legal remedies. The current denunciation of the failures of neoliberalism to deliver sustained economic growth and to address problems of inequality and poverty paved the way for the emergence of alternative ideas to gain authority and legitimacy. As proposed in this book, this process demands further analysis within the framework of domestic politics prevailing now, while simultaneously shaping international governance practices.

The move away from the neoliberal project towards an alternative and more autonomous system of governance in Latin America is still partial and unstable. In particular, the new models of governance are embedded in countries and political cultures that have largely been shaped not only by the recent past of profound economic and political inequality but also by historic legacies of institutional fragility, abysmal gaps between a formal democratic order and the persistent realities of social exclusion, poverty and inequality, and, politically, the entrenched practices of patrimonialism, elitism and corruption. The establishment of truly alternative governance projects will greatly depend on how domestic distributional and political games are resolved, including the ways that civil society organizations and local experts are involved in the construction of consensus and legitimacy, as well as how the IFIs set about the task of serving as a genuine aid to nation-specific development policies.

8
Promoting Governance in Developing Countries: The Need for a New Compromise

For the past 25 years, the neoliberal ideology underpinning the IFIs-sponsored governance reform initiatives throughout Latin America has been both influential and pervasive. The monetarist and neoliberal economic policies which drove the changes in Latin America – from autarchic statism to indiscriminate open economies – during this period carried the expectation that these changes would make the relevant economies more efficient and more effective. However, by the mid-1990s disillusionment with the charms of open markets and of neoliberalism began to creep in. Economic growth in Latin America remained erratic, widespread employment problems were undiminished, new rounds of unpopular adjustment often led to undemocratic practices and social distribution worsened.

The current backlash in Latin America against neoliberalism and its main conveyors, especially the IFIs, and the emergence of alternative models of governance articulated by a resurgence of leftist, nationalist projects in countries like Venezuela, Argentina, Bolivia, Ecuador and to a lesser extent Brazil and Chile suggest that the political and economic tenets supporting neoliberal governance are inevitable in crisis. Changing international economic and political dynamics following the rise of China, India and Venezuela as 'alternative globalizers' are relevant contextual factors behind the emergence of contesting models of governance across the world. Some multilateral institutions, such as the World Bank and the IMF, have seen their reserves shrink as a result of a declining participation in reform processes undertaken by many developing countries together with repayments, international liquidity, debt relief operations and the apparent sense of futility in regard to the legitimacy, credibility and role of the IFIs in the world economy.

This scenario presents the IFIs with an inexorable dilemma in their financial and ideological authority. The increasing bilateral aid that many developing countries now receive from alternative sources is released without conditions in respect of policies and goals. In severely financially dependent countries in Africa, for instance, Chinese aid assistance is displacing that of the IFIs and the loans offered free of conditions on policy and economic goals. In Latin America, funding from Venezuela is also ousting that of the external lending institutions, contributing to a trend of rapid accumulation of foreign exchange reserves by emerging market economies over the last half decade (Mohanty and Turner 2006). The accumulation of cross-border foreign assets opens a whole new spectrum of alternative uses, from repaying external and domestic debts to financing major investment projects including the re-nationalization of previously privatized enterprises. Although these loans can certainly reinforce non-democratic practices in certain contexts, in others they fortify a new political space where alternative models of development and governance can emerge.

In the case of Latin America, there are now clear signs of 'Washington Consensus fatigue' and many Latin American leaders are now piloting a new political project that seeks to reverse the failing market-based mode of governance. The legacy of neoliberalism generated unanticipated consequences and popular dissatisfaction with the policy process associated with it, including the IFIs' modalities of intervention which often entailed pushing through policies via conditional funding negotiated in consonance with like-minded elites in the developing countries. The current search for alternative and autonomous models of development and governance, not exclusively confined to Latin America, is part of a broader process of re-definition of the political tenets of economic management.

This book attempts to understand the implications of the current changes in Latin American political economy – and its search for a more autonomous model of governance – for the (power) relationships between the IFIs and the local actors. It does so by exploring the risks associated with the narrow approach and practices of the IFIs in their promotion of political and economic governance in developing countries. The book takes the lessons of the Argentine crisis and analyses from a broader perspective how the current neoliberal model became discredited and eroded in Latin America and the ways and the extent to which a new model of governance is shaping new social relations involving local and external actors. Four guiding questions are covered in this book: to what extent the IFIs can affect models of the state and development; can 'good governance' be imposed from outside; who is governance good for; and to what extent have the current political and economic trends in Latin America transformed power relationships between donors and recipient countries? In answering these questions, the book explores what 'power' currently means in the relationship between the IFIs and developing countries and the analytical implications for a broader analysis of the tensions between sovereign authority, policy processes and externally driven demands.

The consequences of the disconnection between neoliberalism and social justice, in Argentina as well as in many other developing countries, calls for a re-examination of the various agreements, dynamics and constellations of actors, interests and power resources in the search for governance after neoliberalism. This study devotes particular attention to contesting ideas and power relations, policy processes and prospects of policy change in politically sensitive reforms involving local actors and the IFIs. It illustrates the importance of going beyond deterministic understandings that attribute particular roles and particular power weight to certain actors and emphasizes the need to rethink the articulation of knowledge, funds and power as fundamental to the complex policy process that shapes development policies.

The developing world has provided grounds for the analysis of the relationship with the IFIs, which centred almost exclusively on the huge disparities in levels of power and development which, in turn, shaped the conditions for political and economic outcomes in the region (Phillips 2005). As Chapters 1 and 2 critically manifested, although many substantial accounts, especially within the literature of IPE, focus on complexities of social forces and power relations, including a focus on their system of ideas, most of this work, however, tended to subsume these relationships to a hierarchical and unequal understanding of power relations and ignored the process by which local conveyors of knowledge and ideas can make a telling difference. The empirical evidence presented in the cases of governance analysed in previous chapters suggests that governance can be both an arena of contestation as well as one for political engagement and, even more crucially, that legitimacy derives from the ways local actors are involved in the process of policy change – from agenda setting to the implementation of reforms. This has enormous implications for the modalities of influence of the IFIs in politically sensitive reforms. One of the contributions to critical theory cited in the preceding analysis is thus to discern the contesting forces at the local level, giving autonomy and agency to the local actors *beyond dynamics of co-optation*. As stated in the opening chapters, critical IPE underestimates contestation as often-conflictive relationships between social forces in which the powerful engineer consent centred on a logic of co-optation of local actors and their expertise ('organic intellectuals') to advance change in social institutions to ensure paradigm and global power relations maintenance; in other words, tended to subsume contesting forces and alternative knowledge at the local level to a functional 'transnational managerial class' that acts as a transmission belt for the diffusion of global (capitalist) norms (see Cox 1987; Gill 1990; Sklair 2001; Robinson 2004; Cammack 2006). Likewise, the ideological role played by the IFIs has been greatly overemphasized (see, for instance, George and Sabelli 1994; Williams and Young 1994; Mehta 2001). As such, much of the IPE literature that examines global governance rules and practices has focused on the analysis of the transnational forces and the structural power that sustains international economic policy change.

Acknowledging these caveats, this book draws lessons from power dynamics involving the IFIs and local actors at 'micro-level of relations' – manifested in the formulation and implementation of policy-sensitive governance reforms – to understand the challenges and dilemmas for the IFIs in a context in which Latin America as a region is in search for more politically and economically autonomous models of governance. The study thus begins with a critical analysis of the dynamics of power and knowledge involving the IFIs and local actors in two governance programmes in Argentina, judicial and anti-corruption reforms. It then extends these questions to the post-crisis scenario in a changing context of the regional political economy, where a variety of home-grown ideas and policy projects take a new direction and define the relationships between local and global governance. The nature of the neoliberal crisis and the rhetorical question posed by Dani Rodrik (2002) – 'After Neoliberalism, What?' – makes this an opportune study.

The politics of governance and future challenges for the international financial institutions

Much of what has been observed in the promotion of governance by the IFIs in developing countries has been shaped by 'macro' structural processes of power, illustrated by the financial and intellectual position of the IFIs in the global economy and by the 'micro' relational power involving local and IFIs' staff in the process of policy reform on the ground.

The process of policy change is at the intersection of those macro and micro relations of power. This perception connects levels of analysis and thus spans IPE critical analysis and the models of policy-making depicted in the public policy literature (see Chapter 2). The study of modalities of influence practised by the IFIs and the distinction between the latter as conveyors of policy paradigms or brokers of knowledge and funds, illustrated in the preceding chapters, captures the tensions between local contextual realities and the legal and normative aspects of global governance. It also suggests that it is analytically misguided to assume that local actors simply agree or consent, or are coerced or co-opted, by external financial agencies. The ways in which the IFIs adapt to contesting domestic politics and ideas is critical to the response of the local actors to their promotion of governance forms and practices. This is even more the case in the current scenario of changing international economic and political context. As analysed in previous chapters, the different modalities of engagement of the IFIs has been critical elements explaining the policy outcomes of politically sensitive reforms, such as judicial reform and anti-corruption. This is in fact a current major challenge for the IFIs, and for international actors in general, now confronted with a new 'battle of ideas' in the region.

Crises are always an opportunity for the ideological contestation and accommodation of political and economic projects. New ideas put forward by many Latin American leaders today directly question the tenets of neoliberal governance that supported the IFIs' intervention in the region for over more than two decades. The new repertoire of ideas and practices builds on the notion of the state as a multifaceted actor mediating the relationship between citizens and markets. This relationship between state, markets and civil society is inherently linked to historical and contextual dynamics and thus varies from place to place. Designing institutions and promoting reform cannot be achieved, therefore, based simply upon what works in a certain setting. Designing appropriate institutional arrangements for development is entrenched in the political fabric in any society and thus requires local knowledge and legitimacy.

The type of institutional reform promoted by multilateral organizations such as the World Bank and the IMF has consistently inclined to replicate a modality of 'top-down' transfer of best practices. This modality, as illustrated in the case of judicial reform in Argentina and in other external exigencies in the aftermath of the crisis (Chapters 4 and 6 respectively) assumed that it is possible to determine a unique set of appropriate institutional arrangements and views, and to link up with like-minded elites in developing countries for the affirmation of those policies. These linkages frequently involved the IFIs, governments, influential businesses and financial actors.

Despite the apparent conviction of IFIs' staff that this modality can lead to desirable goals in terms of economic growth by reducing uncertainties for investors and increasing the efficiency of de-politicized institutions, reality indicates that paradigms cannot be transferred uncritically from one setting to another and that local actors are not merely passive recipients of funds and knowledge. Particularly in middle-income countries, like Argentina, where a strong base of local experts, policy think-tanks, consultancies, academic and politically mobilized groups are often involved in policy proposals prior to the arrival of the IFIs in the country, the latter are compelled to avoid the 'best-practice trap'. Politically sensitive reforms, such as governance, are entrenched in a complex policy process in which the dominance of a particular actor or paradigm *vis-à-vis* other contending actors or ideas is not cemented simply by the coercive position of the lender over the borrower, but rather by the lender's capacity to integrate contesting impulses into a broader consensus for policy change. From this perspective, this study demonstrates that the power of the IFIs to implement governance-related reforms is closely related to its capacity act as a norm-broker by engaging in 'pro-reform networks' with local experts, articulating local and external policy paradigms for the design and implementation of policy change. The point of these considerations is that change is context dependent and thus achieving effective institutional change outcomes cannot be achieved by employing the norm of a unique institutional design.

The contextual character of policy reform is also evident in the reconstruction of post-crisis governance in, but not exclusively, Argentina at the turn of the millennium. For instance, the insistence of the IMF on implementing what it considered 'best-practice' in Argentina not only ignored the political implications, and complications, of choices available to post-crisis governments but led in turn to the discredit and isolation of the IMF from the emergent regional financial architecture.

The link between ideas and power in the context of profound economic and political transformation is of paramount importance. The 'technical versus political' dilemma for the IFIs has been to a great extent related to the capacity of their staff to broaden their bases of legitimacy, transforming areas of contestation into areas of engagement. For instance, in the experience of anti-corruption in Argentina, the World Bank staff acknowledged reform as a process of amalgamation and compromise between a variety of actors' interests and knowledge-based proposals for reform (see Chapter 5). In the case of judicial reform, in contrast, policy change was approached as the result of an efficient, cost–benefit decision negotiated between the Bank management and the government (see Chapter 4). As such, while staff from the PREM and the WBI improved the environment for reform by engaging with local actors in networking activities and enhanced the support and capacity of civil society experts to lead reform implementation in the area of anti-corruption, in the case of judicial reform the Bank's Legal Department empowered the government's agenda to advance the reform by following a top-down model that, although reaching agreement at the official level for project approval, in fact not only hampered the implementation of the reform, but also contributed to the increasing discredit of the project and of the Bank's role. This conflicting relationship with the Bank staff engaged in judicial reform – unlike that of the PREM, for instance – mitigated against their involvement with local actors in forums such as *Mesa de Diálogo* for the discussion of post-crisis governance priorities and plans of action. Yet in general, the multilateral development banks did exhibit signs of change and a re-accommodation of their portfolios towards areas of social development that were vital if the government was to recover governance capability. As Chapter 6 explains, unlike the IMF, the support of the World Bank and the IDB for local actors' initiatives in the aftermath of the crisis helped not only the government but also the multilateral banks themselves to regain social trust, legitimacy and relevance in a context of regional political and economic change. The IMF, on the contrary, faces a crisis of its own as many of its members have chosen to follow a policy of 'de-borrowing' by accumulating foreign reserves as a way to avoid subjection to the Fund's prescription. What this suggests is that the capacity of the IFIs to produce and diffuse normative agendas of what constitutes good economic policy is a critical factor pertaining to their structure of power and global scope but is not sufficient to assure policy change at the level of domestic politics. In societies where a strong level of expertise informs policy-making and where that expertise is intertwined with political projects, elite-driven projects of governance are often restrained by antagonistic interests and struggles over the legitimacy of the reform programmes. The challenge for the IFIs is how they adapt to, and endorse, the new local constraints and opportunities in developing and emerging markets.

Theoretically, these trends are bound up with discussions about power relations in a changing global political economy. In concurrence with critical theories in IPE that restore the centrality of organizations and politics in any analysis of social processes and change, local actors and local ideas in developing countries are now issuing new challenges to neoliberal configurations with relations involving the international institutions and local actors. The Latin American political economy is now very different from that of the 1980s and there are a range of elected incumbents who are not only opposing the neoliberal creed but are also willing to advance alternative models of governance in the rejection of externally imposed stabilization programmes. The alternative agenda to neoliberalism is being articulated by a reconfiguration of social actors, ideologies and alliances that, at best, opposes any elite-led project. Several actors are at the centre of public policy in developing countries: workers, local experts and academics, politicians, local businessmen, movements of the unemployed, indigenous populations and the government.

Unlike in the past, when struggles over political and economic stability paved the way for asymmetrical power relations in favour of the exigencies of the IFIs, the current scenario of change in the political economy of Latin America and many other developing countries illuminates a strong rejection of top-down, elite-led models of governance. Popular manifestation and protests in many cities have directly attacked the economic project supported by the IFIs challenging more broadly 'the morality of marketized democracies with an alternative view of state–society relationships' (Grugel 2009).

Yet it is important not to overemphasize the current efforts to move away from neoliberalism in Latin America. Continuity and change are overlapping forces in the redefinition of governance after neoliberalism. In many cases a mix of nationalism and interventionist practices coexist with export-led economies and a commitment to sound macroeconomic and fiscal policies. Of course the process varies across the region. What the post-neoliberal model of governance will look like is still very uncertain. What is certain, though, is that some sense of an alternative path to development is being delineated, and that this project represents a new opportunity for responsive and inclusive political economies. Many observers, although cautious, suggest interpreting the growing number of left-wing governments taking office in many Latin American countries as a new chance for a more encompassing and participatory model of governance (for instance, Hershberg and Rosen 2006: 2). Many questions still arise concerning the regional current political and economic trends. At the national level, the rules of the game in many countries are partial and still unstable. Personalistic politics and the legacies of patrimonialism and clientelism are symptomatic of the difficulties of moving beyond elite-led governance. Moreover, only vague notions as to what a post–Washington Consensus economy can or should look like are uttered; and despite growth, the new political economy in many countries is not meeting the social development deficit that undermined the legitimacy of the neoliberal project of previous decades.

In this context the IFIs can be of significant weight. Despite criticism, some attempts to reconstruct trust among civil society actors confirm the relevance of these organizations in governance practices. Certainly, any intervention by the IFIs has to take on board the lessons of past failures and to capitalize on areas of political engagement such as the challenges of social inclusion and pro-poor policies – areas that even the new left-wing governments are struggling to reconcile. Improvement in popular community action, nationally and intra-regionally, and recognition of the capacity of local experts from think-tanks, academia and other forums of knowledge production to influence the policy stream are also important areas for networking between multilateral organizations and local actors. Equally, the unconditional participation of the IFIs acting as 'gatekeepers', coordinating bilateral donors and developing countries is also a role via which many countries – even those that have 'liberated' themselves from the IFIs' conditionalities through debt write-offs or by paying back debts – may derive benefit.

The emergent political and economic nationalism in Latin America is part of a new diffusion of power and new spheres of autonomy that are currently challenging the global rule and even creating new foundations of global/regional governance. This scenario is transforming power relationships between actors, especially between donors and recipient countries. More than ever before, the IFIs must address the pressing dilemma of being the instrument of the 'old' conservative world or embracing new forms of governance.

References

Abeles, M., K. Forcinito and M. Schorr (2001) *El Oligopolio Telefónico Argentino frente a la Liberalización del Mercado* (Buenos Aires: Universidad Nacional de Quilmes).

Acuña, C. H. (1995) 'Politics and Economics in the Argentina of the Nineties' in W. C. Smith and E. Gamarra (eds.) *Democracy, Markets and Structural Reform* (Florida: North-South Center Press), 17–66.

Acuña, C. H. and W. C. Smith (1994) 'The Political Economy of Structural Adjustment: The Logic and of Support and Opposition to Neoliberal Reforms' in W. C. Smith, C. H. Acuña and E. Gamarra (eds.) *Latin American Political Economy in the Age of Neoliberal Reform* (New Brunswick, N.J.: Transaction Publishers), 17–66.

Acuña, C. H. and F. Tuozzo (2000) 'Civil Society Participation in World Bank and Inter-American Development Bank Programs: The Case of Argentina', *Global Governance*, Vol. 6, No. 4, 433–456.

Acuña, C. and G. Alonso (2003) 'La Reforma Judicial y la Participación de la Sociedad Civil' in D. Tussie and M. Botto (eds.) *El ALCA y las Cumbres de las Américas: ¿Una Nueva Relación Público-Privada?* (Buenos Aires: Biblos), 125–143.

ADC (2003) *Una Corte para la Democracia*, at http://www.adc.org.ar/recursos/521/cortesuprema2003-propuestadereformasinternas. Accessed 17 March 2008.

Akkerman, A. and J. Teunissen (2001) 'Introduction' in A. Akkerman, and J. Teunissen (eds.) *The Crisis That Was Not Prevented: Argentina, the IMF, and Globalisation*, FONDAD, at http://www.fondad.org. Accessed 21 November 2006.

Asselin, R. (1996) *Experiencias Recientes en el Desarrollo de Coaliciones para Promover Reforma Judicial*. Banco Interamericano de Desarrollo, at http://www.iadb.org/sds/doc/sgc-Doc40-1-S.pdf. Accessed 15 May 2004.

Babb, S. (2001) *Managing Mexico: Economists from Nationalism to Neoliberalism* (Princeton: Princeton University Press).

Baldi-Delatte, A. (2005) 'Did Pesification Rescue Argentina?' Paper presented at LACEA Conference, October 2005, at http://www.aup.fr/lacea2005/program/sessions/contributed2/CS53.htm. Accessed 23 November 2006.

Bambaci, J., T. Saront and M. Tommasi (2002) 'The Political Economy of Economic Reforms in Argentina', *Journal of Policy Reform*, Vol. 5, No. 2, 75–88.

Barnes, H. (2005) 'Conflict, Inequality and Dialogue for Conflict Resolution in Latin America: The Cases of Argentina, Bolivia and Venezuela', Human Development Report Office, Occasional Paper (Geneva: UNDP).

Barnett, M. and M. Finnemore (1999) 'The Politics, Power and Pathologies of International Organizations', *International Organization*, Vol. 53, No. 4, 699–732.

Barnett, M. and R. Duvall (2005) 'Power in Global Governance' in M. Barnett, and R. Duvall (eds.) *Power in Global Governance* (Cambridge: Cambridge University Press), 1–32.

Basualdo, E. (2002) 'El Proceso de Privatización en la Argentina: La Renegociación con las Empresas Privatizadas', at http://bibliotecavirtual.clacso.org.ar/ar/

libros/argentina/flacso/no6_ProcesoPrivatizacionArgentina.pdf. Accessed 14 May 2007.

Bertranou, F., R. Rofmanand and C. Grushka (2003) 'From Reform to Crisis: Argentina's Pension System', *International Social Security Review*, Vol. 56, No. 2, 103–114.

Bieler, A. and A. Morton (2001) 'The Gordian Knot of Agency-Structure in International Relations: A Neo-Gramscian Perspective', *European Journal of International Relations*, Vol. 7, No. 1, 5–35.

Bill Chavez, R. (2004) 'The Evolution of Judicial Autonomy in Argentina: Establishing the Rule of Law in an Ultrapresidential System', *Journal of Latin American Studies*, Vol. 36, No. 3, 451–478.

Birdsall, N. (2001) 'Multilateral Development Banks in a Changing Global Economy', *Economic Perspectives*. Electronic Journal of the U.S. Department of State, Vol. 6, No. 1, at http://usinfo.state.gov/journals/ites/0201/ijee/ifis-birdsall.htm. Accessed 14 May 2002.

Birdsall, N. (2005) The *World Bank Under Wolfowitz*, American Enterprise Institute (AEI), Washington, D.C., 7 June, 2005, at http://www.aei.org/events/filter. eventID.1082/summary.asp. Accessed 5 April 2008.

Birdsall, N. and C. Graham (2000) *New Markets, New Opportunities? Economic and Social Mobility in a Changing World* (Washington, D.C.: Bookings Institution Press).

Blair, H. and G. Hansen (1994) 'Weighing in on the Scales of Justice: Strategic Approaches for Donor-Supported Rule of Law Programs'. USAID, at http://www.usaid.gov/our_work/democracy_and_governance/publications/pdfs/pnaax280.pdf. Accessed 12 August 2003.

Blustein, P. (2005) *And the Money Kept Rolling In (and Out): Wall Street, the IMF and the Bankrupting of Argentina* (New York: Public Affairs).

Bøas, M. and D. McNeill (2004) 'Ideas and Institutions: Who Is Framing What?' in M. Bøas and D. McNeill (eds.) *Global Institutions and Development: Framing the World?* (London and New York: Routledge), 206–224.

Boeninger, E. (1992) *Governance and Development: Issues and Constraints*. The World Bank Proceedings of the World Bank Annual Conference on Development Economics 1991 (Washington, D.C.: World Bank).

Bohmer, M. (2004) 'Igualadores Retóricos: Las Profesiones del Derecho y la Reforma de la Justicia en la Argentina', mimeo.

Bräutigam, D. and M. Segarra (2007) 'Difficult Partnerships: The World Bank, States, and NGOs', *Latin American Politics and Society*, Vol. 49, No. 4, 149–181.

Bresser-Pereira, L. (1995) 'Development Economics and the World Bank's Identity Crisis', *Review of International Political Economy*, Vol. 2, No. 2, 211–247.

Buchanan, J. (2001) *Judicial Reform in the Americas*, FOCAL Policy Paper, at http://www.focal.ca/images/pdf/Judicial.pdf. Accessed 10 December 2004.

Burki, S. and G. Perry (1998) *Beyond the Washington Consensus: Institutions Matter* (Washington, D.C.: World Bank).

Burges, S. (2009) 'Governance after Neoliberalism in Brazil' in J. Grugel and P. Riggirozzi (eds.) *Governance after Neoliberalism in Latin America* (Basingstoke: Palgrave/Macmillan), forthcoming.

Buscaglia, E. and M. Dakolias (1996) *A Quantitative Analysis of the Judicial Sector: The Cases of Argentina and Ecuador*. World Bank Technical Paper No. 353 (Washington, D.C.: World Bank).

190   *References*

Buxton, J. (2009) 'The Conundrum of Venezuela: An Alternative to Neoliberalism?' in J. Grugel and P. Riggirozzi (eds.) *Governance after Neoliberalism in Latin America* (Basingstoke: Palgrave/Macmillan), forthcoming.

Cammack, P. (2004) 'What the World Bank Means by Poverty Reduction and Why It Matters', *New Political Economy*, Vol. 9, No. 2, 189–211.

Cammack, P. (2006) 'The Politics of Global Competitiveness', *Papers in the Politics of Global Competitiveness*, No. 1, November, Manchester Metropolitan University.

Cammack, P. (2007) 'Competitiveness and Convergence: The Open Method of Coordination in Latin America'. *Papers in the Politics of Global Competitiveness*, No. 5, Institute for Global Studies, Manchester Metropolitan University, e-space Open Access Repository.

Carothers, T. (2001) 'The Many Agendas of Rule-of-law Reform in Latin America' in D. Pilar and R. Sieder (eds.) *Rule of Law in Latin America. The International Promotion of Judicial Reform* (London: Institute of Latin American Studies), 4–16.

Carrió, A. and A. Garay (1996) *La Corte Suprema y su Independencia. Un Análisis a través de la Historia* (Buenos Aires: Abeledo Perrot).

Casaburi, G., P. Riggirozzi, F. Tuozzo and D. Tussie (2000) 'Multilateral Development Banks, Governments and Civil Society. Chiaroscuros in a Triangular Relationship', *Global Governance* (Special Issue), Vol. 6, No. 4, 493–517.

Castañeda, J. and M. Morales (2008) *Leftovers: Tales of the Latin American Left* (London: Routledge).

Cavarozzi, M. (1994) 'Politics: A Key for the Long Term in South America' in W. C. Smith, C. H. Acuña and E. A. Gamarra (eds.) *Latin American Political Economy in the Age of Neoliberal Reform* (New Brunswick, N.J.: Transaction Publishers), 127–155.

Cesilini, S. (2003) 'Una Iniciativa Experimental en la Construcción de Mecanismos Sociales de Rendición de Cuentas En Argentina' in *Pensando en Voz Alta IV: Innovadores Estudios de Caso sobre Instrumentos Participativos*. Latin America and the Caribbean Region Civil Society Team (Washington, D.C.: World Bank), 79–88.

Chandrasekhar, C. P. and J. Ghosh (2008) 'Shaking up Development Finance in Latin America', *South Bulletin: Reflections and Foresights*, No. 9, February.

Cibils, A. (2003) 'Argentina's IMF Agreement the Dawn of a New Era?' *Foreign Policy in Focus*, October 10, at http://www.fpif.org/commentary/2003/0310argdefault.html. Accessed 27 September 2006.

Cline, W. (2003) 'Restoring Economic Growth in Argentina', *Working Paper N.9/03*, World Bank Office for Argentina, Chile, Paraguay y Uruguay (Washington, D.C.: The World Bank).

Corbalan, M. A. (2002) *El Banco Mundial: Intervención y Disciplinamiento. El Caso Arentino, Enseñanzas para America Latina* (Buenos Aires: Biblos).

Cook, M. (2006) The Politics of Labour Reform in Latin America Between Flexibility and Rights (University Part, Pennsylvania University Press).

Corrales, J. (1997) 'Why Argentines followed Cavallo' in J. Domínguez (ed.) *Technopols: Freeing Politics and Markets in Latin America in the 1990s* (University Park, P.A.: Pennsylvania State University Press), 49–94.

Cox, R. (1986) 'Social Forces, States and World Order: Beyond International Relations Theory' in R. Keohane (ed.) *Neorealism and Its Critics* (New York: Columbia University Press), 204–254.

Cox, R. (1987) *Production, Power and World Order: Social Forces in the Making of History* (New York: Columbia University Press).

Cox, R. (1989) 'Production, the State and Change in World Order' in E. Czempiel and J. N. Rosenau (eds.) *Global Changes and Theoretical Challenges: Approaches to World Politics for the 1990s* (Toronto: Lexington Books), 37–50.

Cox, R. (1993) 'Gramsci, Hegemony and International Relations: An Essay in Method' in S. Gill (ed.) *Gramsci, Historical Materialism and International Relations* (Cambridge: Cambridge University Press), 49–66.

Dakolias, M. (1995) 'A Strategy for Judicial Reform: The Experience in Latin America', *Virginia Journal of International Law*, Vol. 36, No. 1, 167–231.

Damill, M. and R. Frenkel (1993) 'Restauración Democrática y Política Económica: Argentina, 1984–1991' in J. Morales and G. McMahon (eds.) *La Política Económica en la Transición a la Democracia: Lecciones de Argentina, Bolivia, Chile y Uruguay'* (Santiago: CIEPLAN), 37–116.

Damill, M., R. Frenkel and M. Rapetti (2005) 'La Deuda Argentina: Historia, Default y Reestructuración', *Revista Desarrollo Económico*, Vol. 45, No. 178, 187–233.

De Michele, R. (2001) 'The Role of the Anti-Corruption Office in Argentina Lessons on Corruption and Anti-Corruption: Policies and Results', *The Journal of Public Inquiry*, Fall/Winter, 17–20.

De Michele, R. (2004) *Conflicts of Interest an Overview of the Argentine Experience*. Paper presented at the Forum on Implementing Conflict of Interest Policies in the Public Service, 5–6 May (Rio de Janeiro, Brazil: Mimeo).

Dhillon, A., J. Garcia-Fronti, S. Ghosal and M. Miller (2006) 'Debt Restructuring and Economic Recovery: Analysing the Argentine Swap', *World Economy*, Vol. 29, No. 4, 377–398.

Dinerstein, A. (2003) 'Que se Vayan Todos! Popular Insurrection and the Asambleas Barriales in Argentina', *Bulletin of Latin American Research*, Vol. 22, No. 2, 187–200.

Dolowitz, D. and D. Marsh (1996) 'Who Learns from Whom: A Review of the Policy Transfer Literature', *Political Studies*, Vol. 44, No. 2, 343–357.

Dolowitz, D. and D. Marsh (2000) 'Learning From Abroad: The Role of Policy Transfer in Contemporary Policy Making', *Governance*, Vol. 13, No. 1, 5–24.

Domingo, P. (2009) 'Bolivia: Continuity and Change in Post-crisis Governance' in J. Grugel and P. Riggirozzi (eds.) *Governance after Neoliberalism in Latin America* (Basingstoke: Palgrave/Macmillan), forthcoming.

Domínguez, J. (1997) 'Technopols: Ideas and Leaders in Freeing Politics and Markets in Latin America in the 1990s' in J. Dominguez (ed.) *Technopols: Freeing Politics and Markets in Latin America in the 1990s* (University Park, P.A.: Pennsylvania State University Press), 1–48.

Dowding, K. (1995) 'Model or Metaphor? A critical Review of the Policy Network Approach', *Political Studies*, Vol. 43, No. 1, 136–158.

Dowding, K. (2000) 'There Must be End to Confusion: Policy Networks, Intellectual Fatigue and the Need for Political Science Methods Courses in British Universities', *Political Studies*, Vol. 49, No. 1, 89–105.

Easterly, W. (2001) *The Elusive Quest for Growth: Economists' Adventures and Misadventures in the Tropics* (Cambridge, M.A.: MIT Press).

ECLAC (2004) *Latin America and the Caribbean in the World Economy* (Santiago de Chile: ECLAC).

Egan, D. (2001) 'The Limits of Internationalisation: A Neo-Gramscian Analysis of the Multilateral Agreement on Investment', *Critical Sociology*, Vol. 27, No. 3, 74–97.

Ellerman, D. (2001) 'Helping People Help Themselves: Toward a Theory of Autonomy-Compatible Help', *Policy Research Working Paper Series*, No. 2693 (Washington, D.C.: World Bank).

Escude, G. (2002) 'Public Debt and Real Exchange Rate Dynamics in Argentina under Convertibility, Qué?', *Banco Central de la República Argentina*, May, mimeo.

Evans, M. (2001) 'Understanding Dialectics in Policy Network Analysis', *Political Studies*, Vol. 49, No. 1, 542–550.

Evans, M. and J. Davies (1999) 'Understanding Policy Transfer: A Multilevel, Multidisciplinary Perspective', *Public Administration*, Vol. 77, No. 2, 361–385.

Ferguson, J. (1990) *The Anti-Politics Machine: 'Development', Depoliticization and Bureaucratic Power in Lesotho* (Cambridge: Cambridge University Press).

Fernandez, R. and R. Gould (1994) 'A Dilemma of State Power: Brokerage and Influence in the National Health Policy Domain', *American Journal of Sociology*, Vol. 99, No. 6, 1455–1491.

Fernandez-Arias, E. and P. Montiel (1997) *A Decade of Structural Reform: All Pain No Gain? Latin America after a Decade of Reforms*. Office of the Chief Economist, Working Paper 351 (Washington, D.C.: IDB).

Ferreira Rubio, D. and M. Goretti (1996) 'Cuando el Presidente Gobierna Solo. Menem y los Decretos de Necesidad y Urgencia hasta la Reforma Constitucional (Julio 1989–Agosto 1994)', *Desarrollo Económico*, Vol. 36, No. 141, 443–474.

Finkel, J. (2004) 'Judicial Reform In Argentina in the 1990s: How Electoral Incentives Shape Institutional Change', *Latin American Research Review*, Vol. 39, No. 3, 56–80.

Finnemore, M. (1996) *National Interests in International Society* (Ithaca and London: Cornell University Press).

Fitzgerald, V. and R. Thorp (2005) 'The acceptance of economic doctrine in Latin America' in V. Fitzgerald and R. Thorp (eds.) *Economic Docrines in Latin America* (London: Palgrave St. Anthony's Series).

FIEL (1996) *La Reforma del Poder Judicial en la Argentina* (Buenos Aires: FIEL).

Galazo, E. and M. Ravallion (2004) 'Social Protection in a Crisis: Argentina's Plan Jefes y Jefas', *World Bank Economic Review*, Vol. I, No. 18, 367–399.

Gale, F. (1998) 'Cave "Cave! Hic Dragones": A Neo-Gramscian Deconstruction and Reconstruction of International Regime Theory', *Review of International Political Economy*, Vol. 5, No. 2, 252–283.

George, S. and F. Sabelli (1994) *Faith and Credit: The World Bank's Secular Empire* (London: Pan Books).

Gerchunoff, P. and L. Llach (2003) *El Ciclo de la Ilusión y el Desencanto* (Buenos Aires: Ariel).

Germain, R. (2004) 'Globalising Accountability within the International Organisation of Credit: Financial Governance and the Public Sphere', *Global Society*, Vol. 18, No. 3, 217–237.

Germain, R. and M. Kenny (1998) 'Engaging Gramsci: International Relations Theory and the New Gramscians', *Review of International Studies*, Vol. 24, No. 1, 3–21.

Gibson, E. (1997) 'The Populist Road to Market Reform: Policy and Electoral Coalitions in Mexico and Argentina', *World Politics*, Vol. 49, No. 3, 339–370.

Gilbert, C., A. Powell and D. Vines (2000) 'Positioning the World Bank' in C. Gilbert and D. Vines (eds.) *The World Bank. Structure and Policy* (Cambridge: Cambridge University Press), 39–86.

Gill, S. (1990) *American Hegemony and the Trilateral Commission* (New York: Cambridge University Press).

Gill, S. (1995) 'Globalisation, Market Civilisation and Disciplinary Neoliberalism', *Millennium: Journal of International Studies*, Vol. 24, No. 3, 399–423.

Gill, S. (2000) *The Constitution of Global Capitalism*, at http://www.theglobalsite. ac.uk/press/010gill.pdf. Accessed 11 March 2005.

Gill, S. (2005) 'New Constitutionalism, Democratisation, and Global Political Economy' in R. Wilkinson (ed.), *The Global Governance Reader* (New York: Routledge), 174–186.

Gill, S. and D. Law (1988) The Global Political Economy: Perspectives, Problems and Policies (Hertfordshire: Harvester and Wheatsheaf).

Goldman, M. (2005) *Imperial Nature: The World Bank and Struggles for Social Justice in an Age of Globalization* (New Haven, C.T.: Yale University Press).

Görg, C. and U. Brand (2006) 'Contested Regimes in the International Political Economy: Global Regulation of Genetic Resources and the Internationalization of the State', *Global Environmental Politics*, Vol. 6, No. 4, 101–123.

Gramsci, A. (1971) *Selections from the Prison Notebooks*. Trans. Quintin Hoare and Geoffrey Nowell-Smith (London: Lawrence and Wishart).

Grugel, J. (2003) 'Democratisation Studies Globalization: The Coming of Age of a Paradigm', *British Journal of Political and International Relations*, Vol. 5, No. 2, 258–283.

Grugel, J. and P. Riggirozzi (2007) 'The Return of the State', *International Affairs*, Vol. 83, No. 1, 87–107.

Grugel, J. (2009) 'The End of the Washington Consensus: Democratic Renewal from the Left?' in J. Grugel and P. Riggirozzi (eds.) *Governance after Neoliberalism in Latin America* (Basingstoke: Palgrave/Macmillan), forthcoming.

Grugel J. and P. Riggirozzi (eds.) (2009) *Governance after Neoliberalism in Latin America* (Basingstoke: Palgrave/Macmillan), forthcoming.

Grugel, J., P. Riggirozzi and B. Thirkell-White (2008) 'Beyond the Washington Consensus? Asia and Latin America in Search of More Autonomous Development', *International Affairs*, Vol. 84, 3.

Haas, P. (1992) 'Introduction: Epistemic Communities and International Policy Coordination', *International Organization*, Vol. 46, No. 1, 1–35.

Haggard, S. and R. Kaufman (1994) 'Democratic Institutions, Economic Policy and Performance in Latin America' in C. Bradford (ed.) *Redefining the State in Latin America* (Paris: OECD), 69–90.

Hammergren, L. (1998) *Political Will, Constituency Building and Public Support in Rule of Law Programs*. Centre for Democracy and Governance (Washington, D.C.: USAID).

Hanlon, J. and A. Pettifor (2000) 'Kicking the Habit: Finding a Lasting Solution to Addictive Lending and Borrowing and Its Corrupting Side-Effects', at http://www.jubileeplus.org/analysis/reports/habitfull.htm. Accessed 15 February 2005.

Harris, J. and J. Hunter (eds.) (1995) *The New Institutional Economics and the Third World Development* (London: Routledge).

Harris, R. (2000) 'The Effects of Globalization and Neoliberalism in Latin America at the Beginning of the Millennium' in R. Harris and M. Seid (eds.) *Critical Perspectives on Globalization and Neoliberalism in Developing Countries* (Leiden, Boston and Köln: Brill), 139–162.

Harrison, G. (2004) *The World Bank and Africa the Construction of Governance States* (London: Routledge).

Harrison, G. (2005) 'The World Bank, Governance and Theories of Political Action in Africa', *The British Journal of Politics and International Relations*, Vol. 7, No. 2, 240–260.

Hayward, C. R. (2000) *De-facing Power* (Cambridge and New York: Cambridge University Press).

Helmke, G. (2003) 'Checks and Balances by other Means Strategic: Defection and Argentina's Supreme Court in the 1990s', *Comparative Politics*, Vol. 35, No. 2, 213–230.

Hentz, J. (2004) 'The Power of Ideas. Across the Constructivist/realist Divide' in M. Bøas and D. McNeill (eds.) *Global Institutions and Development: Framing the World?* (London and New York: Routledge), 193–205.

Hershberg, E. and F. Rosen (2006) *Latin America after Neoliberalism: Turning the Tide in the 21st Century?* (New York, N.Y.: The New Press).

Hira, A. (2004) 'Paradigmatic Crisis in International Economic Governance: Explaining the Explosion of Protest', *Policy and Society*, Vol. 24, No. 3, 1–16.

Hira, A. (2007) 'Did ISI Fail and Is Neoliberalism the Answer for Latin America? Re-assessing Common Wisdom Regarding Economic Policies in the Region', *Brazilian Journal of Political Economy*, Vol. 27, No. 3, 345–356.

Human Rights First (2000) *Building on Quicksand: The Collapse of the World Bank's Judicial Reform in Peru*, at http://www.humanrightsfirst.org/pubs/descriptions/perubuilding.htm. Accessed 20 July 2005.

Iaryczower, M., P. Spiller and M. Tommasi (2002) 'Judicial Independence in Unstable Environments, Argentina 1935–1998', *American Journal of Political Science*, Vol. 46, No. 4, 699–716.

IDB (2004) *Country Program Evaluation (CPE) Argentina 1990–2002*. Office of Evaluation and Oversight, OVE (Washington, D.C.: Inter-American Development Bank).

IMF (1999) *External Evaluation of IMF Surveillance*. Report by a Group of Independent Experts (Washington, D.C.: IMF), at http://www.imf.org/external/pubs/ft/extev/surv/eval.pdf. Accessed 12 April 2008.

IMF (2001) *Review of the Fund's Experience in Governance Issues* (Washington, D.C.: IMF).

IMF (2004a) *Letter of Intent*, at http://www.imf.org/External/NP/LOI/2004/arg/01/index.htm. Accessed 21 November 2006.

IMF (2004b) *Report on the Evaluation of the Role of the IMF in Argentina, 1991–2001*. Independent Evaluation Office (Washington, D.C.: IMF).

James, O. and M. Lodge (2003) 'The Limitations of Policy Transfer and Lesson Drawing for Public Policy Research', *Political Studies Review*, Vol. 1, No. 2, 179–193.

Kahler, M. (1992) 'External Influence, Conditionality, and the Politics of Adjustment' in S. Haggard and R. Kaufman (eds.) *The Politics of Economic Adjustment* (Princeton N.J.: Princeton University Press), 88–136.

Kapur, D. (1998) 'The State in a Changing World: A Critique of the 1997 World Development Report', *International Monetary and Financial Issues for the 1990s*, Vol. 9 (New York and Geneva: United Nations), 127–140.

Kapur, D. and R. Webb (2000) 'Governance-Related Conditionalities of the International Financial Institutions', *G-24 Discussion Paper Series*, No. 6, August (New York and Geneva: UNCTAD).

Katz, C. (2006) 'Las Tendencias de la Economia Argentina', *Argenpress*, at http://www.argenpress.info/nota.asp?num=027296. Accessed 18 April 2006.

Kaufmann, D., A. Kraay and P. Zoido-Lobatón (1999) *Governance Matters*. *World Bank Policy*, Research Working Paper 2196 (Washington, D.C.: The World Bank).

Kaufmann, D., A. Kraay and P. Zoido-Lobatón (2002) *Governance Matters II: Updated Indicators for 2000/01* (Washington, D.C.: World Bank).

Keck, M. and K. Sikkink (1998) *Activists Beyond Borders: Advocacy Networks In International Politics* (Ithaca, N.Y.: Cornell University Press).

Killick, T. with R. Gunatilaka and A. Marr (1998) *Aid and the Political Economy of Policy Change* (London: Routledge).

Killick, T. (2002) *The 'Streamlining' of IMF Conditionality: Aspirations, Reality and Repercussions* (London: UK Department for International Development).

Korzeniewicz, R. P. and W. C. Smith (2000) 'Growth, Poverty, and Inequality in Latin America: Searching for the High Road', *Latin American Research Review*, Vol. 35, No. 3, 7–54.

La Nación (1998a) 'Menem Va a Washington a Marcar las Diferencias', 1 October, *Economía*: 3.

La Nación (1998b) 'Críticas de Menem a Encuesta sobre Corrupción', 24 September, *Política*: 16.

Landell Mills, P. (2003) 'Coming to Grips with Governance: The Lessons of Experience', *Journal of Contemporary China*, Vol. 12, No. 35, 357–371.

Larkins, C. (1998) 'The Judiciary and Delegative Democracy in Argentina', *Comparative Politics*, Vol. 30, No. 4, 423–443.

Levitsky, S. (2003) 'From Labor Politics to Machine Politics: The Transformation of Party-Union Linkages in Argentine Peronism, 1983–99', *Latin American Research Review*, Vol. 38, No. 3, 3–36.

Levitsky, S. (2005) 'Argentina: Democratic Survival Amidst Economic Failure' in F. Hagopian and S. Mainwaring (eds.) *The Third Wave of Democratization in Latin America Advances and Setbacks* (Cambridge: Cambridge University Press), 63–89.

Levy, D. L. and P. Newell (2002) 'Business Strategy and International Environmental Governance: Toward a Neo-Gramscian Synthesis', *Global Environmental Politics*, Vol. 2, No. 4, 84–101.

Levy, B. and S. Kpundeh (2004) *Building State Capacity in Africa: New Approaches, Emerging Lessons* (Washington, D.C.: World Bank).

Lo Vuolo, R. (2003) *Estrategia Economica para la Argentina* (Buenos Aires: Siglo XXI).

Manzetti, L. (2000) 'Keeping Accounts: A Case Study of Civic Initiatives and Campaign Finance Oversight in Argentine', *Working Paper No. 248*, IRIS Center, University of Maryland, November.

Manzetti, L. (2002) 'The Argentine Implosion', *The North-South Agenda*, 59, at http://www.miami.edu/nsc/publications/Papers&Reports/ArgentineImplosion.html. Accessed 12 May 2004.

Marquette, H. (2001) 'Corruption, Democracy and the World Bank', *Crime, Law &
Social Change*, Vol. 36, No. 4, 395–407.

Marquette, H. (2004) 'The Creeping Politicisation of the World Bank: The Case of
Corruption', *Political Studies*, Vol. 52, No. 3, 413–430.

Marsh, D. (1998) 'The Development of the Policy Network Approach' in D. Marsh
(ed.) *Comparing Policy Networks* (Buckingham: Open University Press), 3–17.

Marsh, D. and M. Smith (2000) 'Understanding Policy Networks: Towards a
Dialectical Approach', *Political Studies*, Vol. 48, No. 1, 4–21.

McElhinny, V. (2007a) *Banco del Sur*, Bank Information Center, at http://www.
bicusa.org/. Accessed 17 February 2008.

McElhinny, V. (2007b) *Descontento, Confusión, Falta de Transparencia: Cómo ser rel-
evante en América Latina*, Bank Information Center, at http://www.bicusa.org/
en/Article.3542.aspx. Accessed 17 February 2008

McNeill, D. (2004) 'Social Capital and the World Bank' in M. Bøas and D. McNeill
(eds.) *Global Institutions and Development: Framing the World?* (New York and
London: Routledge), 108–123.

Meagher, P. (2002) *Anti-Corruption Agencies: A Review of Experience*. IRIS Center,
University of Maryland, at http://www1.worldbank.org/publicsector/
anticorrupt/CoreCourseDec2003/Meagherpaper.doc. Accessed 26 May 2005.

Mehta, L. (2001) 'The World Bank and Its Growing Knowledge Empire', *Human
Organization*, Vol. 60, No. 2, 189–197.

Meltzer Report (2000) *IFIAC (Meltzer) Commission Report and Associated Studies*, at
http://www.house.gov/jec/imf/imfpage.htm. Accessed 16 April 2008.

Ministerio de Economía (1993) *Argentina: A Growing Nation* (Buenos Aires:
Ministerio de Economía, Obras y Servicios Públicos).

Ministerio de Economía (2005) *Informe Económico*, at http://www.mecon.gov.ar/
analisis_economico/nro4/capitulo1.pdf. Accessed 11 July 2006.

Ministerio de Justicia (2001) *Oficina Anti-corrupción, Informe de Gestión*. December
(Buenos Aires: Ministerio de Justicia).

Mohanty, M. and P. Turner (2006) 'Foreign Exchange Reserve Accumulation in
Emerging Markets: What are the Domestic Implications?' Bank for International Settlements, at http://www.bis.org/publ/qtrpdf/r_qt0609f.pdf. Accessed
7 May 2008.

Momani, B. (2007) 'IMF Staff: The Missing Link in Reform Proposals', *Review of
International Organizations*, Vol. 2, No. 1, 39–57.

Moreno Ocampo, L. (1993) *En Defensa Propia: ¿Cómo Salir de la Corrupción?*
(Buenos Aires: Editorial Sudamericana).

Morley, S. (1995) *Poverty and Inequality in Latin America: The Impact of Adjustment
and Recovery in the 1980s* (Baltimore, M.D.: Johns Hopkins University Press).

Mosley, P., J. Harrigan and J. Toye (1995) *Aid and Power: The World Bank and
Policy-Based Lending* (London: Routledge).

Munck, R. (2003) 'Neo-liberalism, Necessitarianism, and Alternatives in Latin
America: There Is No alternative (TINA)', *Third World Quarterly*, Vol. 24, No. 2,
495–511.

Nelson, J. (ed.) (1990) *Economic Crisis and Policy Choice: the Politics of Adjustment
in the Third World* (Princeton, N.J.: Princeton University Press).

Nelson, P. (2000) 'Whose Civil Society? Whose Governance? Decision-making
and Practice in the New Agenda at the Inter-American Development Bank and
the World Bank', *Global Governance*, Vol. 6, No. 4, 405–432.

Newsline (1999) *Gallup Pool*, at http://www.globalethics.org/oldnewsline/private/body.8-23-99.html. Accessed 19 May 2005.

North, D. (1990) *Institutions, Institutional Change, and Economic Performance* (Cambridge and London: Cambridge University Press).

O'Donnell, G. (1994) 'Delegative Democracy' *Journal of Democracy*, Vol. 5, No. 1, 55–69.

O'Donnell, G. (1999) 'Horizontal Accountability in New Democracies' in A. Shedler, L. Diamond and M. Plattner (eds.) *The Self-Restraining State: Power and Accountability in New Democracies* (Boulder: Lynne Rienner), 29 51.

Oficina Anticorrupción (2001) *Informe de Gestión* (Buenos Aires: Ministerio de Justicia).

Oficina Anticorrupción (2003) *Informe de Gestión* (Buenos Aires: Ministerio de Justicia).

Oxhorn, P. (1998) 'Is the Century of Corporatism Over? Neoliberalism and the Rise of Neopluralism' in P. Oxhorn and G. Ducatenzeiler (eds.) *What Kind of Democracy? What Kind of Market?* (University Park, P.A.: Pennsylvania State University Press), 195–217.

Oxhorn, P. and G. Ducatenzeiler (eds.) (1998) 'What Kind of Market? What Kind of Democracy? Latin America in the Age of Neoliberalism' in *What Kind of Democracy? What Kind of Market?* (University Park, P.A.: Pennsylvania State University Press), 3–19.

Palermo, V. and M. Novaro (1996) *Política y Poder en el Gobierno de Menem* (Buenos Aires: Grupo Editorial Norma).

Paliwala, A. (2000) 'Privatisation in Developing Countries: The Governance Issue', *Law, Social Justice and Global Development Journal*, at http://elj.warwick.ac.uk/global/issue/2000-1/paliwala.html. Accessed 17 October 2004.

Panizza, F. (2005) 'Unarmed Utopia Revisited: The Resurgence of Left-of-Centre Politics in Latin America', *Political Studies* 53, 716–734.

Panzardi, R., C. Calcopietro and E. Fanta Ivanovic (2002) *New-Economy Sector Study Electronic Government and Governance: Lessons for Argentina* (Washington, D.C.: World Bank).

Park, S. (2007) 'The World Bank Group: Championing Sustainable Development Norms?', *Global Governance*, Vol. 13, No. 4, 535–556.

Pastor, M. and C. Wise (1998) 'Stabilization and Its Discontents: Argentina's Economic Restructuring in the 1990s', *North-South Agenda*, No. 31 (Florida: North-South Center Press).

Payer, C. (1982) *The World Bank: A Critical Analysis* (New York: Monthly Review Press).

Payne, R. (2001) 'Persuasion, Frames and Norm Construction', *European Journal of International Relations*, Vol. 7, No. 1, 37–61.

Pearson, R. (2003), 'Argentina's Barter Network: New Currency for New Times?' *Bulletin of Latin American Research*, Vol. 22, No. 2, 214–230.

Petras, J. (2004) *Argentina: From Popular Rebellion to Normal Capitalism*, at http://globalresearch.ca/articles/PET406A.html. Accessed 12 March 2006.

Peruzzotti, E. (2001) 'The Nature of the New Argentine Democracy. The Delegative Democracy Argument Revisited', *Journal of Latin American Studies*, Vol. 33, No. 1, 133–155.

Phillips, N. (2005) *Globalizing International Political Economy* (Basingstoke: Palgrave/Macmillan).

Pincus, J. (2002) 'State Simplification and Institution Building in a World Bank-Financed Development Project' in J. Pincus and J. Winters (eds.) *Reinventing the World Bank* (Ithaca and London: Cornell University Press), 76–100.

Plan Fenix (2001) *Hacia el Plan Fenix: Diagnostico y Propuestas*, at http://www.laeditorialvirtual.com.ar/Pages/UBA_Plan_Fenix.htm. Accessed 1 April 2006.

Plan Nacional de Reforma Judicial (1998) *Plan Nacional de Reforma Judicial*, at http://www.reformajudicial.jus.gov.ar/materiales/plannac.htm. Accessed 17 November 2004.

Poder Ciudadano (2005) *Fundación Poder Ciudadano*, at http://www.poderciudadano.org. Accessed 14 February 2007.

Powell, A. (2002) 'The Argentina Crisis: Bad Luck, Bad Management, Bad Politics, Bad Advice', Working Paper 24, Business School, Universidad Torcuato Di Tella, Buenos Aires, Argentina.

Radics, A. (2001) 'Cristal: Transparencia en la Gestión Pública', *Revista Probidad*, Special Edition on Corruption in Argentina. No. 14, May–June, at http://www.probidad.org/revista/014/art14.html. Accessed 27 November 2004.

Razzotti, A. (2003) Case Study: The *Cristal Project* (Argentina). Submitted to the PREM Public Sector Group of the World Bank for the study of '*E- Applications; Overcoming Challenges Inside Government*', mimeo.

Reforma Judicial (2004) *Plan Nacional de Reforma Judicial*, at http://www.reformajudicial.jus.gov.ar. Accessed 9 December 2004.

Reinjfall, T. (2009) 'Continuity and Change in Chile's Political Economy' in J. Grugel and P. Riggirozzi (eds.) *Governance after Neoliberalism in Latin America* (Basingstoke: Palgrave/Macmillan), forthcoming.

Riggirozzi, P. (2007) 'The World Bank as Conveyor and Broker of Knowledge and Finds in Argentina's Governance Reforms' in D. Stone and C. Wright (eds.) *The World Bank and Governance* (Oxon and New York: Routledge), 207–227.

Risley, A. (2003) 'The Political Potential of Civil Society: Advocating for Access to Public Information in Argentina'. Paper presented at the 2003 Annual Meeting of the American Political Science Association, Philadelphia, Pennsylvania, August 28–31.

Ritzen, J. (2005) *A Chance for the World Bank* (London: Anthem Press).

Robinson, W. (1996) *Promoting Polyarchy: Globalisation, US Intervention and Hegemony* (Cambridge: Cambridge University Press).

Robinson, W. I. (2004). *A Theory of Global Capitalism: Production, Class, and State in a Transnational World* (Maryland: John Hopkins University Press).

Rodrik, D. (2002) *After Neo-liberalism, What?.* Paper presented at the Conference 'Alternative to Neoliberalism', May 23–24, at http://www.ksg.harvard.edu/news/opeds/2002/rodrik_neoliberalism_et_11902.htm. Accessed 20 April 2006.

Rodrik, D. (2008) 'Thinking about Governance', mimeo.

Rondinelli, D. and G. Shabbir Cheema (2003) Reinventing Government for the -Twenty-First Century State Capacity in a Globalizing *Society* (Bloomfield: Kumarian Press).

Rupert, M. (2005) 'Class Powers and the Politics of Global Governance' in M. Barnett and R. Duvall (eds.) *Power in Global Governance* (Cambridge: Cambridge University Press), 205–228.

Sabatier, P. A. (1993) 'Policy Change Over a Decade or More' in P. Sabatier. and H. Jenkins-Smith (eds.) *Policy Change and Learning: An Advocacy Coalition Approach* (Boulder and Oxford: Westview), 13–39.

Samoff, J. (1992) 'The Intellectual/financial Complex of Foreign Aid', *Review of African Political Economy*, Vol. 19, No. 53, 60–87.

Santiso, C. (2002) 'Governance Conditionality and the Reform of Multilateral Development Finance: The Role of the Group of Eight', at http://www.G7.Utoronto.ca/G7/Governance/Santiso2002-Gov7.Pdf. Accessed 3 June 2005.

Santiso, C. (2006) 'Banking on Accountability? Strengthening Budget Oversight and Public Sector Auditing in Emerging Economies', *Public Budgeting & Finance*, Vol. 26, No. 2, 66–100.

Schamis, H. (1999) 'Distributional Coalitions and the Politics of Economic Reform in Latin America', *World Politics*, Vol. 51, No. 1, 236–268.

Schorr, M. (2005) 'La Industria Argentina: Trayectoria Reciente y Desafíos Futuros'. Paper presented at the seminar 'Hacia el Plan Fénix II. En vísperas del segundo centenario', Facultad de Ciencias Económicas (UBA), Buenos Aires, Argentina, 2–5 August.

Senderowitsch, R. and S. Cesilini (2000) 'The Country Assistance Strategy in Argentina: How to Make a Consultative Process Work' in M. Anderson (ed.) *Thinking Out Loud II Innovative Case Studies On Participatory Instruments*, Latin America and the Caribbean, Civil Society Team (Washington, D.C.: World Bank), 41–54.

Sending, O. (2004) 'Policy Stories and Knowledge-Based Regimes: The Case of International Population Policy' in M. Bøas and D. McNeill (eds.) *Global Institutions and Development: Framing the World?* (London and New York: Routledge), 56–71.

Sikkink, K. (1991) *Ideas and Institutions: Developmentalism in Brazil and Argentina* (Ithaca: Cornell University Press).

Sklair, L. (2001) *The Transnational Capitalist Class* (Oxford: Blackwell).

Smulovitz, C. and E. Peruzzotti (2000) 'Societal and Horizontal Controls: Two Cases about Fruitful Relationship'. The Helen Kellogg Institute for International Studies (Notre Dame: University of Notre Dame).

Stallings, B. (1992) 'International Influence on Economic Policy: Debt, Stabilization, and Structural Reform' in S. Haggard and R. Kauffman (eds.) *The Politics of Economic Adjustment* (Princeton, N.J.: Princeton University Press), 41–88.

Stewart, F. (1997) 'John Williamson and the Washington Consensus Revisited' in L. Emmerij (ed.) *Economic and Social Development into the XXI Century* (Washington, D.C.: IDB), 62–69.

Stiglitz, J. (1994) 'The Role of the State in Financial Markets', Proceedings of the Annual World Bank Conference on Development Economics (Washington, D.C.: World Bank).

Stiglitz, J. (1998a) *More Instruments and Broader Goals: Moving Toward the Post-Washington Consensus*, WIDER Annual Lecture, Helsinki, at http://www.worldbank.org/html/extdr/extme/js-010798/wider.htm. Accessed 7 May 2002.

Stiglitz, J. (1998b) *Towards a New Paradigm for Development: Strategies, Policies, and Processes*. Prebisch Lecture at UNCTAD, Geneva, Switzerland, October 19, at www.worldbank.org/html/extdr/extme/prebisch98.pdf. Accessed 9 November 2004.

Stiglitz, J. (2000) 'Scan Globally, Reinvent Locally: Knowledge Infrastructure and the Localization of Knowledge' in D. Stone (ed.) *Banking on Knowledge: The Genesis of the Global Development Network* (London: Routledge), 24–43.

Stiglitz, J. (2002) *Globalization and Its Discontents* (London and New York: Norton).

Stone, D. (1996) *Capturing the Political Imagination: Think Tanks and the Policy Process* (London: Frank Cass & Co).

Stone, D. (2000) 'Conclusion: Knowledge, Power and Policy' in D. Stone (ed.) *Banking on Knowledge: The Genesis of the Global Development Network* (London: Routledge), 241–258.

Stone, D. (2001) 'Learning Lessons, Policy Transfer and the International Diffusion of Policy Ideas', University of Warwick, CSGR Working Paper No. 69/01. April.

Strange, S. (1988) *States and Markets* (London: Pinter Publishers).

Strange, S. (1991) 'An Eclectic Approach' in C. Murphy and R. Tooze (eds.) *The New International Political Economy. International Political Economy Yearbook No. 6* (Boulder: Lynne Rienner), 33–49.

Svampa, M. and S. Pereyra (2003) *Entre la Ruta y el Barrio. La Experiencia de las Organizationes Piqueteros.* (Buenos Aires: Editorial Biblos).

Taylor, I. (2004) 'Hegemony, Neoliberal "good governance" and the International Monetary Fund: A Gramscian Perspective' in M. Bøas and D. McNeill (eds.) *Global Institutions and Development: Framing the World?* (London and New York: Routledge), 124–136.

Thirkell-White Ben (2005) *The INF and the Politics of Globalization: From the Asian Crisis to a New International Financial Arquitecture?* (Basingtoke: Palgrave/Macmillan).

Tedesco, L. (2002) 'Argentina's Turmoil: The Politics of Informality and the Roots of Economic Meltdown', *Cambridge Review of International Affairs*, Vol. 15, No. 3, 469–481.

Teichman, J. (2001) *The Politics of Freeing Markets in Latin America: Chile, Argentina, and Mexico* (Chapel Hill: University of North Carolina Press).

Teichman, J. (2004) 'The World Bank and Policy Reform in Mexico and Argentina', *Latin American Politics and Society*, Vol. 46, No. 1, 39–74.

Teichman, J. (2007) 'Multilateral Lending Institutions and Transnational Policy Networks in Mexico and Chile', *Global Governance*, Vol. 13, No. 4, 557–573.

Tenembaum, E. (2004) *Enemigos: Argentina y el FMI* (Buenos Aires: Grupo Editorial Norma).

Transparency International (2005) *Corruption Perception Index*, at http://www.transparency.org/cpi/1998/cpi1998.html. Accessed 2 August 2005.

Trubek, D. (2003) *The Rule of Law in Development Assistance: Past, Present and Future.* Center for World Affairs and Global Economy. University of Wisconsin, at http://www.law.harvard.edu/programs/elrc/events/2002-2003/papers/dtrubek.doc. Accessed 25 November 2004.

Tuozzo, F. (2004) 'World Bank, Governance Reforms and Democracy in Argentina', *Bulletin of Latin American Research*, Vol. 23, No. 1, 100–118.

Tussie, D. (2006) 'Regionalism Adrift: The End of Collective Action?' Paper presented at 'Responding to Globalisation in the Americas' workshop, LSE, 1 June 2006.

Tussie, D. and F. Tuozzo (2002) 'Shooting for Reform: The Interplay of Domestic and External Constraints in Argentina' in H. Hveem and K. Nordhaug (eds.) *Public Policy in the Age of Globalisation: Responses to Environmental and Economic Crisis* (Basingstoke: Palgrave/Macmillan), 23–44.

UNECA (1998) *Economic Report on Africa 1998* (Addis Ababa: UNECA).

USAID (2002) 'Achievements in Building and Maintaining the Rule of Law'. *Occasional Paper Series*. PN-ACR-220. November (Washington, D.C.: USAID).

Verbitsky, H. (1993) *Hacer La Corte: La Creación de un Poder sin Control ni Justicia* (Buenos Aires: Planeta Espejo).

Vreeland, J. (2003) *The IMF and Economic Development* (Cambridge: Cambridge University Press).

Wade, R. (1996) 'Japan, the World Bank, and the Art of Paradigm Maintenance: The East Asian Miracle in Political Perspective', *New Left Review*, No. 217, May/June, 3–36.

Wade, R. (2002) 'US Hegemony and the World Bank: the Fight over People and Ideas', *Review of International Political Economy*, Vol. 9, No. 2, 215–243.

Wade, R. (2007) 'Feature Review: Ngaire Woods The Globalizers: The IMF, the World Bank and Their Borrowers', *New Political Economy*, Vol. 12, No. 1, 127–138.

Weaver, C. (2005) *The Poverty of Reform: Rhetoric and Reality in the World Bank* . Paper prepared for Workshop for Researchers on the World Bank, Central European University, Budapest, April 1–2, 2005.

Weiss, L. (2005) 'The State-augmenting Effect of Globalization', *New Political Economy*, Vol. 10, No. 3, 345–353.

Wendt, A. (1999) *Social Theory of International Relations* (Cambridge: Cambridge University Press).

Weyland, K. (1998) 'Swallowing the Bitter Pill: Sources of Popular Support for Neoliberal Reform in Latin America', *Comparative Political Studies*, Vol. 31, No. 5, 538–568.

Weyland, K. (2002) *The Politics of Market Reform in Fragile Democracies: Argentina Brazil Peru and Venezuela* (Princeton: Princeton University Press).

Weyland, K. (2006) 'External Pressures and International Norms in Latin American Pension Reform', The Helen Kellogg Institute for International Studies, Working Paper Series No. 323 (Notre Dame, Indiana).

Williams, D. and T. Young (1994) 'Governance, the World Bank and Liberal Theory', *Political Studies*, Vol. 42, No. 1, 84–100.

Williamson, J. (1990) 'What Washington Means by Policy Reform' in J. Williamsom (ed.) *Latin American Adjustment* (Washington, D.C.: Institute for International Economics).

Woods, N. (1999) 'Good Governance in International Organizations', *Global Governance*, Vol. 5, No. 1, 39–61.

Woods, N. (2003) 'Unelected Government: Making the IMF and the World Bank More Accountable', *The Brookings Review*, Vol. 21, No. 2, 9–12.

Woods, N. (2006) *The Globalizers: The IMF, the World Bank and Their Borrowers* (Ithaca and London: Cornell University Press).

World Bank (1989) *Sub-Saharan Africa: From Crisis to Sustainable Growth* (Washington, D.C.: World Bank).

World Bank (1992) *Convenio Constitutivo* (Washington, D.C.: World Bank).

World Bank (1994) *Governance: The World Bank's Experience*. Washington, D.C.: World Bank.

World Bank (1996a) *The World Bank Participation Sourcebook* (Washington, D.C.: World Bank).

World Bank (1996b) *Country Assistance Strategy Review*. Report No. 15844. OED (Washington, D.C.: World Bank).

World Bank (1997a) *OED Précis*. Operations Evaluation Department, No. 137, March (Washington, D.C.: World Bank).

World Bank (1997b) *World Development Report 1997: The State in a Changing World* (Washington, D.C.: World Bank).

World Bank (1997c) *Helping Countries Combat Corruption: The Role of the World Bank* (Washington, D.C.: World Bank).

World Bank (1998a) *Project Appraisal Document. Model Court Development Project.* Report 17459-AR. PREM and Argentina, Chile, Uruguay Country Management Unit. Unpublished document (Washington, D.C.: World Bank).

World Bank (1998b) *Project Appraisal Document. Year 2000 Technical Assistance Project. Report 18521* (Washington, D.C.: World Bank).

World Bank (2000a) *Reforming Public Institutions and Strengthening Governance: A World Bank Strategy. A World Bank Strategy.* November. Public Sector Group and PREM (Washington, D.C.: World Bank).

World Bank (2000b) *Country Assistance Strategy for the Argentine Republic*, Report No. 20354 (Washington, D.C.: World Bank).

World Bank (2000c) *Anti-Corruption Diagnostic for Argentina: An Overview of Three Reports and General Recommendations.* Report No. 20133-AR. PREM and Argentina, Chile, Uruguay Country Management Unit (Washington, D.C.: World Bank).

World Bank (2001a) *World Development Report 2002: Building Institutions for Markets* (Washington, D.C.: World Bank).

World Bank (2001b) *Argentina. Legal and Judicial Sector Assessment.* Legal Vice Presidency (Washington, D.C.: World Bank).

World Bank (2002a) *Reforming Public Institutions and Strengthening Governance: A World Bank Strategy. Implementation Update Part 2* (Washington, D.C.: World Bank).

World Bank (2002b) *Project Appraisal Document on a Proposed Loan in the Amount of US$600 Million to the Argentine Republic for the Jefas y Jefes de Hogar* (Heads Of Household), Report No: 23710-AR, October 22 (Washington, D.C.: The World Bank).

World Bank (2003) *Report No. 26127, Argentina. Crisis and Poverty 2003 A Poverty Assessment, Volume I: Main Report*, PREM (Washington, D.C.: The World Bank).

World Bank (2004a) *2003 Annual Review of Development Effectiveness: The Effectiveness of Bank Support for Policy Reform.* OED (Washington, D.C.: World Bank).

World Bank (2004b) *Mainstreaming Anti-Corruption Activities in World Bank Assistance: A Review of Progress Since 1997.* Report No. 29620. OED (Washington, D.C.: World Bank).

World Bank (2005) *Inclusive Governance: Empowering the Poor and Promoting Accountability in Latin America and the Caribbean Region.* Regional Framework and Strategy for Engaging Civil Society. Latin American and the Caribbean Region, Civil Society Team (Washington, D.C.: World Bank).

World Bank (2006) *Country Assistance Strategy for the Argentine Republic* (Washington, D.C.: World Bank).

World Bank Institute (2002) *Legal and Judicial Reform and the Control of Corruption in Latin America and the Caribbean. A Distance Learning Program for Bolivia, Colombia, Ecuador, Guatemala, Mexico and Peru*, at http://www.worldbank.org/wbi/governance/judicial-lac.htm. Accessed 22 May 2005.

Index

Abeles, M., 106
Acuña, C., 11, 12, 32, 50, 51, 52, 54,
    56, 108
Africa
    Chinese aid in, 180
    IFIs failures in, 3, 4
African Women's Economic Policy
    Network, 4
Akkerman, A., 61, 133
ALBA, see Bolivarian Alternative for
    the Americas (ALBA)
Alberto Fujimori, 129
Alfonsín, Raul (1983–1989), 50–3
Alianza, 70, 81, 89, 109
*Alianza por el Trabajo, la Justicia y la
    Educación* (Alliance for Work,
    Justice and Education), 60
    Crisis, 60–4
    Governance reforms, 64–71
    Impact of, 131
    Lack of legitimacy, 137
    Legitimacy and crisis resolution,
        150–1
Alternative Bolivariana para las
    Americas, *see* Bolivarian
    Alternative for the
    Americas (ALBA)
Alonso, G., 108
alternative globalizers, 160–1, 179
Alvarez, Carlos, 61
*Annual Review of Development
    Effectiveness*, 78
Anticorruption Diagnostic for Argentina,
    112
Anti-Corruption Office, 111, 116
Anti-Corruption Office Programme,
    100, 116–18
anti-corruption programmes, 3, 66–8,
    99–124
    civil society participation, 116–18
    Fernando de la Rúa presidency,
        109–11
    international agenda, 108

NGO involvement in, 66–8
Poder Ciudadano, 66, 107
PREM, 17, 70, 102–3, 107, 113,
    115–21, 130, 185
World Bank involvement in, 16, 20,
    33, 66–70, 101–3; brokerage
    role, 120–1
a-political stance of IFIs, 6, 15, 17, 21,
    45–6, 59, 69, 72, 74, 77, 81–3, 88,
    97, 104, 129–30, 151, 167
ARGENJUS, 91–2
Argentina, 1–3, 15, 21, 40, 47–73,
    74–98, 99–124, 125–54, 161, 174,
    179, 184
Argentine Industrial Union (UIA),
    135–6
Asselin, R., 80
authoritarian governments, 49
autonomous developmental model,
    search for, 163–5
Axel van Trotsenburg, 136

Babb, S., 8, 42
Baldi-Delatte, A., 136
Bambaci, J., 51, 52, 79
Banco del Sur (Bank of the South),
    172, 174
Bankruptcy Law, 138
Barnes, H., 149
Barnett, M., 2, 8, 16, 35, 40
Basualdo, E., 55
Bertranou, F., 55
best-practice trap, 7, 15, 17, 24, 38, 45,
    70, 75, 92, 101–4, 158, 162,
    166–7, 184
Bieler, A., 36
bilateral trade, 27, 168–9, 180
    see also intra-regional cooperation
Bill Chavez, R., 57, 81
Birdsall, N., 4, 76, 145
Blair, H., 65, 79, 80
Blustein, P., 61
Bøas, M., 31, 36, 38, 39, 76

203